RADICAL THEORIES

This book aims to reclaim and rediscover the range of radical, democratic and socialist alternatives to capitalism. Darrow Schecter argues that whilst the collapse of the Soviet Union has seen the failure of one type of Socialism, it has presented the left with the chance to re-evaluate the contribution of thinkers and movements obscured by the hegemony of Marxism-Leninism.

Schecter surveys the range of radical alternatives, both from the early years of Socialism and from contemporary political theory. Revolutionary Syndicalism, Anarchism, Council Communism, Guild Socialism, Market Socialism and Green, post-industrial Socialism all come under his critical gaze. He argues that the key to new socialist politics lies in the recognition and re-politicisation of Civil Society.

RADICAL THEORIES

Paths beyond Marxism and social democracy

DARROW SCHECTER

MANCHESTER UNIVERSITY PRESS

Manchester and New York

distributed exclusively in the USA and Canada by St. Martins Press

Published by Manchester University Press
Oxford Road, Manchester M13 9NR, UK
and Room 400, 175 Fifth Avenue, New York, NY 10010, USA

Distributed exclusively in the USA and Canada
by St. Martin's Press, Inc., 175 Fifth Avenue, New York, NY 10010, USA

British Library Cataloguing-in-Publication Data
A catalogue record is available from the British Library

Library of Congress Cataloging-in-Publication Data
Schecter, Darrow, 1961–
    Radical theories : paths beyond Marxism and social democracy /
Darrow Schecter.
        p.   cm.
    Includes bibliography references (p.   ) and index.
    ISBN 0–7190–3618–6 (hardback). — ISBN 0–7190–4385–9 (paperback)
    1. Socialism.   2. Radicalism.   3. Syndicalism.   4. Anarchism.
    5. Communism.   6. Civil society.   I. Title.
    HX73.S34   1994
    335.4—dc20   93–50584

ISBN 0 7190 3618 6 hardback

ISBN 0 7190 4385 9 paperback

Photoset in Linotron Joanna
by Northern Phototypeseting Co. Ltd, Bolton

Printed in Great Britain
by Biddles Ltd, Guildford and King's Lynn

Dedication

To Fernand Avila, Jeff Bourns, Bart Elsbach, Axel Elbeshausen, Wynne Greenhalgh, Richard Jemmett, Luca Lavatori, Immanuel Luc, Glenn Paterson, Carole O'Reilly, Mand Ryaira, Jaroslav Skupník and Frank Smyth because the next revolution will need new ideas and the creative power of the imagination.

Contents

Acknowledgements

The following book is the result of a long meditation on the possibilities of outlining the contours of a society that is at once socialist and libertarian. Many have said and will continue to say that this is an impossible task, but I hope that this book will convince them otherwise. Whatever the result may be, I learned a great deal during the research and writing, and had immense pleasure in discussing the ideas with friends, students and colleagues.

At a time when research money is constantly under threat, the British Academy is a source of hope and inspiration. Their Post-Doctoral Fellowship during 1990–92 enabled me to lay the theoretical groundwork for the book and to travel to libraries in Berlin, Rome and Paris.

From an intellectual standpoint it would be impossible to thank everyone who has helped me clarify my ideas. I owe a special thanks to the students and faculty of the University of Sussex. I benefited greatly from the ideas of Mick Dunford, Mathew Gandy, Maggie Günsberg, William Outhwaite and Neal Stammers. The most important contribution came from Luke Martell and John O'Neill, who read the entire draft and commented on each chapter. It is no exaggeration to say that without their help this book would have been less fun to write and would be less enjoyable to read. John's departure to Lancaster is a sad loss for Sussex – we will miss him greatly.

Let me also thank Adam Buick for his comments and criticisms, Mary Clarke for all her help, and the students of my summer 1993 Politics, Planning and Society seminar and of my 1993–94 Modern European Mind seminar. Their contribution has also been indispensable.

Richard Purslow and Celia Ashcroft have provided the encouragement and patient support that makes my continued collaboration with Manchester University Press so productive. I hope to have the pleasure of working with them in the future.

Finally, let me say to Jackie and Jarret that your warmth and humour have been more powerful than any political argument I have ever encountered – I guess some truths cannot be demonstrated!

Abbreviations

General
GIC   Group of International Communists

France
BFCC   French Bank of Co-operative Credit
CGT   French General Confederation of Labour
PCF   French Communist Party
PSF   French Socialist Party
SCOP   Workers' Co-operative Production Society

Germany
AAUD   General Workers' Union of Germany
FAUD   Free German Workers' Union
KAPD   German Workers' Communist Party
KPD   German Communist Party
SED   East German Communist Party
SPD   German Social Democratic Party
STASI   East German Security Police

Italy
CGT/CGIL   Italian General Confederation of Labour
CI   Italian Factory Committees
FIOM   Italian Metal Workers' Union
ON   *Ordine Nuovo*
PCI   Italian Communist Party
PDS   Italian Democratic Party of the Left
PSI   Italian Socialist Party
USI   Italian Union of Syndicalists

Spain
CGT   Spanish General Confederation of Labour
CLP   Basque Casa Laboral Popular
CNT   Spanish National Confederation of Labour
FAI   Spanish Anarchist Federation
UGT   Spanish Socialist Trade Union Federation

Russia
CPSU   Communist Party of the Soviet Union

USA
IWW   International Workers of the World

Introduction

What is the relevance today of ideas about socialist democracy and self-management in the light of everything that has transpired in Eastern Europe and the Soviet Union since the fall of the Berlin Wall? It would seem to be the case that Socialism is everywhere on the retreat. The Italian Communist Party's transformation into the Democratic Party of the Left in 1990 seemed to be a conscious effort of the Party leadership to distance itself from any association with the atrocities committed in the name of Socialism, even though the Party had always reaffirmed its commitment to parliamentary democracy since the Salerno declaration of 1944.[1] Other socialist parties which either do not follow the Italian Party's example or do not substantially modify their programmes are ridiculed as vestiges of a long outdated tradition of authoritarian 'workerism' which refuses to accept that capitalism and democracy simply 'go together'. The aim of this book is to demonstrate that there exits a neglected tradition of radical socialist theory and practice which need not be abandoned with the undeniably negative characteristics of life under the socialist dictatorships in Europe, Asia and elsewhere. Indeed, by rejecting the centrally planned economy and the subordination of social life to the control of a single vanguard party, this tradition stands in marked opposition to the worst aspects of life under those dictatorships. This chapter will briefly analyse some of the theoretical problems with Marxism which became glaring realities during the years of 'existing socialism'. The discussion will serve as an introduction to the analysis of the radical socialist tradition that has been overshadowed by the frequent assumption that revolutionary

---

[1] Ginsborg, *A History of Contemporary Italy*, pp. 42–4.

Socialism is by and large covered by the term 'Marxism-Leninism'.[2] Until now currents which fall outside of this category have been too easily dismissed as marginal, as in the case of Guild Socialism, or utopian, as is the case with Anarchism. Finally, it will be argued that the thinkers considered here can perhaps offer some insights for the future of the left at a time when socialists appear unable to construct a vision which differs considerably from the relatively bland doctrines of Social Democracy and Keynesianism, on the one hand, and strategies which have already been tried and are unlikely to arouse much enthusiasm such as nationalisation, on the other. Chapters 4, 5 and 6 on Guild Socialism, Market Socialism and Green Socialism attempt to contribute to a re-thinking of a radical socialist alternative. In the conclusion I will argue that in order to achieve this alternative we must work towards the construction of a socialist Civil Society. This chapter introduces the concept of Civil Society, while subsequent chapters explore the possibilities of a radical transformation of the civil sphere.

First, very briefly, what is inadequate about Social Democracy, and second, what are the presuppositions of a socialist Civil Society? The literature on the former is overwhelming and space here is limited, so I will restrict myself to a few general remarks. One of the obvious problems with Social Democracy is that it has addressed but not solved the persistent problems of inequality in wealth, power and life-chances that continue to plague those western industrialised countries where it has become the institutional norm and assumed the role of the dominant ideology. To the extent that it can boast some success, Social Democracy has humanised capitalism and used the State to moderate wealth imbalances. Technocratic management has been employed to attenuate the economic and social effects of recessions and to attempt to curb the perennial problem of unemployment. The countries of Western Europe, Japan and the United States have tried various forms of progressive income tax to counter the inequalities

---

[2] There is no doubt that the term 'Marxism-Leninism' is misleading insofar as it suggests that there are not substantial differences between the ideas of Marx and Lenin. On this point see both volumes of R. N. Hunt, *The Political Ideas of Marx and Engels*. I use the term primarily to denote the Bolshevik appropriation of Marxism, which historically was often accomplished only with great distortion to the letter and spirit of Marx's work, especially the socialist humanism of Marx's early writings. Indeed, some of the writers discussed in the following chapters seek to rescue precisely that element of Marx's work from the practice of the Soviet Union and other countries which have justified repressive political practices by citing Marx as an authority.

that uncontrolled capitalism inevitably produces. The implementation of such reforms has varied tremendously from one country to the next. But periodic rioting and exploding social tensions, especially in the United States, casts some doubt on the success of the overall project. The Welfare State has attempted to provide decent housing and medical care for those who found out the hard way that the market does not allocate resources according to need. Again, however, various attempts in the 1980s and 1990s to dismantle the Welfare State and its imperilled existence during times of recession cast doubt on its continued viability.[3]

Contrary to the case with the State Socialism of the former Soviet Union and similarly governed countries, the verdict on Social Democracy is still open. Yet it remains to be seen whether Keynesian techniques will continue to be effective in terms of minimising unemployment and ensuring economic growth. Increasing government spending has led to high levels of inflation, with the resulting problems of capital flight and under-investment. Right-wing governments which doubt the Keynesian approach and seek to revive economic growth by fighting the inflationary effects of government spending find themselves faced with high levels of unemployment and the attendant social tensions that massive redundancies cause. The future of Social Democracy may thus be less than sanguine, auguring drastic reversals between Keynesianism and Monetarism, declining economic growth and persistent unemployment. Moreover, the room for political manoeuvre of social democratic governments remains to a significant extent restricted by the movement of private capital. This phenomenon suggests a permanent tension between market freedom on the one hand, and the democratic ideal of holding power accountable, on the other. The problem of holding private interests accountable to the public sphere continues to plague western industrial societies, and is a central concern for the theorists to be considered here.[4]

Who are these theorists? Let us say that the thinkers to be examined in this book share the premise that a society cannot be

---

[3] Miller, *Market, State and Community*, pp. 8–9; Parkin, *Class Inequality and Political Order*, chapter 4. Parkin provides a concise account of the problems encountered by social democratic governments in tempering the inequalities generated by capitalism. Although written in the early 1970s, the problems he diagnoses are as relevant now as then.

[4] This problem has been recently given a cogent exposition by M. F. Dunford in 'Theories of Regulation', pp. 308–19. On the tension between the interests of private capital and long-term regional political and economic development, see Dunford's *Capital, the State and Regional Development*.

characterised as democratic simply because its most powerful government posts are elected. It is conceivable that a republic could function well as an elected government despite major class inequalities.[5] But for our theorists the principle of democracy requires that wherever in society power is exercised it must be shared and held closely accountable. This is especially the case with regard to the vital sphere of the production and control of society's resources in the widest sense, that is, in industry, education, health, culture, etc. Theorists in this tradition insist that power in both the government and the economy must be decentralised and controlled by participatory institutions, and that this is incompatible with any kind of authoritarian State. If there is a single common thread uniting the different theorists we will consider which sets them apart from the Marxist-Leninist tradition, it is the recurrent anti-statism and anti-centralism pervading their writings. However, this does not signify a wholesale abandonment of democratic economic planning on their part, as we shall see in later chapters.

This is not to deny that some of the ideas of Marx and Lenin are also highly critical of the authoritarian State. This is especially true of the young Marx, Marx the defender of the Paris Commune, and Lenin the champion of the workers' Councils, or Soviets, in *The State and Revolution*. But as we will see in this chapter, there was sufficient ambiguity in Marx's writings to enable Lenin to portray him as a centralist. Lenin thus used Marx's remarks on the dictatorship of the proletariat to legitimate repressive measures against the Workers' Opposition and other groups who demanded shopfloor power for the working class and less power for the Communist Party. Those who defended the ideas of socialist democracy against the centralising tendencies of Bolshevism saw that the power of the Party-State was being used *against* the working class. Thus our theorists have almost without exception been fierce opponents of Leninism in power. Future chapters will be dedicated to drawing out all of the implications of these theories. First we must begin by looking at Marx's ideas on Civil Society and democracy to see how they were transformed in Soviet practice.

---

[5] While Machiavelli actually cites class conflict as promoting a necessary balance of forces in the Roman republics, modern observers such as Toqueville and Arendt regard the attempt to create social equality as detrimental to the political liberty necessary in a flourishing republic. In fact, Rousseau is unusual amongst the theorists in the republican tradition by insisting that social and economic equality are indispensable in any republic.

Marx, Lenin and the State

Marx developed his initial ideas on the State in his *Critique of Hegel's Philosophy of Right*. Hegel had seen that contrary to ancient Greece or feudal Europe, modern industrial democracies were riven by class inequalities, poverty, and social conflict militating against the most basic level of social cohesion. But Hegel argued that these conflicts could be confined to the sphere of social interaction he called Civil Society. In Hegelian philosophy the civil sphere is governed by the interaction of various private interests. These could be interests related to the buying and selling of labour and property, or they might be expressed as divergent political viewpoints found in newspapers and other forums of discussion. Hegel was most concerned with the buying and selling of labour as a commodity in accordance with the demands of the free market. He acknowledged that these exchanges were usually conducted to the detriment of the working classes forced to sell their labour for survival. The replacement of the medieval Guild system by modern industry often deprived workers of their previous training as skilled craftsmen and artisans. There thus emerged a mass of amorphous workers who had little bargaining power in market exchanges, which often led to their pauperisation. Moreover, all relationships in the civil sphere were governed by contracts that were quickly formed and as easily dissolved from the moment one of the parties saw no further utility in the deal. But in an elaborate argument Hegel maintained that the undeniably centrifugal forces in the civil sphere could be reconciled in the political community of the State. Life in Civil Society negated the unconditional and immediately affective bonds of the family. In the State these bonds were reconstituted in a more complexly articulated unity of forces than was possible at the level of any individual family. Thus the modern State could absorb and harmonise the clash of interests deriving from modern forms of industry and commerce.[6]

In *On the Jewish Question* and the *Critique of Hegel's Philosophy of Right* (both of 1843), Marx praised Hegel for recognising the separation of the State and Civil Society as one of the hallmarks of modernity. But he refused to accept Hegel's argument that the tensions in Civil Society were reconciled in the higher unity of the State. Marx began elaborating a critique of the democratic parliamentary State, praising it as an advance over feudal arrangements, but condemning it as

[6] Hegel, *Philosophy of Right*, paragraphs 260 and 261, pp. 160–2; Hunt, *The Political Ideas of Marx and Engels*: Vol. I, p. 56.

incapable of providing the institutional basis for a truly harmonious and democratic society. Hence he began to speculate about the possibility of a social order in which the State and Civil Society were merged in a higher synthesis, and the conflict between public and private interests was effaced. Marx followed Rousseau and the young Hegel in admiring the fundamental unity between the citizen and the State characteristic of political life of the Greek polis. As of 1843, however, he had not yet envisaged how the State and Civil Society might be re-united. He used Ludwig Feuerbach's transformative method to 'stand Hegel on his feet', and to argue the modern State was a complex of institutions mediating the conflicting interests of Civil Society – not resolving them. Indeed, rather than transcending and uniting particular interests, the modern State protected the interests of private property against the real interests of the entire community.[7]

Marx maintained that in modern Civil Society the legal equality of citizens was offset by the reality of competing private interests. While in the Middle Ages private associations such as Guilds, estates, and corporations had political functions, the revolutions of the eighteenth century placed the private individual in an unmediated relationship with alienated political power:

> The political revolution therefore abolished the political character of civil society . . . But the consummation of the idealism of the State was at the same time the consummation of the materialism of civil society. The bonds which had restrained the egoistic spirit of civil society were removed along with the political yoke. Political emancipation was at the same time the emancipation of civil society from politics, from its even having a semblance of a general content.[8]

The French Revolution constituted the apex of this movement separating communal from general interests. By destroying all intermediate political associations such as the Guilds, estates, and corporations, Civil Society was stripped of its political functions and authority. This resulted in two decisive features in the anatomy of modern industrial democracies. First, rather than abolishing social conflict, conflict was confined to a separate and ostensibly non-political sphere. Second, the State arrogated the previously held political functions of Civil Society to itself, and removed itself from popular accountability, participation and control. Marx described

---

[7] Marx, On the Jewish Question, in Tucker (ed.), pp. 44–6.
[8] Marx, On the Jewish Question, in Tucker (ed.), p. 45; Hunt, The Political Ideas of Marx and Engels: Vol. I, pp. 60–2.

this process and its apogee in *The Eighteeth Brumaire of Louis Bonaparte* of 1852.

From the moment Marx seized upon the separation of the State and Civil Society as the distinctive feature of modern politics, he began searching for a non-parliamentary solution to the divorce between an individual's existence as a citizen and their existence as a producer. He thus set about outlining what new social institutions could possibly protect the essential unity of the human individual as worker, citizen, and legislator. The work of the political revolution would have to be completed with a total, *human* revolution. Marx argued that the primary activity in Civil Society was production, and that all members of society could not individually share in legislative power if the civil and political spheres were separated. Thus the aim of the next revolution had to be the abolition of representative power extraneous from production, and thereby make all individuals legislators in some capacity. Here pure democracy and Socialism would converge.[9] As we shall see, this is precisely what the syndicalists, Council communists and Guild socialists would attempt to do: by setting up democratic decision-making institutions in the workplace, they hoped that the rift between the citizen and worker could be abolished in one stroke.

While Marx's early writings hint at the possibility of achieving such a total human emancipation, it was not until the events of the Paris Commune that he was able to give clear expression to what he had in mind. When the Prussians had crushed the French in the war of 1871, they were dismayed to find that Paris was not ready to yield to foreign invasion, and instead the people of the city set up their own government based on radically democratic principles. The event fired Marx's imagination, not to mention the intense loyalty of future generations of socialist militants. In a letter of 12 April 1871, Marx affirmed that the revolution that was in the offing would not be won by transferring State power from one set of oppressors to another. The State in its present form would have to be dismantled, so that political power could be wielded by the people organised at the local level. However, this was not to be achieved in the old medieval corporations, but by locating a new collective body capable of mediating between producer functions and citizen functions. Thus in *The Civil War in France* Marx affirmed that 'One thing especially was proved by the Commune, viz., that the working class cannot

[9] Marx, *Critique of Hegel's Philosophy of Right*, in the *Collected Works of Marx and Engels* (MECW), Vol. 3, p. 119.

simply lay hold of the ready-made State machinery and wield it for its own purposes.'[10]

For Marx, the great merit of the Commune was to have abolished the political realm as a separate, alienated sphere of unaccountable political power. Instead, the Parisian Communards set up a system of 'recall on demand': representatives of the people could be relieved of office from the moment a majority of their electors deemed that their views were no longer being accurately defended. Executive and legislative activities were fused, such that those who made the laws also had to carry them out. Under these conditions, Marx maintained, one could avoid the bureaucratic nature of parliamentary lawmaking and the uselessness of idle parliamentary debate. In addition, the standing professional army was replaced by a people's militia, so that all citizens were now able to make laws, execute them, and defend the polity that they had gone to such great lengths to establish. Recall on demand was of primary importance, however, since it ensured that government officials could not become career politicians and thereby deny the average citizen their right to participate in public affairs. Marx had always held the notion of the professional politician in contempt and as inadmissible in a true democracy. Such a professional cast was only possible where people were gullible enough to believe or forced to accept the Hegelian notion of the bureaucracy as the 'universal' class.[11] Marx thus concluded that it was possible for the Commune to be the standard form of government for the smallest country town, and that it was the ideal polity to accompany the 'self-government of the producers'. The Commune, in short, was 'the political form at last discovered to work out the economic emancipation of labour'.[12]

However, the Commune writings, which were extensively cited by Lenin as the primary source of inspiration for his own ideas, raise a number of important questions which became tremendous problems during the years of Soviet rule. Marx's previous emphasis on human liberation faded from discussion, while he concentrated on his critique of the undemocratic aspects of Bonapartism and the modern State in general. For Marx, the events of the spring of 1871 demonstrated how Civil Society might re-appropriate the political functions of the State within a decentralised federation of Communes. Yet Marx also states that centralised planning will be the

---

[10] Marx and Engels Selected Works in 1 Volume (MESW 1 Vol.), p. 32.
[11] Marx, Critique of Hegel's Philosophy of Right, MECW, Vol. 3, p. 50.
[12] MESW 1 Vol., p. 290.

logical solution to end the exploitative nature of capitalist Civil Society:

> Yes, gentlemen, the Commune intended to abolish that class-property which makes the labour of the many the wealth of the few ... If co-operative production is not to remain a sham and a snare; if it is to supersede the Capitalist system; if united co-operative societies are to regulate production upon a common plan, thus taking it under their own control, and putting an end to the constant anarchy and periodical convulsions which are the fatality of Capitalist production – what else, gentlemen, would it be but Communism, 'possible' Communism?[13]

If co-operative production is to be regulated by a common plan, the question then becomes, who will have the power to preside over its formulation? Will it be a body of technical experts, or will it be the chief task of a political elite organised as the vanguard of the working class? We might suppose that the organisation of production by an expert body of planners is to be combined with the elimination of the essential attributes of a capitalist economy – wage labour, commodity production, private property and market forces. Would such a situation result in the self-government of the producers? In the highly complex industrial economy capable of producing the levels of abundance Marx presupposes as the necessary condition for Communism, planning functions would be entrusted to a small number of experts. The majority of the working class would then be left with the task of reaching the production targets called for by the planners. Ironically, the planners have now acquired the position of the 'universal' class in the *Philosophy of Right* that had inspired Marx's original critique of Hegel.

Marx's followers continually returned to two essential tenets of *The Civil War in France*: (1) the existing State machine could not be seized and wielded in the interests of the working class, and therefore had to be smashed and replaced with a network of Communes; (2) the organisation of production according to a central plan must accompany the smashing of the State. But how would a federation of decentralised Communes based on the Paris model be combined with a centrally planned economy? Command planning under the supervision of a small body of experts would require new directive political bodies to co-ordinate resource allocation functions once performed by capitalist enterprises competing on the market. The Commune was by its nature decentralised and thus inappropriate for this task. A vanguard Party could preside over the

---

[13] MESW 1 Vol., pp. 290–1.

political direction of the economy. But by taking over the State in this way, the Party would be a major obstacle to the institution of the radical participatory democracy of the Paris Commune. In *The State and Revolution* Lenin called for a centralised vanguard, a planned economy, and a Commune style government, perhaps thinking that any contradictions would work themselves out in practice. Lenin argued that in any case Marx had himself inveighed against the elaboration of detailed blueprints of the future as utopian, and the revolution would produce its own forms of struggle in accordance with the needs of the masses.

Bolshevism in power

In the Russian Revolution this dilemma was solved at the expense of the organs of grassroots democracy, or Soviets, as they were called in Russia. Despite the eloquent praise of popular democracy in *The State and Revolution*, Lenin had no misgivings about interpreting Marx as a centralist:

> Marx disagreed both with Proudhon and Bakunin precisely on the question of federalism (not to mention the dictatorship of the proletariat). Federalism as a principle follows logically from the petty-bourgeois views of anarchism. Marx was a centralist. There is no departure whatever from centralism in his observations just quoted. Only those who are imbued with the philistine 'superstitious belief' in the State can mistake the destruction of the bourgeois State machine for the destruction of centralism![14]

As we shall see in chapter 2, Proudhon and other anarchists had substantial differences with Marx's conception of Communism long before the Bolsheviks abandoned the call for 'all power to the Soviets' in *The State and Revolution* and instead consolidated all power in the hands of the Communist Party. And as the above quotation suggests, anarchists and other non-Bolshevik socialists would have no truck with Marx's notion of the dictatorship of the proletariat. Lenin prepared himself for the attacks of those critics who would point out that the message of Marx's Paris Commune writings was essentially that the State was to be smashed by democratising it. Lenin's response was quite simple. Whether polemicising with the leader of the German Social Democratic Party, Karl Kautsky, or with Rosa Luxemburg and other defenders of workers' institutions,

---

[14] Lenin, *Collected Works*, Vol. 25, p. 429.

Lenin stated that the new State would indeed resemble the Commune to the extent that it was based on Soviets. However, Lenin was able to exploit Marx and Engels's somewhat contradictory interpretations of the Commune. In the Preface to the 1891 German edition of the *Communist Manifesto*, Engels, not Marx, referred to the Paris Commune as a practical example of the dictatorship of the proletariat. It is true that Marx also employed this term, but in a completely different context and with reference to a completely different event – the Gotha Programme of the German Workers' Party (1871). In this latter usage by Marx the term dictatorship of the proletariat was clearly intended to indicate a transition to the higher stages of Communism, whereas the Commune was a permanent alternative to the parliamentary State. Lenin was thus able to say that the Soviet State, like the Paris Commune, was a proletarian *democratic* dictatorship, with all the centralisation that the term dictatorship implies. Any resemblance to the structures of popular participation lauded in *The Civil War in France* were quickly dismantled. Thereafter, the Bolsheviks justified their authoritarian rule as the only feasible way to defend the revolution against reactionaires and counter-revolutionaries.

The first casualties of the Bolshevik dictatorship were the Soviets and Workshop Committees. The Soviets were units of local democracy in which workers, soldiers, peasants and other opponents of the regime organised their opposition to the Czar. The Workshop Committees were factory-based workers' Councils in which workers challenged the authority of management by demanding a right to participate in decisions on production and distribution. In terms of the conflict between the grassroots democracy of workers' organisations and the monopoly of power by the Communist Party, the fate of the Workers' Opposition and the Kronstadt Soviet are especially noteworthy. Bolshevik manipulation of the Russian trade union movement gave rise to the formation of a dissenting faction in the Party calling for worker management of the economy. This faction, the Workers' Opposition, argued that in order to realise Socialism, the effective running of the economy would have to be in the hands of the trade unions and factory committees. The Bolsheviks could have an important supervisory and ideological role, but the leaders of the Opposition warned that any inordinate role for the vanguard would result in catastrophe for the workers' capacity to become self-governing. Opposition leader Alexandra Kollontai predicted that if the Bolsheviks did not quickly confer power on workers' organisations, the Russian Revolution would deteriorate into the authoritarian rule of the bureaucracy.

The Workers' Opposition challenged the resolutions of previous national trade union congresses which demanded the incorporation of the trade unions into the State. There had indeed been a vigorous debate on whether these resolutions were calling for State control of the unions, or the co-operation of unions and the State. The Workers' Opposition reminded their Bolshevik opponents that Point 5 of the Party programme ratified at the Eighth Party Congress in March 1919 approved the motion that trade unions should control the management of the entire Russian economy. Kollontai maintained that the final goal of a worker-managed economy and State depended on the thorough participation of the unions in laying the groundwork for the new Communist economic system.[15] The Workers' Opposition demanded that economic power be vested in a delegation of Russian producers which would elect a Central Committeee from its ranks. Producers were to be represented both at the local level (according to trade) and the federal level (according to region). There was also to be a horizontal structure in which trade union congresses would elect representatives to aid in the management of various industrial sectors. These new institutions would have wide-ranging jurisdiction, and the Opposition also added that technical experts would be subject to the same democratic controls as ordinary workers. At the shopfloor level, elected workers' Councils were assigned the task of running daily operations, while the Party – albeit a far less hierarchically organised one than the Bolshevik Party – would continue to serve as an important ideological guide. At the Tenth Bolshevik Congress of March 1921, Kollontai's colleague Shlyapnikov assured the Party that its role would not be usurped, but rather modified, in order to accommodate the increasingly popular bases of the new State. The Workers' Opposition was prepared to accept that the new economic bodies managing the economy should be staffed by Party members or at least have the approval of comrades in the local branch of the Party. The main target of Opposition reforms was the Party-State fusion which threatened the original aims of the revolution, that is, the self-government of the masses.[16]

While many Opposition proposals were in consonance with Lenin's ideas in *The State and Revolution*, he ridiculed the Opposition

[15] Sirianni, *Workers' Control and Socialist Democracy*, pp. 232–3; Bunyan and Fisher, *The Origins of Forced Labour*, p. 49.
[16] Sirianni, *Workers' Control*, pp. 233–5; Shapiro, *The Origins of the Communist Autocracy*, p. 294.

programme as syndicalist and a complete deviation from Marxist principles. Lenin was now firmly against trade union and other forms of popular control of the economy, since it was only the Communist Party which could safeguard the revolution from a degeneration to the defence of local craft interests. Party members had acquired the most conscious awareness of the long-term interests of the entire working class, while trade union leaders still worked on the basis of their experiences under capitalism. Lenin insisted that the Party would first have to educate the masses in the skills of self-management before it could relax its grip on the economy and State.[17]

Lenin had raised some valid objections to the Opposition programme, citing a lack of analysis of the role of the peasants in the Russian economy as one of its major flaws. But he also used the Tenth Party Congress to indefinitely postpone the crucial question of worker control. The majority of Bolsheviks would not accept anything less than Party control of the economy, which became regulated according to the targets set in the New Economic Policy (NEP, 1921–27) and the successive Five Year Plans which followed the NEP years. The NEP was initiated as a measure intended to increase food supplies and meet peasant grievances. But its implementation quickly affected all aspects of the Soviet economy, including financial and budgetary concerns. By attempting to increase production through material incentives to the peasants, the 'Nepman' appeared, acting as a private intermediary between suppliers and purchasers. Many of the nepmen used this position to gain large profits which were in turn taxed by the State. G. D. H. Cole, observed that under NEP the USSR returned to the practices of capitalist industry and finance, albeit with the difference that the State controlled the main industrial operations and foreign trade. Indeed, most alarming to the Workers' Opposition was the almost total control of the State in determining the conditions under which this hybrid form of State capitalism was to operate.[18]

Was the move to State capitalism inevitable under the circumstances facing the country at this time? The Bolsheviks shared the Opposition's view that the issues of the party and State would have a crucial significance for the future of the new socialist economy. During the initial period of War Communism (1918–21) immediately prior to the NEP years, a number of modest reforms had been made. These included the nationalisation of some industries,

---

[17] Sirianni, *Workers' Control*, pp. 235–7; Lenin, CW, Vol. 27, pp. 49–50, 245–51.
[18] Cole, *A History of Socialist Thought. Vol. IV*, pp. 555–63.

redistribution of nationalised land amongst the peasants, and the institution of limited forms of workers' control of industry and an eight-hour work day. The Opposition demanded that the reform process be pushed further, while the Bolsheviks claimed that this was impossible in the prevailing conditions of scarcity and disorganisation. Moreover, the revolution itself was under attack from forces still loyal to the Czarist regime that enjoyed material support from the capitalist West. Lenin argued in favour of greater economic centralisation, labour discipline and wage incentives, in order to arrive at some temporary compromise with the peasantry and certain financial interests in the country that had not yet been expropriated.[19]

The onslaught of the civil war required more drastic measures. The ensuing years of War Communism were marked by the nationalisation of almost all large industry in the country. The resulting inflation precluded any extensive increase in the printing of money as an immediate strategy. Relations with the peasantry came under severe strain when the government simply demanded that the peasants produce more in order to provide the State with revenue. Meanwhile in the cities, the Bolsheviks appointed their own trade union officials to impose discipline in the factories. Both Trotsky and Bukharin backed Lenin's moves in this direction. By 1921 it became clear that neither the workers or peasants could stand such a regime for long. The NEP, which began in March 1921 and lasted for seven years, replaced the system of direct State requisition with a tax in kind which allowed the peasants to keep a fixed share of their surplus. Such measures were accompanied by the reintroduction of regulated market relations between agriculture and industry, and the de-nationalisation of some small industries. After the devastation of War Communism, the NEP years symbolised the desirability of good relations with the peasantry in an overwhelmingly agrarian society. It seemed that there was no other way of securing peasant support for the next step of the revolution, that is, rapid industrialisation. The Workers' Opposition opposed what they saw as the simultaneous strengthening of the Party and introduction of State capitalism, but their proposals were denounced at the Tenth Party Congress of 1921.[20]

At this Congress Lenin went as far as calling for formal censure and shortly thereafter demanded a ban on all organised factions in the Party. Despite the strength of the Workers' Opposition in the

[19] McLellan, Marxism after Marx, pp. 115–16.
[20] McLellan, Marxism after Marx, pp. 118–21.

national metal workers' union, they lacked a firm basis for mobilising workers in other industries. Towards the end of 1920, currents championing an ideology of radical democratic self-management hostile to the Bolshevik approach were waning quickly. Moreover, as the Bolsheviks marshalled their forces against their civil war opponents, they increased their control of the unions at all levels, and won support for Bolshevik views on factory democracy and political pluralism. Opposition to Bolshevik centralisation culminated with protests in Moscow, Petrograd and other cities. Finally, the Red Army crushed the Kronstadt Soviet on 17 March 1921, thus backing with force Lenin's statement that Soviets not controlled by Bolsheviks were potential enemies of the revolution. Nonetheless, the Party boldly proclaimed its adherence to the ideals of socialist democracy by staging a celebration of the fiftieth anniversary of the Paris Commune the very next day.[21]

The ravages of the civil war and the subsequent drive to construct the industrial base necessary for Socialism in Russia, combined with the triumph of Lenin's theory of the party, resulted in a general acceptance of the Bolshevik strategy within the international communist movement. In its essentials this strategy consisted of striving for rapid industrialisation and capital accumulation through State capitalism directed by the communist vanguard. After Lenin's death in 1924 and Stalin's ascent to uncontested power shortly after, the hierarchical and dictatorial tendencies inherent in this strategy became increasingly obvious. The hegemony of the Bolshevik model was further bolstered by the Russian Party's control of the Communist Third International, or Comintern, founded in March 1919. At the Second Plenum in June 1922, condition for entry to the Comintern became adherence to the famed Twenty-one Points, which aimed at Bolshevising the entire international communist movement. Given the enormous prestige they accrued from seizing power in Russia, the Bolsheviks were able to do this without much effective resistance.[22]

As time passed it proved to be the case that it was in the developing world and not, as Marx had prophesied, in the most advanced capitalist countries that Socialism would flourish. Since this looked like the most obvious path to modernisation, the Leninist and Bolshevik model of rapid industrialisation under a

---

[21] Sirianni, *Workers' Control*, pp. 237–9; Avrich, *Kronstadt, 1921*, pp. 111, 136; Berti, Introduction to the *Quaderni*, pp. 22–4; Lenin, CW, Vol. 32, pp. 35, 51–2, 61, 68; Paggi, *Gramsci e il moderno principe*, pp. 247–9.

[22] Hulse, *The Forming of the Communist International*, pp. 205–11.

single Party was widely emulated. Lenin had been greatly impressed by what appeared to be capitalism's ability to organise the productive forces according to the strictest criteria of rationality and efficiency. He initially argued that the secret of Socialism's success would be its capacity to combine capitalist principles of organisation and efficiency, on one hand, with socialist planning and distribution, on the other. In this respect he admired the ideas of Frederick Taylor, whose time and motion studies in the workplace were designed to discipline the workforce in the service of higher profits. Thus in 1918 Lenin argued that:

> The Taylor system, the last word of capitalism in this respect, like all capitalist progress is a combination of the refined brutality of bourgeois exploitation and a number of the greatest achievements in the field of analysing mechanical motions during work, the elimination of super-fluous and awkward motions, the elaboration of correct methods of work, the introduction of the best system of accounting and control, etc. The Soviet Republic must at all costs accept all that is valuable in the achievements of science and technology in this field. The possibility of building socialism depends exactly on our success in combining the Soviet power and the Soviet organisation with the up to date achievements of capitalism. We must organise in Russia a study and teaching of the Taylor system and systematically try it out and adapt it to our own ends.[23]

Given that Marx in *Capital* had himself envisaged communist society as a large factory of co-ordinated productive activities, Lenin's ideas on Taylorism do not seem to be such a major concession to capitalist methods. In practice, the legacy of the Paris Commune became increasingly obscured. It was replaced by the one-party State coupled with the capitalist factory system, equipped with merely symbolic forms of worker participation in decision making. Even these were abolished, when Stalin outmanoeuvred his opponents to gain control of the Party–State apparatus soon after Lenin's death in 1924. Announcing his programme for the construction of 'Socialism in one country', Stalin's ostensible goal was the quickest possible industrialisation of the Soviet economy, to be paralleled by the greatest possible collectivisation of agriculture. The first Five Year Plan was announced in 1929, two years after the end of the NEP. During 1929 to 1930 the number of agricultural workers on collectivised farms rose from 4 to 58 per cent of the agrarian workforce. This figure fluctuated during the following years, as Stalin's war on the petit bourgeois class of *Kulaks* was resisted by various strata of the

[23] Lenin, CW, Vol. 27, p. 259.

agricultural population. Yet by 1934 seventy-five per cent of farms had been collectivised. The ensuing chaos and mismanagement prepared the way for some of the worst famines in Russian history, resulting in the death of millions of people. The year 1934 also marked the assassination of Kirov and the beginning of the show trials, which culminated with the execution of Bukharin in 1938. Little can be said to accurately convey the scale of violence and exercise of arbitrary power that resulted in the death of at least three million people. Whereas Lenin had sanctioned the persecution of 'class enemies' and political opponents, Stalin actually turned this violence against members of the Bolshevik Party itself. A mere 3 per cent of delegates to the 1934 Party Congress survived; 70 per cent of Central Committee members elected in that year were shot.[24]

In the meantime, the industrial bases of the future Soviet economy were set in place. The rigidity with which the entire economy was planned from above contributed to the massive inefficiency and corruption that earned the system its subsequent infamy. But as Trotsky pointed out after his exile, it was entirely false to equate nationalised property with worker-controlled property. In fact, Soviet society was highly stratified and inegalitarian. The pyramidal structure of the planning bureaucracy was matched by unequal access to the best apartments, holiday homes and a vast quantity of other privileges reserved for the 'vanguard' and members of their families. Moreover, the economic system was based on a combination of compulsion and incentives. Such incentives came in the form of material rewards for the ministers of the most productive industrial sectors and their plant-level managers and workers. This system – Stakhanovism – basically complemented the Taylorian system of management with equally capitalist notions of reward. Trotsky characterised the resulting inequalities as indicative of the tension between the partial socialisation of the means of production, on one hand, and bourgeois norms of distribution, on the other. He presciently argued that this transitional form of political economy would eventually have to culminate in either the completion of the socialist revolution or the rebirth of capitalism. With the 'velvet revolutions' of 1989 behind us, we now know that it was State Socialism that could not last. The Chinese gerontocracy now argues that there is also an evolutionary path back to capitalism. This, we are now told, is the ineluctable fate of all non-capitalist

[24] McLellan, Marxism after Marx, pp. 131–4.

social formations, thus bringing us to the 'end of history'.[25]

The end of history?

Trotsky was not completely innocent of the charges of political
authoritarianism himself. He helped suppress the Kronstadt Soviet,
and was a defender of the power of the Party until it turned against
him. But he was entirely correct to argue that Socialism conceived as
the self-government of the people is incompatible with both the
economic and political privileges of a Party bureaucracy and the
leadership cults characteristic of 'existing Socialism'. It is this version
of radical thought that inspired *The Civil War in France* and *The State and
Revolution*; it was tragically lost with the degeneration of the Russian
Revolution. This became true not only of the Soviet Union and
Eastern Europe, but also of communist States around the globe like
China and Cuba claiming to adhere to Marxist-Leninist ideology.[26]
Equally menacing to those who remained faithful to Marx's early
ideas, however, was that these States not only failed to live up to the
promise of human emancipation that inspired them. They even
lacked the progressive aspects of the capitalist societies they were
supposed to bury. Workplace democracy was abolished in all but
name, while important freedoms of association, press, and opinion
which were extinguished in the Soviet Union also perished in the
other countries of 'existing socialism'. Naturally there were important differences in the degree of repressiveness between one
country and the next, but the general picture has been quite dismal.
Thus the 'velvet revolutions' of 1989 proceeded with the overwhelming support of the citizens of those countries. However,
rising levels of crime and unemployment in former East Germany
and other Eastern European countries is leading to the general
realisation that capitalism brings its own set of far-reaching problems. This has prompted the widespread feeling in the former
German Democratic Republic that, viewed retrospectively, the
choice between Honnecker and Kohl was in fact no real choice at
all.[27]

---

[25] Elliot, 'The Cards of Confusion', pp. 3–12; McLellan, *Marxism after Marx*, pp. 137–9;
Kornai, *The Socialist System*, pp. 53–61.

[26] Braverman, *Labour and Monopoly Capitalism*, pp. 11–13; Brus, *Socialist Ownership and
Political Systems*, pp. 35–6. The great exception is the Yugoslav attempt at Market
Socialism, which we shall examine in chapter 5.

[27] Gysi, 'Wird es einen demokratischen Sozialismus in der DDR geben?', and
Bahro, 'Alles kommt auf eine ökologische Alternative an', in Blohm and Herzberg

This brings us to the final point of our introduction. The history of Bolshevism and its variants in power has given the apologists of capitalism and the strong State an all too easy 'straw man' to demolish. Despite the fact that persistent inequalities in economic, political and social power continue to destabilise the industrial democracies of Europe, Japan and the United States, the left appears unable to challenge the political elitism and environmental degradation that characterise the advanced capitalist countries. But the end of State Socialism does not signify the end of history or that there are no alternatives to capitalism. The recurrent tendency of communist countries to deteriorate into one-party dictatorships was denounced by a number of non-Bolshevik left-wing currents. This tradition of libertarian socialist thought pre-dates the Bolshevik Revolution, and, it will be argued here, survives its demise. The aim of subsequent chapters will be to show what was lost with the consolidation of Bolshevism and its variants as the only concrete example of Socialism in power. In concluding, we will examine in what measure the theorists considered here can contribute to a revitalisation of the left today.

Such a revitalisation requires a refusal to concede ground to vacuous ideas about history coming to an end. The historical process is forever marked by the possibility for creative political intervention, that is, the desire to take an active role in consciously shaping our collective future. In doing so, we have no better guide than the mistakes of the past. With the collapse of the Soviet Union and its allies, it has become fashionable to argue that the path towards greater freedom and democracy lies in the rediscovery of Civil Society. Indeed, it seems reasonable that in order to combat an authoritarian State it is necessary to empower the forces of the civil sphere. It is certainly true that oppositional groups in the USSR and Eastern Europe did challenge and eventually defeat their governments in this way. But the harsh realities of post-Communist Eastern Europe reveal that the strategy to combat a Leviathan is not sufficient for building something positive in its place. Nonetheless, we are now assured that with the dismantling of socialist authoritarianism, we need only place our faith in competitive market struggle. Such measures shall supposedly allocate resources in a just and efficient way, and at the same time protect individual liberty against the State. Many such pleas suggest that we can restore the civil sphere with the

(ed. and intro.), *Nichts wird mehr so sein, wie es war*, pp. 64–75, and pp. 99–116. These are perhaps the most important essays, but the entire volume contains valuable contributions to a possible democratic socialist alternative in Germany.

pristine innocence it enjoyed prior to Hegel's diagnosis.[28] The massive dislocations witnessed in the East demonstrate that this is not the case. If dominated by market competition and the clash of private interests, Civil Society will be no more democratic or free in post-communist Europe than it was in the past. To this extent Marx's critique of Hegel retains its validity for us. We also know from Soviet history that the State cannot be trusted to harmonise the competing interests in the civil sphere. Civil Society – and most importantly the economy – must itself be democratised. The theorists and movements we will examine in the following chapters show that there are theoretical and practical reasons to believe that this can be done.

Needless to say, in global terms there has been a plethora of left-wing opponents of Bolshevism and Marxism-Leninism. In terms of the feasibility of this study, I have had to limit myself to an assessment of European currents. The fact is, however, that historically there have been numerous and important movements for revolutionary Socialism in the United States, Algeria, India and Israel, to name but a few. Moreover, in order to keep the focus of the study on the political economy of alternative conceptions of Socialism, I have had to omit Feminism and a number of important New Social Movements. However, each of these merit a study in their own right, and I could not hope to do justice to their contribution to political theory in the space provided by this book. Indeed, leaving aside the aforementioned movements, all the theories to be examined here deserve a far more lengthy analysis than the individual chapters of this book can provide. My hope is that this book will provide the stimulus for such studies in the future.

---

[28] This is the thrust of Robert F. Miller's introduction to Miller, *The Developments of Civil Society*, pp. 1–5, 9–10. Miller's is just one of many arguments of this kind that have followed the collapse of State Socialism.

1

Revolutionary Syndicalism

It will be recalled from our Introduction that Lenin and his followers argued that Marx's economic theories and his ideas on the Paris Commune implied the necessity of a violent overthrow of the parliamentary-democratic State and its substitution with the dictatorship of the proletariat. This dictatorship would control State power until all of the enemies of the revolution had been vanquished. Ruthless suppression of suspected class enemies was considered a small price to pay in return for safeguarding proletarian power. However, a significant number of socialists replied that the Bolshevik strategy was itself a deviation from Marxist theory, to the extent that: (1) Marx argued that the most developed capitalist countries (not Russia) would produce the first socialist revolutions, and indicate to the less developed countries their ineluctable future path of development; (2) Marx had shown that the capitalist economy was governed by 'iron laws', and interventionist political interventions could actually retard the revolution; (3) Marx and Engels admitted that in the most developed capitalist countries it was quite feasible that once the working class had become sufficiently aware of its mission, it would 'win the battle of democracy', as the *Communist Manifesto* states. That is, Socialism could be legislated from the ballot box: after all, the Paris Commune represented the extension of democracy, not its abolition. These became the fundamental positions of reformist Socialism, which is the precursor of many contemporary brands of Social Democracy. The revolutionary syndicalists were equally opposed to both Bolshevik and reformist conceptions of Socialism. Thus a quick look at the basic tenets of the reformists will allow us to see what the syndicalists were reacting against and what they proposed as an alternative. While syndicalist currents sprang up all across Europe, this chapter will focus on the two countries where the movement had its most developed theoretical articulation, in France and Italy.[1]

The strategy of creating a socialist society through the parliamentary democratic State was first given significant impetus in Germany with the writings of Eduard Bernstein and Karl Kautsky, as well as the gradualist approach of the German Social Democratic Party (SPD). In *Evolutionary Socialism* (1899) Bernstein challenged Marx's analysis of the inevitable fall of capitalism by marshalling a mass of empirical statistical evidence to show that capitalism was not moving towards either class polarisation or homogenisation of the class structure. In essence, Bernstein's claim was that without the political support of non-proletarian social classes, the working class would never by itself be strong enough to attain State power. The middle classes were proliferating and contributing to Germany's economic growth in medium and small enterprises. Moreover, across Europe peasant strata continued to flourish. Such tendencies were likely to continue for the foreseeable future. In the meantime, the only viable political strategy was to mount a steady though gradual attack on capitalism with progresive reforms aiming at public ownership of the means of production and the democratisation of the State. This approach was encapsulated in Bernstein's dictum that in the struggle for Socialism, 'the movement is everything'.[2]

Kautsky did not share Bernstein's optimism concerning the ability or even desirability of the working class forging alliances with other social classes. In fact, Kautsky argued, accumulation crises and underconsumption disequilibria would force large sections of the bourgeoisie into reactionary political positions. Marx had been correct to argue that capitalism would not be able to sustain itself, though it was not the task of the party to make the revolution. When the contradictions of capitalism brought the system to its knees, the

[1] Thus I will not be discussing the important ideas of British syndicalists like Tom Mann. It is also true that Revolutionary Syndicalism was a potent force in Spain. However, Annamaria Andreasi points out that if English, French and Italian revolutionary syndicalists regarded the trade union as both a means of struggle against capitalism as well as the basis of the future proletarian society, the Spanish were less exclusively concerned with the emancipation of the working class. They sought the conditions for the liberation of humanity as a whole, which separated them from their counterparts elsewhere in Europe. This made them much more receptive to Anarchism, as we shall see in the next chapter. See Andreasi, *L'Anarchismo*, p. 74. For the following discussion of syndicalist ideas in France and Italy I am indebted to Jeremy Jennings and David D. Roberts, who have provided the two major contributions to our understanding of the subject in English. I thus advise any interested student to read Jennings, *Syndicalism in France*, and Roberts, *The Syndicalist Tradition and Italian Fascism*. Jennings's book also examines reformist Syndicalism, which will not be dealt with here.

[2] McLellan, *Marxism after Marx*, pp. 22–6.

SPD would be ready to take over. This was the view put forward in *The Road to Power* of 1909. While Bernstein advocated gradual reforms, Kautsky seemed to be saying that the revolutionary process had its own logic that was not to be interfered with. Kautsky's position on the mass strike was symptomatic in this regard. While on the one hand he had since 1905–1906 advocated workers of all trades to simultaneously go out on strike, on the other hand he never specified when they should do this. He also adduced a series of preconditions that were not always likely to be present in a potentially revolutionary situation. Until the great day, however, Kautsky advocated parliamentary reform to heighten working-class consciousness and militancy; in this respect his views resembled Bernstein's.[3]

Variants of Bernstein's and Kautsky's positions represented the predominating strains of socialist thought throughout the period of the Second International (1889–1914). Though Kautsky's position was ostensibly more revolutionary, he relied heavily on Marx's notion that the development of capitalism would create the conditions of its own demise. Moreover, he believed that parliamentary democracy was an adequate vehicle for the socialisation of the means of production and popular control of the State. Though he stressed that the State, especially the executive, should be democratised, he had no vision of an alternative to the State like the Paris Commune.[4] When the Soviets appeared on the scene in the Russian Revolution, it seemed to many socialists that the radical democracy of the Commune had been brought to life once again. Kautsky, however, had a far more cautious assessment, chiding Lenin that either the Bolsheviks would jettison their particularly Jacobin interpretation of the dictatorship of the proletariat, or the Soviets would never survive. This led to a vitriolic exchange between Kautsky and Lenin in their respective works, *The Dictatorship of the Proletariat* and *The Proletarian Revolution and the Renegade Kautsky*. With the benefit of hindsight, it appears that Kautsky was correct on one fundamentally important point: there is a strict incompatibility between the presuppositions of a self-governing Civil Society, on one hand, and a single-party dictatorship in charge of the State and the economy, on the other. Thus the suppression of the Workers' Opposition and

---

[3] McLellan, *Marxism after Marx*, pp. 33–7.
[4] Kautsky, *The Class Struggle*, pp. 185–1; Hindess, 'Marxism and Parliamentary Democracy' in Hunt, *Marxism and Democracy*, pp. 22–5; Pierson, *Marxist Theory and Democratic Politics*, pp. 62–9.

Kronstadt came as no surprise to Kautsky and others who distrusted the Bolshevik dictatorship.[5]

French Revolutionary Syndicalism

Revolutionary Syndicalism was born in France as a critique of reformist Socialism. While the doctrine provided a sustained critique of more ostensibly revolutionary positions like Kautsky's, it also anticipated many of the problems inherent in the Bolshevik approach. The French revolutionary syndicalists rejected the reformist policies of socialist parliamentarians such as Jean Jaurès, Jules Guesde and Alexander Millerand, who at the turn of the century argued that the State would become the vehicle of working-class emancipation. These politicians maintained that the power of the bourgeoisie would be gradually eroded through proper education and social legislation, reflecting their faith in the Enlightenment ideals of reason and progress.[6] Such a view corresponded neatly with the widespread belief that the contradictions between the forces and relations of production were slowly but surely pushing society towards Socialism anyway. This approach carried two dangers: (1) that the working class might believe that it could passively wait for Socialism to be legislated by benignly disposed bourgeois politicians; (2) that bourgeois education and increased material gains within the capitalist system would convince workers that their highest aspirations lay in attaining a middle-class standard of living, with its attendant values of utilitarianism and leisure.[7]

Fernand Pelloutier was among the first to reject Millerand's conception of Socialism as a series of State-sponsored reforms. Born in 1867, Pelloutier moved from Republicanism to Marxism before deciding that Revolutionary Syndicalism was the doctrine of working-class emancipation. While his most well-known journalistic activity took place in his review *L'Ouvrier des deux mondes* (*The Worker of the Two Worlds*) between February 1897 and June 1899, his participation in the Bourses du Travail (Labour Exchange) will be remembered as his most lasting contribution to the syndicalist cause. His defence of the Bourses stemmed from his belief that if the proletariat sought to protect its interests in reigning institutions like the State and socialist political parties, the inexorable tendency to

---

[5] Salvadori, *Kautsky e la rivoluzione socialista, 1880–1938*, p. 253; Steenson, *Karl Kautsky, 1854–1938*, pp. 9–10, 204–6.

[6] Horowitz, *Radicalism and the Revolt against Reason*, p. 26.

[7] Hughes, *Consciousness and Society*, pp. 165–71.

reach compromises would deprive it of its vital moral fibre. In order to retain its independence from both the bourgeoisie and the State, the working class needed its own educational institutions which at the same time addressed the daily reality of the workers as pro-ducers. Pelloutier regarded the Bourses as the germ cell of a new proletarian civilisation. It was created in 1892 as a working-class educational institution. Educational services ranged from the setting up of libraries, museums of labour history, technical colleges, and schools for the education of workers' children. Under Pelloutier's leadership the Bourses quickly took on additional functions, such as providing information on how to find work, how to enter the *syndicats* (unions) and co-operatives, and how to battle employers in the event of strikes. General propaganda was also one of their major functions. Thus where possible the Bourses were to publish their own newspapers, and disseminate their information about the labour market to any interested proletarian organisations.[8]

Thus the Bourses strove to make the working class independent, dynamic, and morally pure, and to aid in the construction of a new centre of social authority outside of and in opposition to the existing State. Workers schooled in the Bourses represented the image of the future socialist individual – the producer – which the reformist socialists had abandoned in their search to integrate the working class into mainstream decadent and materialist French society. Pelloutier hoped that once educated in their own institutions, the producers would forge a new system of values which had nothing in common with the bourgeois lust for wealth. Technical skills, discipline and sacrifice were valued over wealth, comfort and leisure. The 'revaluation of existing values' was linked to the project of constituting a new social authority distinct from the existing coercive bureaucracy. The leaders of the producing class would form a technical elite capable of educating the whole of society in the duties demanded by the rigours of a producer's civilisation. Pelloutier was also concerned to distinguish the authority of the Bourses from a new form of collectivist State; the rights of individual producers were to be respected at all times. The Bourses were a superior form of political organisation which virtually eliminated the gulf separating the State and Civil Society, characteristic of parliamentary regimes.[9]

[8] Jennings, *Syndicalism in France*, pp. 19–21; Julliard, *Fernand Pelloutier*, pp. 13–14; Howe, *Radicalism and the Revolt against Reason*, pp. 26–8.

[9] Howe, *Radicalism and the Revolt against Reason*, pp. 28, 30–1, 36; Pelloutier, *Histoire des Bourses du Travail*, pp. 85–7, 159–71, and especially 168–71.

Pelloutier maintained that although both the trade unions and
Bourses were indispensable for the realisation of the self-
government of the producers, they were distinct institutions with
separate functions. The unions had the task of establishing the
material basis of a democratised Civil Society. In addition to co-ordinating production within a given sector of the economy, the unions
would send representatives to the Bourses. The Bourses, in their
turn, had the task of co-ordinating efforts between different sectors
of production. Thus in economic terms they functioned like
decentralised planning bodies. Within this form of democratic planning the Bourses were in charge of gathering and disseminating
information on production matters and consumer interests, thus
giving the producers an overarching view of the production process
in its entirety. But in practice it proved impossible to separate the
two institutions. When Pelloutier died in March 1901 he was succeeded by Georges Yvetot, with Paul Delesalle as his assistant. The
year 1901 also marked the election of Victor Griffuelhes to the head
of the French confederation of trade unions, the General Confederation of Labour (CGT, founded in 1895), with Emile Pouget as
his deputy. The next year the Bourses and the CGT merged. Yvetot,
Delesalle, Griffuelhes and Pouget thus became the leaders of a united
syndicalist movement, whose principal ideas they disseminated in
books, newspapers, pamphlets and CGT conferences. They were
not always theoretically consistent, nor did they succeed in producing a detailed account of the functioning of the capitalist
economy characteristic of much Marxist analysis. But as Jennings
notes, they displayed enormous courage – all but Delesalle were to
spend some time in prison.[10]

In an important sense, the syndicalist failure to produce their
own equivalent of *Capital* was not as serious a lacuna as it might seem.
The syndicalists stressed that proletarian action – not analysis –
would bring down the capitalist system. As the Bourses began to fade
in importance, the union became the central focus of the aspiration
for concerted proletarian action. Delesalle argued that, unlike political parties, which grouped people according to opinions and beliefs
that could change at any time, the unions were rooted in the daily
lives of the workers as producers. The goal was to make the workers
realise their power as world makers who refashioned the raw stuff of
nature in accordance with human needs. To this extent, the associated producers had no need of the capitalists nor the politicians,

socialist or otherwise. The capitalists simply owned the tools and raw materials that the workers transformed into useful products. The politicians were superfluous chatterboxes who did not understand production matters, but rather, made their careers on the backs of those who actually contributed to society's productive enterprise. This was no less true of Guesde and Millerand than it was of the representatives of the bourgeoisie. Indeed, anyone who saw Millerand fraternising with General Gallifet, who helped suppress the Paris Commune, could see that career politicians were to be mistrusted.[11]

French Revolutionary Syndicalism bequeathed its clearest statement of principles and aims in the Charter of Amiens. This document was drawn up in accordance with the decisions of the Amiens Congress of 1906. At Amiens the syndicalists declared their hostility towards parliamentary reform, socialist politicians, anarchists and all other 'sects' outside of the revolutionary trade union movement. Three currents were represented at the Congress: (1) reformist trade unionists such as Auguste Keufer, who argued for a strict separation of union and political activity and a concentration of union activity on professional security; (2) 'political' syndicalists such as Victor Renard who argued that trade union activity was unavoidably political and believed that in order to maximise the gains of the labour movement as a whole, it was necessary to strengthen ties between the French Socialist Party and the CGT; (3) revolutionary syndicalists who argued for the complete autonomy of the working class organised in trade unions, seeking the overthrow of the capitalist regime through the General Strike. The revolutionaires won a resounding 834–9 victory, approving Griffuelhes's motion. Despite the many crises which the CGT was to undergo, the ideas of the Charter of Amiens remained the guiding principles of the movement. Writing in the daily newspaper of the French Communist Party L'Humanité in 1920, Griffuelhes affirmed that it was at Amiens that Syndicalism, as a revolutionary ideology and movement distinct from Socialism, Marxism and Anarchism, was born. Two articles from the text of the Charter are of particular importance:

> In the daily fight, Syndicalism pursues the co-ordination of workers' struggles, and the increase of working class welfare through the achievement of immediate reforms such as a decrease in the hours of the working day, increased salaries, etc. . . . But this task is only one aspect of

[11] Louzon, Introduction to *Georges Sorel*, pp. 30–35; Jennings, *Syndicalism in France*, p. 38.

Syndicalism, which also prepares the ground for complete emancipation. This can only be realised by the expropriation of the capitalists
through the General Strike. The trade union, which today is a defensive
institution, will be, in the future, the basis of production, distribution,
and the re-organisation of society.[12]

In the pursuit of these immediate and long-term goals, the
syndicalists spurned not only socialist politicians, but political
parties in general. This was not to say that they ignored the problem
of leadership and the need to generate a new set of elites to replace
the politicians. Hostility towards professional politicians extended
to the notion of parliamentary democracy itself, which Pouget and
Hubert Lagardelle regarded as the rule of the all too easily manipulated mass electorate. The producers, by contrast, were an elite
group representing the most healthy and vital elements in society, in
a struggle against all the parasitic elements – the clergy, the army and
the bureaucracy. Universal suffrage, championed in the French
Revolution as an inalienable right, was used by the ruling class to
dupe the population into sacrifices for these parasites in the supposed interests of la patrie – the country. In reality, however, the
exploited everywhere had a vital interest in overthrowing the
exploiters. In this sense the syndicalists were advocating a return to
the class struggle as 'the alpha and beta of Marxism'. This essential
tenet had been lost due to the pernicious influence of reformist
politicians like Bernstein and Millerand on the one hand, and
metaphysicians and charlatans who distorted Marxism into an
abstract positive science, on the other. By stressing historical
inevitability, the pseudo-scientists had deprived Marxism of its
ability to inspire heroic intransigence, moral strength, and proletarian violence. As the leading theorist of Revolutionary
Syndicalism, Georges Sorel sought to restore these virtues to the
cause of proletarian self-emancipation.[13]

Born in 1847, Sorel was an engineer by profession. He retired
early, however, so that he might dedicate all of his time to writing
about the various subjects that impassioned him – science, art,
politics and philosophy. His first major foray into political theory
came near the turn of the century, when he participated in the 'crisis
of Marxism' debates with Bernstein, Benedetto Croce, Antonio
Labriola, and F. S. Merlino. The apparent discrepancy between

[12] Maitron, Histoire du mouvement anarchiste, p. 296; Julliard, Autonomie ouvriere, pp.
199–222.
[13] Louzon, Introduction, p. 41; Jennings, Syndicalism in France, p. 40; see also Jennings,
Georges Sorel, pp. 122–4.

Marxism's claim to be a science of society on one hand, and the failure of its most important predictions on the other, sparked a raging controversy throughout Europe. Sorel was initially attracted to Marxism as an epistemology with direct relevance to the methodology of the natural sciences. He also hoped that Marxism might offer the groundwork for a new morality appropriate for the machine age and the decline of religion. Since he believed that this new morality could not be provided by the decadent middle classes, Sorel had great hope that the working classes would create a new producers' society with its own forms of art, politics, and morality. In 1896 Sorel began his contribution to Le Devenir Social (The Social Process). During the months of October to December of that year he wrote his 'Study of Vico', where he sought to supplement the theory of historical materialism with Vico's conception of history as a cyclical process in which dominant and subaltern groups struggled to impose their way of life on the entire society. This was acccomplished not only with the use of force, but through symbolic rituals and mythical representations. From his reading of Vico's New Science, Sorel drew the conclusion that myth was a more powerful force than reason in moving people to action. This insight had direct implications for the proletarian aspriration to self-government.[14]

As Sorel became increasingly doubtful about the scientific status of Marxism, the labour theory of value and the theory of causality suggested by the base-superstructure model, he insisted that the working class must abandon rational-legal approaches to Socialism in favour of a mythical-poetic approach. As in the example of Christianity, the birth of new civilisations came about as the result of revolutions. But replacing bourgeois parliamentary representatives with socialist parliamentary representatives was completely insufficient to achieve the scope of change Sorel had in mind. The revolution would have to be an intellectual and moral reform which affected the daily existence of each individual producer. This entailed transformation not only of political and economic structures, but also of ways of looking at art, conceiving friendship and understanding death. The proletarian revolution would change our most basic understanding of the world, i.e., our 'common sense'. In order to achieve such dramatic change, the proletariat had to remain completely separate from the bourgeoisie and all its institutions, which had become thoroughly corrupted with the values of utility and strictly material forms of enrichment.[15]

[14] Sorel, 'Etude sur Vico', pp. 1033–4; Vico, La Scienza Nuova, pp. 391–415.
[15] Portis, Georges Sorel, pp. 74–80.

In a series of articles first published in *L'Humanité nouvelle* near the turn of the century under the title 'The Socialist Future of the Unions', Sorel asserted that the key to the foundation of a proletarian civilisation lay in a return to the healthy spirit of primitive man, which had not yet learned to see the world in terms of profit and self-interest. The right institutions and myths could recreate this primordial vitality. The working class thus needed its own myth – the General Strike – to return to the human race, albeit in a modern industrial context, its recurrent instinctual and intuitive understanding of reality. We will return to the idea of the General Strike when discussing the Italian revolutionary syndicalists, who borrowed their ideas on the subject from Sorel. For now let us simply say that for Sorel and his followers in France, Italy and elsewhere, the myth of the General Strike was the purest expression of the proletariat's will to irrevocably break with the bourgeois social order and establish its own system of law and morality.[16]

In 'The Socialist Future of the Unions', Sorel stressed that the morality of the producers could only be protected by securing the material foundations to support proletarian autonomy. He thus hoped for maximum expansion of the power of unions, workers' co-operatives and credit associations in order to develop an alternative economy within capitalist society. Eventually this network would make the workers completely independent of both capitalism and the parliamentary State. Such independence was the essential prerequisite of a new mode of production, that is, of revolution. In terms of day to day political strategy, union leaders had to take every possible opportunity to contest capitalist control of the production process. In terms of more long-term strategy, the unions had to co-ordinate their efforts with co-ops and other working-class institutions in order to imbue them with a distinctly proletarian morality. This morality had immmediate economic consequences:

> The *syndicats* can exert a great influence on the co-operatives to the point of dictating the direction they will take, especially at the moment of their formation. It is up to the *syndicats* to animate them with the proletarian spirit, to keep them from turning into simple economic relief societies and to encourage the elimination of anything which smacks of capitalist enterprise from them. What is really essential to elicit from the co-operatives is the development of new juridical conceptions. For example, conceptions such as 'seller-buyer' and 'loaner-borrower',

[16] Sorel, 'L'Avenir socialiste des syndicats', pp. 14–16, 77–85; Pastori, *Rivoluzione e continuità in Proudhon e Sorel*, p. 145.

which dominate the lives of workers in their relations with shopkeepers, should give way before conceptions involving co-operation and solidarity.[17]

Sorel shared the young Marx's view that there can be no real equality where people can be represented abstractly as equal citizens in the political sphere, while in their life as producers they are exploited in the civil sphere. The parliamentary State asked for a sum total of individual votes, as if society was comprised of separate atoms, each with their own interests. Within this framework majorities could theoretically decide to legislate major changes in the economic system and society's class structure. In reality, however, the socialist, as a materialist, should insist that social classes are the constituent elements of any given mode of production. As Marx explained in his *Introduction to the Preface of the Critique of Political Economy*, the mode of production is the key to understanding forms of political repre-sentation, social structure, ideology and morality. Reformist socialists like Kautsky and Guesde continually erred in believing that one could achieve a more just society by occupying positions of power within the existing State apparatus. At some point a socialist majority in parliament would then legislate Socialism into existence. But how could parliamentary Socialism be superimposed on the existing capitalist economy? Surely this ignored the vital point that the State apparatus was created to preserve the relations of power particular to a specific mode of production. Sorel was con-vinced that the unions, co-ops and other working class institutions could act in concert to create a new mode of production, and with it new forms of politics, ideology, art and morality would also be created.[18]

Thus socialist politicians and Marxist intellectuals prevented the working class from attacking the question of political power by the roots. They should have stressed the virtues of proletarian autonomy as the precondition of a new mode of production and new forms of social solidarity. Instead, they sought to integrate the working classes into the machinery of the capitalist economy and the parliamentary State. With the monopolisation of 'orthodox Marxism' by socialist politicians of one bent or another, Sorel aban-doned the doctrine in favour of Revolutionary Syndicalism. The deformation of Marxism by bourgeois intellectuals deprived it of any revolutionary value it once may have had. Sorel ridiculed the

[17] Sorel, 'L'Avenir socialiste des syndicats', in Portis, *Georges Sorel*, p. 78.
[18] Portis, *Georges Sorel*, pp. 84–7.

reformist attempt to control the bourgeois State by electoral or Blanquist means as 'the decomposition of Marxism'. His views on Marxism and his conversion to Revolutionary Syndicalism were given full expression in three important works of 1908: The Decomposition of Marxism, The Illusions of Progress, and his most famous work, Reflections on Violence. The Reflections were initially a series of articles, though it was not until 1908 that they were collected and published as a book. In the Reflections Sorel argued that as the revolutionary ideology of an entirely new civilisation, Syndicalism was irreconcilably opposed to its two rivals: parliamentary socialists of all kinds and humanitarian reform-minded capitalists, who sought to sap the proletariat of its moral strength by integrating it into bourgeois society with material comforts. Proletarian myths were necessary to prevent such incorporation. Myth was not to be confused with utopia, however; the latter was a product of the intellect and thus could be judged according to empirical canons of verification and refutation. Thus in the 'Defence of Lenin' of September 1919, Sorel expressed his unequivocal support for the Soviets in the Russian Revolution as purely proletarian organs of self-government:

> Lenin's discourse of May 1918 on the problems of power for the Soviets has no less importance than Marx's study of the civil war of 1871. It is possible that at the end of the day the Bolsheviks may surrender their arms . . . but the ideology of a new form of proletarian State will not perish. It will survive and attach itself to the myths that will take shape in the form of popular tales of the struggles of the Soviet Republic against the coalition of powerful capitalist interests.[19]

Despite the marginalisation of syndicalist currents in France after World War I, Pelloutier and Sorel bequeathed a powerful patrimony of ideas to militant workers across Europe. Revolutionaries in Italy, in particular, were particularly receptive to syndicalist ideas for reasons we shall now see.

Revolutionary Syndicalism in Italy

The conception of a democratised Civil Society capable of founding new forms of proletarian authority and morality was developed in Italy by Arturo Labriola, Enrico Leone, Sergio Panunzio and Paolo Orano. They were confident that Sorel offered an alternative to the

---

[19] Sorel, 'Plaidoyer pour Lénine' (September 1919) now in Réflexions sur la violence, fifth edition, pp. 442–3.

reformist strategy pursued by the leader of the Italian Socialist Party (PSI), Filippo Turati. The Italian revolutionary syndicalists maintained that the PSI strategy of gradual reform would lead to some species of State Socialism which differed little from capitalism. In Italy the syndicalist argument against the State borrowed ideas from Sorel and applied them to the perennial problem of the Italian south, or Mezzorgiorno. For Labriola, Leone, and other syndicalist theorists, many of whom were of southern origin themselves, the Italian proletariat had to follow the lessons of the Paris Commune, that is, that the working class could not lay hold of the ready-made State machinery and wield it in its own interests. Rather, it was the Italian State which maintained the alliance of northern industrialists and large southern landowning interests which undermined a truly popular-democratic outcome of the Risorgimento – the Italian unification movement which culminated in 1861.

The syndicalists challenged the general orientation of the PSI by citing Sorel's notion that the basis of a new society was contained within the trade union. They agreed that pleading with the State for reform of the existing socio-economic system would only produce passivity amongst the workers. But with the formation of the Italian Confederation of trade unions (CGL) in 1906 and its formal separation from the PSI, Italian Socialism in practice amounted to CGL demands for reform of capitalism's excesses, which the PSI would then seek to enact in the form of parliamentary legislation. Thus while the PSI formally claimed adherence to Marxist ideas, it appealed to the State for redistributive measures. In theory, it should have been seeking the 'withering away' of the State. Thus the Party posed no effective challenge to Prime Minister Giovanni Giolitti's strategy of preventing the emergence of rival centres of authority which could compete with the weak post-unification State. In so doing, the PSI acknowledged the legitimacy of formulating national policy in accordance with the electoral strength of the various interests which had parliamentary representation. This was not so much of a problem for the northern working class, which was defended by the PSI. But the southern peasants were badly organised and thus had virtually no parliamentary representation, even though they comprised the overwhelming majority of the population. Industrialisation of the north proceeded apace while the *Questione Meridionale* (Southern Question) continued to haunt all those who still cherished Giuseppe Mazzini's dream of a democratic nation with unity of purpose.[20]

In his book The History of Ten Years 1900-1909, Arturo Labriola gave a cogent account of how the Mezzogiorno became a virtual colony for the raw material and manpower needs of the industrial north. He explained that the south was assailed by four chronic problems: illiteracy, poor communication and transportation links between regions and between the urban centres and the countryside, the continuing existence of a mass of poor peasants, and, most importantly, the virtually uncontrolled domination of the large landowners, or latifundisti. Rather than solving these problems, the State passed palliative measures which slightly alleviated the misery, but never challenged the right of the landowners to exploit the peasants. Giolitti had guessed correctly that if workers' wages in the north could be kept artificially high through tariff protection, the revolutionary demands of the industrial working class could be channelled within the non-revolutionary PSI. The fact that such tariffs made it difficult for the southern peasants to export their products was not a problem, as long as Giolitti could somehow secure adequate profits for the latifundisti. The government thus made deals with the landowners in return for taxes on southern products and especially on southern grain to raise the revenue to keep the Giolitti regime in power. Though this made it extremely difficult for the peasants to sell their agricultural products to foreign buyers, they lacked adequate organisation. They might occasionally resort to brigandage, but when acting without the support of the industrial working class the peasants were incapable of mounting a political challenge to the regime. It thus became clear to Labriola, Leone and other syndicalists that the real political questions of the day were being resolved in terms of alliances between different powerful economic interests. The bourgeois-liberal notion of a legislature whose principal aim was to arrive at a universally acceptable formulation of the common good was purely chimerical. Indeed, the real politics of the country were taking place outside of and against the legislature. Given the realities of the Italian situation, the very idea of a parliamentary road to Socialism was simply pathetic.[21]

The syndicalists regarded the Questione Meridionale as the most urgent problem of the post-unification State.[22] Gaetano

[20] Gentile, Il mito dello Stato nuovo, pp. 5–9; Gentile, La Voce e l'età giolittiana, pp. 7–9.
[21] Labriola, Storia di dieci anni 1899–1909, p. 305; Soldani, La struttura del dominio, pp. 26–37; Marucco, Arturo Labriola, pp. 131–3.
[22] Labriola, Storia di dieci anni 1899–1909, pp. 305–6; Romano, Storia della questione meridionale, pp. 51–5; Salvadori, Il mito del buongoverno, pp. 90–1.

Salvemini and other defenders of the South argued that the right kind of federal system would limit the power of both the bureaucratic central State and powerful economic interests. This could provide a national solution to the problem of regional diversity. Salvemini agreed with Labriola that the problem of the Italian State preceded the related problem of abolishing capitalism. But in opposition to both Salvemini and reformist socialists, the syndicalists argued that the State was the product of social conflicts engendered by capitalism. However, this would not be altered by State Socialism. Both the State and capitalism had to be replaced by new political and economic institutions. Here the Italian syndicalists fashioned a synthesis of the ideas of Marx and Sorel. The political form for the economic emancipation of labour was the Commune, as Marx had said. In opposition to Marx's proposals for a planned economy, however, the economic content of a re-politicised civil sphere was to be realised in the working-class trade union, as Sorel had said.[23]

The synthesis of Marx and Sorel found its most complete expression in Labriola's works. Labriola saw that the experience of the Paris Commune had to be joined with Proudhon's economic ideas. The key issue was who controlled the means of production. State ownership signified the reign of the bureaucracy, hence the domination of a group of intellectuals over the working class – not the abolition of classes. Labriola emphasised that Proudhon's genius lay in demonstrating that the power of the State was equally as menacing as the power of capital. Syndicalism thus represented a pre-Bolshevik critique of what would later become Marxism-Leninism. The Italian syndicalists envisioned a producers' society in which groups of workers collectively controlled the means of production of their particular enterprises. Resources would be allocated by supply and demand, not the State planning apparatus. In this way, producers could respond to consumers' needs. Thus in addition to anticipating problems with Bolshevism, the Italians were direct precursors of the market socialist critique of State Socialism (chapter 5). In *Syndicalism and Reformism* of 1905, Labriola expressed his misgiving about the State socialist vision thus:

> But the substitution of State ownership for private ownership does not abolish the capitalist system of production. This system is distinguished by the separation of owners of the means of production and wage-

---

[23] Salvemini, *Scritti sulla Questione Meridionale*, pp. 152–3; Labriola, *Sindacalismo e riformismo*, pp. 14–16; Leone, 'L'azione elettorale e il socialismo', pp. 17–22; Panunzio, 'Socialismo, liberismo, anarchismo', pp. 72–4.

earners. Instead, Socialism seeks to create an autonomous and worker-controlled system of production which eliminates the distinctions between producers and owners of the means of production. With the passage of private industry to the state, the State bureaucracy replaces the capitalist and the worker remains a wage-earner.[24]

The syndicalists reasoned that if the new socialist economy was left to self-managed firms, local communes could tend to the political needs of the community. These Communes would have little in common with existing government bodies, since for the most part social life would be centred on the trade union. Like Sorel and Pelloutier in France, the Italians thought that once the State was abolished, workers' organisations in Civil Society would re-absorb most of the political functions of the central State. The unions would no longer fulfil the defensive tasks they performed in opposition to capitalism. They would become centres of education, technical training and the cultivation of new forms of industrial art. The Italians also followed Lagardelle, Pouget and other French syndicalists in rejecting the political party as a vehicle for the radical transformation of society. For revolutionary syndicalists everywhere, the Party was a symptom of the separation of State and Civil Society they sought to overcome. The overcoming of this separation was not to be accomplished through the Leninist Party-State, however, but rather through the reinvigoration of Civil Society and its principal institution – the trade union. Writing in the Italian journal *Il Divenire Sociale* (*The Social Process*, like its French equivalent) in 1906, Panunzio expressed the syndicalist position thus:

> in the syndicalist conception the trade union is not only an economic organism, but is also a 'political' and juridical organism. In opposition to those that only acknowledge the economic, corporative and apolitical character of the workers' trade union, we affirm that in the trade union the workers perform a wide range of social activities, not just economic ones. Thus they perform their multi-faceted intellectual, moral, juridical, political and artistic activities in the trade union ... they harmonise the needs of the individual with that of the collectivity of which they form a part.[25]

While the French, and Pelloutier in particular, affirmed that there were affinities between anarchist and syndicalist visions of the new

---

[24] Labriola, *Sindacalismo e riformismo*, pp. 15–16. See also Orano, 'Perché il sindacalismo non è popolare in Italia' in *Il Divenire Sociale*, II, (1907), pp. 225–7; Labriola, 'L'onesta polemica', pp. 185–200; Labriola, 'Sindacati e socialismo', pp. 259–61; Cavallari, *Classe dirigente*, pp. 27–32.
[25] Panunzio, 'Socialismo, liberismo, anarchismo', p. 73.

society, the Italians insisted on the differences between the two doctrines. Panunzio claimed that the syndicalist revolution would not abolish authority as such. Authority would be transferred from the abstract, bureaucratic and authoritarian power of the State to the intimate relation between fellow producers working within the trade union.[26] Rather than seeking gradual change through parliamentary bodies distant from the daily lives of ordinary citizens, Labriola and his followers proposed a revolutionary alliance between northern industrial workers and southern peasants outside of parliament. Once again they applied Sorel's ideas to the Italian situation, calling for a General Strike in order to shatter the existing alliance between industrialists and southern landowners.[27]

In September 1904 the the General Strike was launched, indicating the degree to which workers and peasants were alienated from their parliamentary representatives. Syndicalist support grew throughout Italy, as the year also recorded the highest number of strikes in the history of the unified State.[28] The events of 1904 gave further testimony to the gulf between the masses and reformist politicians. While there was a discernible shift of opinion to the right within the parliamentary Party, support for Revolutionary Syndicalism increased in the unions and the Chambers of Labour, which were the Italian equivalent of the French Bourses. According to the analysis of the Neapolitan journal *La Propaganda*, Italian socialists would have to choose between German style Social Democracy, or combining political, economic and social goals in a revolutionary programme that would attract mass support. Unfortunately, the division of the Italian labour movement into the PSI and CGL militated against any such general project of revolutionary change. This organisational structure would have to be superseded, in conjunction with a more precise formulation of the objectives of the General Strike. It was also necessary to co-ordinate trade-based and regional action by clearly delimiting the respective functions of the trade federations and the Chambers of Labour, whose past relations had been marred by rivalry and conflict. The syndicalist arguments against centralisation were bolstered by the fact that CGL tended to be dominated by reformists who sought to limit strike action at the national level. By contrast the local union leadership and Chambers frequently led offensive strikes and wildcat strikes in support of

[26] Panunzio, *La persistenza del diritto*, pp. X–XXII, pp. 1–64; Prezzolini, *La teoria sindacalista*, pp. 103–13.

[27] Arfe, *Storia del socialismo italiano*, p. 15; Furiozzi, *Sorel e l'Italia*, pp. 151–73.

[28] Procacci, *La lotta di classe*, pp. 375–400; Riosa, 'Alcuni elementi', pp. 75–6.

other striking workers. In January 1905 a Secretariat was established in Genoa to resolve these issues. But the Genoa Congress left important issues unresolved. The relationship between offensive and defensive strikes and the crucial issue of defining the spheres of action of the federations and Chambers were not settled.[29]

The publication of Arturo Labriola's *Reform and Social Revolution* accompanied the General Strike of 1904, thus marking the diffusion of Sorel's ideas in Italy. Following the Genoa Congress of January 1905, Enrico Leone and Paolo Mantica founded the syndicalist journal *Il Divenire Sociale*. Syndicalist theory and practice became dominated by the issue of the General Strike and the problem of developing a distinctive syndicalist world-view. This world-view was shaped by an excoriation of the bourgeois elements in the PSI, and an attempt to synthesise the ideas of Marx, Sorel, Proudhon, Merlino, Nietzsche and Bergson into a new revolutionary ideology of the producers.[30]

The General Strike was hailed as the most pure expression of proletarian heroism, and the only force capable of combatting the moderate bourgeois elements which corrupted parliamentary socialist politics. While Sorel and Labriola provided a devastating theoretical critique of reformism, the practical task was to discover new forms of struggle in which the proletariat could acquire the capacity for self-government. Both Sorel and Labriola emphasised the productivist basis of the proletarian revolution, which was to be a revolution against parasites as much as it was a revolution against capitalism. Thus the producers' revolution presupposed both an intransigent proletarian morality and an extremely high level of technical education among all workers. The General Strike was to rally workers with different capacities who had been in competition for jobs under the old regime. The new morality of solidarity would supplant the bourgeois notion of competitive individualism. In the process, friction between formerly antagonistic groups such as the Chambers of Labour and the trade federations would be eliminated. Anticipating Leninist type objections, the syndicalists held that what looked like a purely economic struggle, in reality addressed the political exigency of uniting all workers, regardless of wage and skill

---

[29] Riosa, 'Alcuni elementi', pp. 78–85; Procacci, *La lotta di classe in Italia*, pp. 255–63.
[30] Roberts, *The Syndicalist Tradition and Italian Fascism*, chapters 3, 7, 9 and 10. Roberts gives a cogent account of the originality and shortcomings of this attempted synthesis. See also Furiozzi, *Sorel e Italia*, pp. 165–73, and Riosa, 'Alcuni elementi', pp. 85–90.

differentials, in the concerted action necessary to construct a socialist economy from below.[31]

Revolutionary syndicalist support for the General Strike clashed with Turati's view that the effectiveness of strike action depended on wisely choosing when to strike. In most cases, however, the strike was to be reserved for exceptional circumstances, however, and even then only to give the parliamentary party more bargaining power in its quest for reforms. In contrast to the reformist view, the syndicalists praised strikes for the possibilities of spontaneous action they offered. Leone frequently articulated this view during his period as chief editor of Il Divenire Sociale between 1905 and 1910. Leone argued that the General Strike of 1904 and other instances of proletarian action proved that the working class would no longer participate in Giolitti's game of class compromise, a game in which Turati had been an all too willing player.[32] Reformists and revolutionary syndicalists battled for the leadership of the PSI until 1908, when the General Strike was declared dangerous and Syndicalism was denounced as contrary to the social democratic programme of the Party. The years immediately following the 1904 General Strike witnessed the consolidation of Turati's wing even in Sicily, where peasant revolts were frequent and often extremely violent. With Turati's aid, Giolitti managed to isolate the syndicalists. By maintaining the fragile alliance binding the economic interests of northern industrial workers with the political interests of northern industrialists and southern latifundisti, the revolutionary potential of the Italian proletariat was defused.[33]

Frustration with the PSI led a number of important syndicalists to seek alliances with nationalist elements during the Libyan war of 1911. Continued dissatisfaction with the PSI after World War I actually led some prominent syndicalists to compromise with Mussolini and Fascism. Emphasis on the General Strike faded given the imperative of supporting the War effort. Nonetheless, a core of syndicalist themes remained constant, all of which aimed at avoiding the most obvious mistake of parliamentary Socialism: accepting capitalism and parliamentary democracy just because they occasionally raised the material welfare of the proletariat. The syndicalists regarded this capitulation as evidence that gains made within the

---

[31] Soldani, La struttura del dominio, pp. 45–54.
[32] Leone, Il sindacalismo, pp. 8–15; and 'Per uno secondo congresso sindacalista', p. 101.
[33] Romano, Storia della questione meridionale, pp., 55–60; Melis, Introduction to Sindacalisti italiani.

system – even in the name of revolutionary doctrines – could not solve fundamental problems linked to modernity such as urban alienation and social atomisation. In this context syndicalists argued that the individual emancipation sketched in Marx's *German Ideology* was also inadequate. Marx envisaged the arrival of the solitary individual who hunts in the morning, fishes in the afternoon and writes poetry in the evening. The syndicalists argued that both Socialism and liberalism's emphasis on materialism, with its precedents in the works of Hobbes, Locke and Marx, were incapable of finding the bases of a more social and communal individuality. In this sense they were searching to ally their exaltation of the producer with existential themes about the nature of social existence. David Roberts has correctly underlined the 'metapolitical' elements in syndicalist writings, which can be traced to Sorel's positive assessment of the myth as a galvanising and unifying phenomenon.[34]

In syndicalist society, political participation would be more extensive and immediate than the traditional liberal divisions between public and private allowed. In Italy political life would be decentralised in response to the specific problems which plagued the Italian state, which was too weak to govern a fragmented and atomised Civil Society. The State was compelled to compensate for its lack of popular support with authoritarian and arbitrary interference in the civil sphere. To effectively deal with particular problems such as the *Questione Meridionale* and lack of political legitimacy, Labriola and Panunzio argued that it was necessary to socialise the individual in a corporate structure, and at the same time diffuse political power. Thus the trade unions were attractive as intermediate bodies in opposition to the prevalent individualism in bourgeois Civil Society and the authoritarian State. Panunzio and Olivetti stressed that this concern to diffuse rather than abolish authority in workers' organisations distinguished the syndicalist from the anarchist position. Producers organised in trade unions would manage economic enterprises collectively. They argued that it was necessary to have direct links between producers' unions, and to protect individual rights within the union itself. The autonomy of the union could only be safeguarded when free to govern its own affairs. Like the Yugoslav reformers we will examine in chapter 5, the Italian syndicalists insisted on the market as a means of defending

[34] Roberts, *The Syndicalist Tradition and Italian Fascism*, pp. 172–4; Panunzio, 'Per la revisione di socialismo, pp. 83–6, and X–XII (1917), pp. 139–42; Mantica, 'Mentre si attua, p. 1; Olivetti, 'Il manifesto dei sindacalisti', pp. 143–5, 158–9; Orano, 'Decentramento e lotta di classe', pp. 321–4.

producers' organisations from the interference of extraneous political bodies such as the Leninist Party-State.[35]

Italian Marxists such as Antonio Labriola and Amadeo Bordiga after him were also concerned to find solutions to problems like alienation and anomie. But Arturo Labriola and Leone in particular were much more perceptive than their Marxist counterparts of the problems connected with creating a cohesive and participatory Civil Society, without resorting to the authoritarian State to provide this cohesion. For Sorel the role of the Soviets in the Bolshevik revolution seemed to provide the key to Marx's original problem, the separation of the State from Civil Society and the attendant inequalities resulting from it. Hence in the 'Syndicalist Manifesto' of May 1921 in *Pagine Libere (Free Pages)*, A. O. Olivetti wrote that:

> The bourgeois revolutions champion the liberty of man and citizen, but the ideology that inspired them considers abstract man and the theoretical citizen, neglecting to consider man and citizen in his practical function as producer. Theoretically all men were proclaimed equal, but in effect the enormous inequality of fortunes and initial conditions prevented the exercise of freedom in the integral sense, and the citizen-worker became the proletarian.[36]

However, Olivetti goes on to explain that the mistake of Bolshevism, including its Italian variants, was to seek an end to economic inequality through a proletarian Leviathan, which could only result in a new form of bureaucratic collectivism. Lenin's castigation of the Workers' Opposition and the instituting of the Five-Year Plans presaged the absorption of Civil Society into the State, and the consequent loss of all producer autonomy to the State-level planners.[37] Syndicalist criticism of the Bolshevik revolution focused on the argument that the revolution was led by a vanguard of non-proletarian intellectuals rather than a mature industrial proletariat. In relatively backward countries like Russia and Italy this could only result in a partial revolution which forced the proletariat into alliances with other social groups whose class interests were not necessarily socialist. In the aftermath of their expulsion from the PSI, some syndicalists conceded that given prevailing economic conditions in Italy, the socialist project would have to be a long-term struggle. The news from Russia confirmed these suspicions, and added force to the syndicalist belief that the socialist revolution

---

[35] Olivetti, 'Ripresa', p. 2; Panunzio, 'Il socialismo in ritratto', pp. 293–4; Labriola, Storia di dieci anni, pp. 197–8.
[36] Olivetti, 'Il manifesto dei sindacalisti', pp. 146–7.
[37] Olivetti, 'Il manifesto dei sindacalisti' pp. 143–5.

in Italy could not be considered until the working class developed superior moral, political and technical capacities.[38]

In light of the manifest problems encountered by the Bolsheviks in Russia, the syndicalists were not inclined to the opinion that Italian capitalism was a spent force. The Italian revolution might more realistically take shape as the revolt of productive capitalists and highly-skilled workers against finance capital, corrupt politicians, the bureaucracy and the clergy. It was becoming clear that Italy was riven by a plethora of social problems; some were direct results of the capital–labour conflict, others were not. The international communist movement founded the Comintern in Moscow in March 1919 to further the cause of world revolution. But the syndicalists clamoured that the Comintern's tendency to trace all problems in all countries back to class conflict had to be modified in terms of Italian history and culture. As it became clear that the Comintern was to become an instrument of Russian foreign policy, many syndicalists called for a return to the ideals of Mazzini. Mazzini was an Italian revolutionary who appeared to offer an alternative to both liberalism and Bolshevism. The idea was that by rekindling national-popular revolutionary traditions one could build a sense of community in Italy. Mazzini rejected the French Revolution as the source of abstract conceptions of liberty and individualism. Yet he was equally convinced that though class conflict could tear a country apart, a revolutionary's main task was to build anew. Class struggle would have to be supplemented with new constructive myths.[39]

During the years 1917–19 Sergio Panunzio attempted an original synthesis of Marxism and liberalism highly characteristic of the Italian syndicalist attempt to infuse social theory with new ideas. In a series of articles in the journal *Vie Nuove* (*New Ways*) he maintained that the Marxist-Leninist understanding of the political as an epi-phenomenon of the class struggle precluded an accurate picture of the complexity of social life. Marx's system shared the defects of all systems, that is, to explain away phenomena that were difficult to account for within the parameters of the system as unimportant or transitory. In reality, however, various social struggles took place within national political cultures which could not be reduced to the relations of production. Like Labriola and Leone, Panunzio argued that class interests coexisted with the interests of individuals as

[38] Orano, 'Il controllo operaio', pp. 473–6; Lanzillo, *La rivoluzione del dopoguerra*, pp. 141–2; Roberts, *The Syndicalist Tradition and Italian Fascism*, pp. 154–6.
[39] Roberts, *The Syndicalist Tradition and Italian Fascism*, p. 169; Olivetti, 'La fiaba del governo', p. 420.

members of a community, and that these could come into conflict. This multi-faceted aspect of reality required new forms of political organisation which reduced man to neither the bourgeois citizen nor the proletarian producer. Such complexity was an ineluctable feature of any modern society riven on several different axes. Labriola, Leone, Panunzio and others disagreed with the Marxist view that the tension between producer and citizen could be abolished. Instead, new forms of economy and social solidarity in Civil Society might usher in new forms of participatory democracy that did not share the atomistic presuppositions of parliamentarism.[40]

Concluding remarks

The syndicalist analysis of modern society obviously left many questions unanswered. First, even if several syndicalist theorists acknowledged that conflict occurred in many areas of social life, the overwhelming thrust of their analysis was directed at liberating the *producers*. They had very little to say about consumers, members of the local community and unemployed people like the elderly. A more radical approach would have been to insist simultaneously on worker control of the production process within individual enterprises, coupled with decentralised forms of political control of the economy at the local, regional and national levels. Obviously the specific form and scope of political control would depend on the sector of production in question. Railways, utilities, communication networks and other such large-scale industry would be best regulated at a national or even international level. Democratically-managed small and medium-sized enterprises could produce for more regional and local markets. As we shall see in chapter 4, the Guild socialists realised that other sections and interests in society had to have their own machinery of government existing alongside the system of industrial democracy. This continues to be an urgent practical and theoretical issue in contemporary debates that is explored in the conclusion to this book.[41]

For a time the French syndicalists also seemed to have a structured dialogue between producers, consumers and citizens in mind. They argued that under capitalism workers had to buy the products of their own labour on a market over which they had no control. This was to take the odious example of workers having to buy their

---

[40] Panunzio, 'Per la revisione del socialismo', p. 141, and XIII–XIV, (1917), pp. 170–3; Soldani, *La struttura del dominio*, pp. 55–60.
[41] Glass, *The Responsible Society*, p. 5.

basic necessities from the company store, and to transfer the example to the level of the economy as a whole. The syndicalist alternative was to entrust major production decisions for individual sectors of the economy to the confederation of revolutionary trade unions (CGT). At the same time, the Bourses du Travail would co-ordinate the activities of different sectors of production. The Bourses also had extensive informational, educational and cultural functions connected to libraries, museums, restaurants and workers' co-ops. In this way the unions and Bourses enlarged their sphere of activity into fields stretching far beyond what people today would typically associate with 'trade unionism'. Pelloutier and Sorel correctly perceived that when pursuing the distinct aims for which they were ideally suited, the unions and the Bourses constituted an alternative economy that was autonomous from capitalism. It was this autonomy that potentially freed the workers from the authoritarian State which regulated the capitalist economy. But, tragically, the Bourses and the CGT merged in 1901, and shortly thereafter the Bourses quickly faded in importance. Pelloutier's untimely death in 1901 accelerated this highly inauspicious trend in the French labour movement. Then in 1906, the Charter of Amiens ascribed all of the previous functions of the Bourses to the CGT, when the confederation was simply not capable of performing such a wide range of activities.[42]

The Italian syndicalists never reached the same level of sophistication as Pelloutier, Sorel and the militants of the Bourses du Travail. They argued simply that the market was to be used to establish direct links between producer groups and thereby keep the State at bay. They thus neglected the wider educational and informational issues that the Bourses sought to champion. Moreover, Marx and other economists had been correct to see that market competition produced monopolies which would eventually undermine the producer autonomy the syndicalists valued so highly. Panunzio and others affirmed that monopoly could be prevented by the authority of some new form of State. Yet beyond an appeal to resurrect the Paris Commune, it remained unclear how this State might function, and how much autonomy the trade unions would enjoy within its territory. As we shall see in chapter 5, these political and economic problems with markets remain of vital importance in contemporary debates about Market Socialism.[43]

[42] Julliard, Fernand Pelloutier, pp. 142–3; Portis, Georges Sorel, pp. 67–74.
[43] Christopher Eaton Gunn, Workers Self-Management, pp. 191–2; Baldassarre, Introduction to Baldassarre, I limiti della democrazia, pp. xviii–xix.

As the syndicalist movement foundered in Italy, Panunzio and others accepted the subordination of the unions to the Mussolini's Corporate State. Many of the syndicalist themes on the need to combat anomie and to give a greater social dimension to individual's lives within a participatory State were compatible with Italian fascist ideology. In this context the adherence of a number of important syndicalists like Panunzio, Orano and Olivetti to Italian Fascism was not altogether surprising.[44] In concluding, we could say that both French and Italian syndicalists attempted to combine their stress on producer autonomy with ethical themes conspicuously absent in both Marxism and parliamentary Socialism. If the excessive praise of the trade union marks one of Syndicalism's crucial limitations, it is also the stress on the inadequacies of political parties and the dangers of the State which reserves Syndicalism a place in the family of revolutionary alternatives to Bolshevism, Jacobinism and Social Democracy. While all the other conceptions of Socialism we will look at derived an enormous amount of inspiration from the syndicalist distrust of parties and the State, this was particularly true of the anarchists, to whom we now turn.

---

[44] It should be noted that some prominent Italian syndicalists such as Enrico Leone did not support Fascism, and others, such as Arturo Labriola and Cesare Longobardi actively fought against it. A more controversial subject is the role of syndicalists like Hubert Lagardelle in French Fascism. For an analysis see Sternhell, *La Droite revolutionnaire* and *Ni droite ni gauche*.

2

Anarchism

Anarchism has too often been dismissed as either utopian or senselessly violent. On the one hand it is certainly true that its stormy legacy is closely connected to a history of bombings and assassinations. On the other hand it is also the case that the anarchists have posed and continue to pose theoretical and practical questions that have not been satisfactorily answered by more widely accepted political doctrines. By challenging the arguments for the sanctity of private property and the legitimacy of government, the anarchist tradition has called the major premises of the social order into question. In discussing the legitimate claims of government the liberal political philosopher Joseph Raz has admitted that:

> Our conclusions are modest. They are so modest that some may find them disconcerting. Those who consent to the authority of reasonably just governments or respect their laws are subject to their authority and have an obligation to obey their laws. But not everyone does consent . . . Those who do not are not necessarily guilty of any wrongdoing.[1]

Anarchist thinkers and militants have successfully expanded the sense in which people in the above cited quotation are 'not necessarily guilty of any wrongdoing' into a coherent attack on all forms of unaccountable power, whether it be that of capital or government. Moreover, in the Spanish Civil War of 1936–39, the socio-political protests of May 1968, and contemporary resistance to the dominant forms of political organisation, Anarchism has time and again shown itself to be a libertarian alternative to the political movements inspired by Marxism-Leninism. By stressing that the social revolution must be the work of grassroots organisations rather than vanguard political parties, anarchists have often been confused with

---

[1] Raz, *The Morality of Freedom*, p. 99. For a convincing account of how anarchist arguments can be used to refute the claims of political authority, see Wolff, *In Defence of Anarchism*.

revolutionary syndicalists, thereby obscuring the originality of the anarchist critique of both liberalism and Marxism. In chapter 6 we will see that contemporary Communitarian Anarchism fundamentally departs from syndicalist ideas on productivism and the unquestioned hegemony of the working class in the new order. The present chapter will show that while there is some overlap between anarchist and syndicalist ideas on the organisation of production in a liberated social order, anarchist ideas are distinct in a number of important respects which need clarification. This historical perspective provides an introduction to the anarchist tradition, while the second section of chapter 6 focuses on current anarchist debates on the appropriate economy for a self-governing Civil Society. We will look first at anarchist arguments against the syndicalist's unqualified celebration of the trade union, before going on to a more general exposition of anarchist ideas on production and society.[2]

Anarchism and Syndicalism

It will be recalled from the last chapter that in the Charter of Amiens of 1906, French revolutionary syndicalists declared that the trade union, far from being a merely defensive institution appropriate for workers' struggles within the capitalist system, was actually the ideal form of organisation for the overthrow of capitalism and the establishment of a producers' society.[3] The Amiens Congress was followed by the Amsterdam Congress of August 1907, where several prominent anarchists contested the claims of Revolutionary Syndicalism. Chief amongst the anarchist contingent were the Italian Errico Malatesta and the Russian prince Peter Kropotkin. By this time Malatesta was already 53 years old, and a legend, due to his heroic feats dating back to the First International. Malatesta's opponent was the 25-year-old editor of *La Vie Ouvriere (The Working Life)* Pierre Monatte, who, after reading Pelloutier's history of the Bourses du Travail, switched his allegiance from Anarchism to Syndicalism. Monatte

---

[2] Once again, in order to keep the focus on the political economy of non-Bolshevik conceptions of Socialism, I have had to leave out the important contributions of anarchist thinkers whose primary concern was justifying unconditional individual liberty. But those interested in such individualistic conceptions of Anarchism are urged to read the works of William Godwin and Max Stirner, to name but a few of such revolutionaires. There are also distinctly capitalist forms of Anarchism, but these will not be discussed here. Interested readers should consult chapter 3 of Miller, *Anarchism*.

[3] Alfred Rosmer, *Le mouvement ouvrier pendant la guerre*, p. 34; Dolleans, *Histoire du mouvement ouvrier*, Vol. 2.

argued that Syndicalism was the most appropriate response to the anarchist tendency to become absorbed in abstract philosophical debates on absolute liberty, when in fact only proletarian action could transform the world. Malatesta replied that while he was in no way against militant trade unionism, such activity could only be considered a means to more general revolutionary ends. Organising workers on the basis of their various trades encouraged them to conflate the interests of their particular branch of industry with the social revolution as a whole. Within a capitalist framework, railway workers could go on strike, but only at the expense of miners who needed to sell coal via the railway network in order to make a living. In fact, Malatesta warned, the future anarchist society would depend vitally on the capacity of workers in various industries to co-ordinate their efforts in the construction of a non-capitalist and non-statist economy. As for the General Strike, he argued that it too was useful as a means to rally workers together, but that the idea that the capitalists would relinquish their power simply because the workers refused to work was an absurdity. The workers were obviously much poorer than the bosses, and would eventually be starved back into the factories and fields. Again, a truly revolutionary programme would necessarily stress the need for workers of different industries to collaborate – not to concentrate on the material interests of any one sector at any one time.[4]

The anti-syndicalist current in French anarchist circles had already been taking shape at the turn of the century and in the years leading up to the Congress of Amiens. Writing in journals such as Le Libertaire and L'Anarchie, anarchist militants decried the tendency of the trade union movement to improve the living conditions of the working class, thereby decreasing its instinct for revolt. Moreover, far from representing the germ cells of an egalitarian society, the unions were themselves organised hierarchically. Thus rather than liberating the individual from social oppression, the union actually disciplined the worker with the promise of a steady wage within capitalism. Writing in L'Anarchie in October 1905, Andre Lorulet expressed the anarchist position:

> For us, there are no classes, we only recognise individuals. Among these individuals, some are disposed towards good relations with us. To them we respond with reciprocity, since they are anarchists, while the rest contribute to the functioning of the society that oppresses us. They support this society with their adherence to its laws, by voting, by

---

[4] Maitron, *Histoire du mouvement anarchiste*, pp. 302–4; see also Malatesta, *Scritti, Vol. I*, pp. 346–8, and Cerrito's Introduzione to Malatesta, *Scritti scelti*, p. 34.

joining unions, and obeying its general principles: they are our enemies. Whether they are workers or bosses is of no consequence . . . We address our propaganda to both.[5]

Lorulet echoed recurrent themes in the work of Malatesta and the Russian anarchist Michael Bakunin, arguing that regardless of their position in the division of labour, many workers regarded the union as the best vehicle to attain higher living standards, increased consumption, and power over other groups in society – most notably women, the unemployed, and even other groups of workers in less prospering industries. Bakunin insisted that one of the chief weaknesses of Marxism was its inordinate stress on the leading role of highly skilled industrial workers, when these were the individuals most likely to emulate bourgeois lifestyles. He was convinced that the peasants and urban poor had retained their instinct of revolt, and would therefore be more useful to the revolution than Marx's class-conscious proletariat. Only those who had no material or moral stake in the present system could be counted on to rebel against it. Yet Bakunin was also aware of the need to develop alternative economies within capitalism until revolutionary consciousness spread to all oppressed social strata. He argued that producer and consumer co-ops and proletarian credit societies were better suited to this task than the large trade union federations. The latter simply organised the workers according to the needs of capital.[6]

Jean Grave observed that the trade union had undeniably led to the improvement of working class living standards, but at the very high price of creating a 'labour aristocracy' between the working class and the capitalists. In order for the union to effectively protect the workers of a given trade, it had to impose stringent conditions on who could join, such that many of the unskilled and semi-skilled were left outside of union organisation. High fees for entry to the union and a long period of apprenticeship were often used to restrict mass access. For Grave this was merely a logical consequence of the fact that the union's task was to secure a high price for the commodity of labour, which could only be done by restricting the labour supply. For the considereable number of workers who did not have the necessary skills or family connections to enter a trade union, the results were often disastrous. In the long run this form of organisation would only serve to protect the interests of some

[5] Andre Lorulet quoted in Maitron, *Histoire du mouvement anarchiste*, p. 256; Jennings, *Syndicalism in France*, pp. 24–6.
[6] Bakunin, *Marxism, Freedom and the State*, pp. 47–9; Dolgoff (ed.), *Bakunin on Anarchy*, p. 173; Cahill, 'Co-operatives and Anarchism', pp. 235–43.

favoured members of the working class at the expense of the rest, thereby dividing the class as a whole and jeopardising the revolution.

These objections to the syndicalist position were first cited by Pierre-Joseph Proudhon (1809–65), the founder of Anarchism, and the originator of the idea of self-management. Proudhon's ideas are particularly important for our purposes, since he envisaged an alternative to capitalism and State Socialism which at the same time allocated a major role to market competition. To this extent his arguments foreshadow ideas that we will return to in the context of more contemporary debates about Market Socialism in chapter 5.[7]

Anarchism as justice: Mutualism and Federalism

Proudhon is perhaps most remembered for his remark that 'property is theft'. In reality, however, he was not against property ownership as such. In fact, his theory of Anarchism aims at establishing a framework for a just distribution of property, based on the idea of the exchange of equivalents between bargaining units with equal power. Under capitalist forms of ownership, workers were forced to sell their labour for far less than it was worth, forcing them further and further into a state of dependence and subservience. In the meantime, the capitalist accumulated the fruits of the worker's labour. Proudhon advocated a radical redistribution of property in order to ensure that each individual could exchange the equivalent of labour time for property with any other individual, with the aggregate result being that everyone possessed the same amount of property – provided that they had worked the same number of hours. Since the market would now be balanced by different trading partners exchanging equivalents, no one partner could gain enough leverage to buy any other, and a state of perfect equilibrium would quickly be reached and maintained. While the individual worker-exchanger was Proudhon's ideal, he also realised that under modern conditions of production, workers of different trades combined their efforts in the *atelier*, or worshop. Thus he advocated that the various workers in these workshops form trading firms, or, as he called them, mutualist associations.[8]

Proudhon envisaged three sectors of production. In the agricultural sector production would be the work of individual proprietors. In the artisanal sector individual productive efforts

[7] Grave, L'Anarchisme, pp. 242–5; Bancal, Proudhon, Vol. II, p. 17.
[8] Proudhon, De la capacité politique, (CP), pp. 75–84.

would be balanced by voluntary joint efforts performed by several workers. Mutualist firms were to undertake production in the industrial sector, where large-scale industry was useful in promoting efficiency. Regardless of whether it was individuals, small groups or mutualist firms that were exchanging, producers sold their goods on the market. However, rather than letting price be determined by the typical competitve equilibrium between supply and demand, price was to be fixed by the labour-hours necessary to produce a given product. To this end money would be abolished, and a People's Bank would issue notes to each worker for the number of hours they had spent in production. Thus notes indicating labour hours spent could be traded for the equivalent in goods and services. The People's Bank would provide credit without interest to help mutualist firms buy the necessary tools for their enterprise. While workers would thus have access to land and property, they would not be able to earn money by renting land or machinery – all income was derived exclusively through labour.[9]

For Proudhon the following conditions of membership should obtain within each mutualist association:

1 Each individual member had the same rights as any other active member.
2 Each member had to assume their share of the less rewarding tasks.
3 Each member should have a number of important technical skills which would allow them to contribute in several areas of production and give him or her an overall view of the productive enterprise as a whole.
4 All functions were to be allocated on the basis of elections, the rules for which had to be approved by the membership of the firm as a whole.
5 Remuneration was to be awarded on the basis of the nature of the task a worker performs, the skill required to do the job, and the sphere of competence to which it extended. Each member is entitled to remuneration in proportion to their contribution.
6 A member of the mutualist association can leave the firm at any time, demanding their final payment and giving up all further say in the operation of the firm.

[9] Miller, *Anarchism*, pp. 10–11; Joll, *The Anarchists*, pp. 47–8. For an incisive analytical discussion of Marx's criticisms of Proudhon's theory of value and his other concepts, see Paul Thomas, *Karl Marx and the Anarchists*, pp. 204–14. For an account of the brief history of the People's Bank which Proudhon did actually manage to set up, see Dolleans, *Proudhon*, pp. 175–202.

7 The workers in the firm elect their managers and accountants on
   the basis of demonstrated ability and experience, who will in turn
   provide the greatest possible instruction to all less knowledgeable
   workers.[10]

It has often been observed that within Proudhon's mutualist
framework there is a great emphasis on pluralism. He believed that
in order to put an end to the unequal bargaining power of capitalists
and workers it was necessary to set up a network of heterogeneous
forces, thus creating relations of mutual interdependence and
reciprocity between them. If it were the case that each mutualist firm
supplied something that another needed, no single unit could gain
the upper hand over the others. Proudhon believed that in such a
society individual needs would multiply, so that in addition to
economic diversity there would also be a flourishing of different
ideas, personalities and talents. It has been observed that the
emphasis on pluralism, bargaining and reciprocal need that figures
so strongly in Proudhon is conspicuously absent in Marx. Where
Marx seems to have relied on little other than social pressure to
ensure compliance with the norms of a harmonious socialist society,
Proudhon stressed bargaining, debate, and compromise between
social and economic units.[11]

Proudhon's moral outrage against capitalism took on political
and economic dimensions in the aftermath of the revolutionary
upheavals which swept Europe in 1848. His social theory began with
a critique of the very idea that the State, as some vaunted
embodiment of reason, could rightfully discharge society's most
essential functions through the service of career politicians and
bureaucrats. While this form of *étatisme* reached its pinnacle with the
French Revolution, the revolutions of the nineteenth century indicated to Proudhon that Civil Society was gaining consciousness of its
separate identity and independence from the State. As consciousness and moral revolt against the State grew, the civil sphere would
demand greater and greater autonomy for its network of mutualist
associations and Communes. But by 1857, the number of self-
managed firms which had sprung into existence with such fervour in
1848 had declined from several hundred to a mere twenty. Proudhon denounced the reigning proclivity of the firms towards
narrowly self-interested behaviour, thus lending credence to Marx's

[10] Proudhon, CP, pp. 84–104; Guerin, L'Anarchisme.
[11] Thomas, Karl Marx and the Anarchists, pp. 180–2; Ritter, The Political Thought of Pierre-
Joseph Proudhon, pp. 126–38, and Anarchism, p. 50.

depiction of Civil Society as a commercial battlefield. Mutualist firms were internally marked by the hierarchy and privilege characteristic of capitalist firms: managers and the highly skilled exploited their advantages without scruple. Proudhon's sober assessment of these developments led him to modify his initial ideas on mutualism. In his last book, *On the Political Capacity of the Working Classes*, Proudhon states that the principle that he calls Mutualism in the economic sphere is nothing other than Federalism in the political sphere.[12]

In this work of 1864 Proudhon conceded that perhaps he had been wrong to think that the economy could be set up as a complex equilibrium of forces between equally powerful bargaining units. Some mutualist firms would certainly be more successful than others in selling their products and reaching high levels of growth. The inevitable discrepancies in the performances of the various firms would cause tensions in the system requiring coordination of some kind – though *not* that which could be secured through the State. Socialists like Louis Blanc, and later Marx, correctly perceived that Proudhon's proposals sought to combine the contradictory principles of competition and solidarity. Proudhon acknowledged that these principles were, in fact, in conflict. He retorted that the just society would find the most libertarian means possible to attenuate – not abolish – the great tension between freedom and order. The State socialist approach was not a solution, but a cancellation of the most crucial element of the equation: freedom. Writing in 1864 with remarkable foresight Proudhon exclaims that centrally planned Communism would in practice be:

> A compact democracy having the appearance of being founded on the dictatorship of the masses, but in which the masses have no more power than is necessary to ensure a general serfdom in accordance with the following precepts and principles borrowed from the old absolutism: indivisibility of public power, all-consuming centralisation, systematic destruction of all individual, corporate and regional thought (regarded as disruptive) and inquisitorial police.[13]

Proudhon's book was inspired by the Manifesto of the 60, written in 1861 as an electoral manifesto by a group of workers whose ideas were similar to his own. Following Babeuf's *Manifesto of the Equals* and *The Communist Manifesto*, Proudhon hoped to establish mutualism and federalism as the founding principles of a self-governing Civil Society. He called for an economy organised as an agrarian-industrial

[12] Proudhon, CP, p. 144; Guerin, *L'Anarchisme*, pp. 56–7.
[13] Proudhon, CP, translated and quoted in Buber, *Paths in Utopia*, p. 31.

federation of mutualist firms, interpenetrating with a political structure based on the division of authority, and the maximum autonomy
for regional associations and Communes. To counter the parochial
tendencies characteristic of some of the mutualist firms he observed,
Proudhon now argued that it would be necessary for the Communes
to lend out the means of production to the various economic enterprises within its territory. In this way the enterprises would understand that although they enjoyed the use of such instruments, they
did not own them. In keeping with his insistence that economic
justice required the fair exchange of equivalent amounts of labour,
Proudhon maintained that political justice demanded the proper
balance between freedom and order. In the federalist State, the
authoritarian concept of government would be superseded by the
much more flexible notion of contract. However, Proudhon's
notion of contract is very different from the social contract theory we
normally associate with Hobbes and Locke. For the latter theorists,
especially Hobbes, once the citizenry has vested the government
with power, it renounces its right to self-government; the State
becomes a completely separate and autonomous set of institutions.
For Proudhon, the political units in his federal State were to be
comprised of free and equal individuals who had reached
agreeement spontaneously. As such, any agreements could be ter-
minated from the moment one of the parties decided to contract out
of its obligations.[14]

In Proudhon's scheme any organised group can ally itself with
another and thereby constitute a unit of the State. Units are not
ordered hierarchically, and all relations with larger units require
express contractual consent. Thus if within a given region a local
Commune decides not to join the regional government, the regional
government has no authority over the Commune. Individual Communes could come together to accomplish a given task such as
building public transport systems, and then return to their former
status as independent political units. Importantly, all mutualist firms
working within a given territory were in no way compelled to
recognise the authority of local political units. They might choose to
do so, though at all times reserving the right to terminate any such
relationship. There is no Hobbesian State to act as an all-powerful
adjudicating force to settle disputes between mutualist firms and
local Communes. Proudhon believed that once educated and aware

[14] Comisso, *Workers' Control*, pp. 25–6.

of the virtues of such a system, bargaining, discussion, and compromise could reconcile a plurality of viewpoints and interests.

However, this left important theoretical issues unresolved which have been real problems in the actual practice of self-management around the globe. On the one hand Proudhon argued that the Communes should lend out the means of production to the various economic enterprises within its territory. On the other, he maintained that all mutualist firms working within a given territory were in no way compelled to recognise the authority of local political units. Thus Proudhon evaded the tension between liberty and authority rather than solving it, as he had claimed against Marx. Moreover, it is clear that in Proudhon's scheme the worker who produces more popular goods will earn their firm consistently higher rewards than firms with less fortunate workers. While the most successful firms amass large fortunes the others stagnate and decline; meanwhile there is no recognised State to redress the balance. Perfect competition would no longer obtain, and many of the supposed virtues of the system would be sacrificed. In *On the Political Capacity of the Working Classes* Proudhon admits that:

> the superior worker who conceives and executes more radidly, secures a greater yield and a better quality product than another, who knows how to combine his technical talents with the genius of management, thus exceding the average, will receive a greater salary. He will be able to earn the equivalent of one and a half, twice, or three days of work in a day . . . If justice disregards no one, it does not disregard talent either.[15]

Unsurprisingly, this formulation was not acceptable to a number of anarchists who saw that, in practice, Proudhon's system could well produce the kinds of inequalities it was designed to abolish. Several came to the conclusion that true liberation could only be accomplished by *abolishing market competition while retaining market exchange*. The communitarian anarchists argued that this idea could guide the construction of a non-statist economy designed solely for the satisfaction of individual need.

---

[15] Proudhon, CP, pp. 95–6; Ritter, *The Political Thought of Proudhon*, pp. 137–8; Guerin, *L'Anarchisme*, pp. 59–60. George Crowder argues that inegalitarian outcomes are indeed likely within Proudhon's system. Crowder maintains that despite this problem, Proudhon's emphasis on fair exchange and justice provides a means of avoiding the vast inequality that is the source of corruption and domination in capitalist societies. See Crowder, *Classical Anarchism*, pp. 108–9. For a convincing critique of Crowder's views, see Ruth Kinna, 'George Crowder's *Classical Anarchism*, pp. 51–8.

Anarchism as community

In *Ideas on Social Organisation* (1876), Bakunin's friend and comrade James Guillaume argued that it would be possible to abolish commerce altogether. He envisaged the creation of a Bank of Exchange in each Commune, which would receive all the goods produced within its territory. The value of the goods would be determined not by labour-hours, but by committees comprised of local trade unionists and Commune members on the basis of statistical information on production costs, relative scarcity, etc. In return for depositing the goods produced, individual workers would receive vouchers entitling them to what they needed, which would be valid throughout the federation of Communes. Some vouchers would be for goods to be consumed within the Commune where the worker lived, while others would allow the individual to obtain things from other Communes. Builders and other workers who did not turn out immediately usable products were to receive longer-term vouchers corresponding to the probable duration of the projects they worked on. Likewise, people working for the Commune performing administrative services would obtain similar vouchers. The Bank of Exchange in each Commune thus had to store all the goods produced in its territory, as well as maintain communication with the Banks of other Communes to determine what it needed to import from them in terms of food, raw materials, or finished products of any nature. Guillaume believed that as the different Banks of Exchange and Communes co-ordinated their activity to an ever greater extent, exchange itself would give way to distribution on purely needs-based criteria. It would probably be necessary, at least temporarily, to restrict the distribution of scarce goods. But eventually technological innovation – now freed from the distortions of an economy based on greed and profit – would create a situation where all the basic necessities would be distributed on demand, and most other goods and services would be readily available.[16]

The abolition of all vestiges of the wages system was central to the political thought of Peter Kropotkin, who went further than even Bakunin in articulating the possibility of a completely needs-based Communitarian Anarchism. Kropotkin began his analysis with the premise that remuneration according to performance was not only likely to encourage egotism and inequality, but that the very notion was incoherent. In 1899 he launched an attack on this principle in *The Wage System*. First, Kropotkin argued that despite its history in

---

[16] Guillaume, *Idées sur l'organisation sociale*,, pp. 349–52.

State socialist circles as a great model of the future proletarian model of government, the Paris Commune of 1871 represented a deviation from communist ideals. The Commune erred in deciding to pay the members of the Communal Council substantially more than the national guards on the ramparts. This was to distinguish between the significance of the distinct but equally important contributions made by the various workers to the defence of the Commune. When the revolution made the appropriation of all socially created wealth a reality, such bourgeois norms of justice would have to be abandoned in all spheres of human activity. Kropotkin demanded to know who deserved the highest wages deriving from the working of a mine: was it those who had made the initial investment, those who realised that coal was likely to be found on the chosen site, those who had actually gone into the pits, or those who transported the coal to all the centres of industry where it was needed? Since all are indispensable to the process as a whole, all should have equal reward for their labour. Any attempt to differentiate the contribution of each worker was bound to become submerged in futile calculations that did not correspond to the basic fact that all had different skills, but all were equally needed:

> Service rendered to society, be it labour in factory or field, or moral service, cannot be rendered in monetary units. There cannot be an exact measure of its value, either of what has been improperly called its value in exchange or in its value in use. If we see two individuals, both working for years, for five hours daily, for the community, at two different occupations equally pleasing to them, we can say that, taken in all, their labours are roughly equivalent. But their work could not be broken up into fractions, so that the product of each day, each hour, or minute of the labour of one should be worth the produce of each minute and each hour of that of the other . . . We cannot take what one man has done during any two hours and say that this produce is worth exactly twice as much as the produce of one hours's work from another individual and reward each proportionally.[17]

In his most famous works, The Conquest of Bread (1892), Fields, Factories and Workshops (1899), and Mutual Aid (1902), Kropotkin maintained that neither representative government nor the wages system were compatible with a truly democratised economy and society. The abolition of individual property would launch society into completely new directions which could not fail to modify the daily relations between individuals and transform previous conceptions of justice. The lesson of the Paris Commune was not merely that 'the working class cannot simply lay hold of the ready-made State machine and wield it for its own purposes'. Self-government had to be extended and enriched, that is, applied on more than a simply territorial basis to embrace the individual in his or her existence as a producer and participant in all the activities required for the life of a community to function: education, the family, environmental protection, etc.[18]

The Conquest of Bread is Kropotkin's manual for the anarchist transformation of society, while Mutual Aid outlines his ideas on social organisation. Fields, Factories and Workshops contains three key ideas of particular relevance to our discussion of the economic bases of a radically democratised Civil Society. In this book Kropotkin tells us that: (1) there is no technical reason why industry and agriculture must necessarily be large-scale operations; (2) as the most basic of necessities, food in particular could be produced plentifully for local markets through intensive farming techniques; and (3) in more general terms, decentralised production for local consumption is entirely feasible. Kropotkin linked these points with the imperative of changing the education system. In order for his decentralised communitarian vision to work, all members of society would need a strong grounding in the technical/practical sciences of agriculture and industry. Both Mutual Aid and Fields, Factories and Workshops stressed that each person could choose which producer and civic groups they wanted to join. In this way no individual or group could be forced to work full time in unpleasant or alienating employment. As a consequence, people would spontaneously work together in the productive and civic associations of their choice, donating the fruits of their collective activity to the Commune, from where it was freely available on the basis of need. The resulting society would be highly decentralised, self-sufficient and community oriented. To accomplish large-scale projects, such as the construction of railway networks, workers within a given territory could federate with workers of other regions, though Kropotkin continually stressed the virtues of autarky. This was because small-scale enterprise gave people an overall view of the productive needs of the community which was denied to them under the normal conditions of factory production. This would also enable the community to maintain its independence from the hostile forces that would no doubt attempt to subvert its 'dangerous experiment'.[19]

[18] Pengan, 'Anarcho-Communism', pp. 70–6.
[19] Ward, Introduction to Kropotkin, Fields, Factories and Workshops, pp. 9–14. Ward has

In order to make an economy whose founding principle was distribution according to need possible, groups of workers would deliver their products to the local Commune for distribution. Kropotkin was confident that once private property and the barbaric specialisation of modern production was abolished, people would organise amongst themselves and decide what to produce on the basis of their interests and talents. As naturally creative beings, there would no longer be any need to provide people with ridiculous incentive schemes, which essentially boiled down to encouraging them to be greedy and self-centred. That was a vestige of the capitalist system, in which the 'fortunate' exercised their right to give up independently chosen work in exchange for steady wages, high status, and mental labour, while the unfortunate were condemned to a life of continual economic uncertainty, low status, and extremely tedious labour. Decentralisation and self-sufficiency would enable individual Communes to adjust producer and consumer interests without too much difficulty. As a geographer of considerable renown, Kropotkin amassed a wealth of data on agricultural production around the world to support his argument. He cited the example of the gardeners in the suburbs of Paris, who made their own soil from manure, and managed to cultivate fruits and vegetables in great abundance. This was possible without artificial fertiliser, on small plots, and with such success that it was possible not only to feed Paris but export the surplus to England. It is in this sense that Kropotkin has been seen as precursor of organic farming and gardening. He favoured a harmonious integration of the agricultural and industrial sectors of each country, so that no country would be dependent on another. He argued further that contrary to what Marx believed, it was no longer possible for a country to develop as England had. England was able to benefit from the raw materials of other countries to construct its industrial base, while the countries that merely supplied raw materials were forever dependent on their ability to export. Kropotkin was correct in asserting that the division of the world into industrial and agrarian nations would inexorably lead to wars for the capture of new markets and cheap labour.[20]

In 'Modern Science and Anarchism' (1913), Kropotkin

put together a highly useful abridged version of Kropotkin's original text with the title *Fields, Factories and Workshops Tomorrow*. For a Kropotkin-inspired vision of modern anarchist practice, see Ward's *Anarchy in Action*.

[20] Kropotkin, 'Anarchist Communism', pp. 48–52, 77–8; Marshall, *Demanding the Impossible*, pp. 326–7; Miller, 'Kropotkin', pp. 323–4; Capouja and Thomas (eds), Introduction to *The Essential Kropotkin*, pp. X–XI.

expressed his disagreement with Proudhonian schemes based on labour cheques and competitive incentives, and outlined his own version of what he called 'free Communism'. His objections to Proudhon can be summarised as follows: since the aggregate wealth and skill on hand in any community or country was the result of the collective efforts of countless past generations, it was pointless to award people differential wages as if individual contributions could be disentangled from the immense collective enterprise of housing, clothing, feeding and educating an entire society. Moreover, such differentiations would justify existing barriers and perpetuate the educational and hereditary privileges which had always accompanied discrepancies in wealth. Of course Kropotkin encountered the time-worn objection that without wage differentials no one would work. We have seen that he did not consider this a problem – once people had been freed from the shackles of the present division of labour. The present system condemned the vast majority to years of uncreative, physically demanding labour, while those who had been lucky in one way or another had access to the most interesting and lucrative work. Under such conditions it was unsurprising that it was difficult to make people work! By contrast, in the anarchist society, work would be selected in relation to what interested the worker, who would naturally find partners who shared similar proclivities. Echoing Kropotkin's ideas at the turn of the century, Alexander Berkman declared that in reality there is no such thing as laziness:

> What we call a lazy man is generally a square man in a round hole. That is, the right man in the wrong place. And you will always find that when a fellow is in the wrong place, he will be inefficient or shiftless. For so-called laziness and a good deal of inefficiency are merely unfitness, misplacement. If you are compelled to do the thing you are unfitted for by your inclinations or temperament, you will be inefficient at it; if you are forced to do work you are not interested in, you will be lazy at it.[21]

There would still be the need to dispose of waste, clean the streets, etc., but this could be done by everyone in their neighbourhoods. In this way no one would have to spend their entire life as a sanitation worker. In any case, once people had to clean up after themselves they would be much more aware of the problem, and not childishly say 'that's not my job'. Obviously priority would have to be made for supplying the basics – food, shelter, health and education. But

---

[21] Berkman, *What is Communist Anarchism?*, p. 198. See also Berkman's *ABC of Anarchism*.

Kropotkin reasoned that modern technology made such provision possible on a highly reduced working schedule, thus opening up considerable time for the cultivation of the arts and sciences, recreation, etc. For the obstinate few who refused to work under these conditions, social pressure would be applied. If this did not work, as a last resort measure a recalcitrant person could be banished from the community. In no case, however, would this unpleasant task be performed by the State or its penal institutions.[22]

For Kropotkin, the State had shown itself to be remarkably incompetent in satisfying basic human needs. He claimed that in any case, apart from the landowners, capitalists, police, army and members of the church hierarchy, the authority of the State had always been contested by the majority of people in Civil Society. Following the decline of the medieval city and the subsequent rise of the modern State, a variety of new social institutions sprang into existence in the civil sphere. Such mutual aid societies performed the essential tasks of co-operation that the State was too remote and bureaucratic to attend to on a daily basis. As we shall see in chapter 6, a number of contemporary anarchists have modelled their ideas on the theory of mutual aid in Kropotkin's later writings. He argued that if a species is to survive and evolve in a positive direction in the face of environmental challenges, it will develop various means of helping its members. Contrary to competitive applications of the theory of evolution such as those of Herbert Spencer, Kropotkin argued that the survival of the human species depended on its ability to develop higher forms of social co-operation corresponding to the growing complexity of human needs. Once physical needs had been satisfied, there was the entire range of emotional, creative and intellectual needs which atrophied under the oppressive and inegalitarian conditions of industrial capitalism. In 'Anarchist Communism' Kropotkin reminds us that while we have recorded every minute of parliamentary proceedings, we know remarkably little about the history of co-operation, which, despite State encroachments, continues to flourish. Indeed, Kropotkin argued that we could learn a great deal more from the history of voluntary associations like the Lifeboat Association than we could from the dreary register of parliamentary bills. For most people it was as if the State did not exist: millions of human beings lived and died with only the slightest contact with the State, since their day-to-day transactions depended on the far more immediate need to keep their word in

[22] Kropotkin, 'Modern Science and Anarchism', p. 173; Miller, 'Kropotkin', pp. 325–7.

any exchange of goods or services. In order for such transactions to continue and for both parties to an agreement to benefit, there was mutual interest in maintaining the confidence of the members of the community that one dealt with every day. Again, those who refused to co-operate would simply not enjoy the fruits of co-operative life: food, clothing, shelter, association, etc., which would in most cases reform even the most obstinate free riders.[23]

Can Civil Society actually realise co-operative forms of decentralised production and distribution along the lines advocated by Guillaume, Bakunin and Kropotkin? To answer this question we must look briefly at the practical achievements of the anarchist movement in the Spanish Civil War and elsewhere.

Anarchism in practice: Spain and beyond

Like Proudhon in France, opponents of centralised political authority in Spain applauded the ideals of the French Revolution – liberty, equality and fraternity – while disagreeing violently with the Jacobin attempt to realise these aspirations from above. Spain's long history of intensely held local allegiances and regional traditions naturally tended to generate opposition to the general centralist trend across Europe that followed 1789. In the 1830s and 1840s, Pi y Margall, a lower middle-class Catalan working in a Madrid bank began reading Proudhon and decided that the Frenchman's ideas on Federalism actually fit quite well with Spanish realities. His translation of Proudhon's *On Federalism* became a kind of manifesto for the Spanish federalist movement, which began gaining momentum in the 1860s. The federalist impulse was then given a dramatic anarchist turn in 1868 with the arrival in Spain of Bakunin's supporters Giuseppe Fanelli and Elie Reclus. Bakunin had just founded the semi-clandestine anarchist Alliance for Social Democracy, and Fanelli and Reclus were sent to explore the possibilities of attracting members among the radical Spanish peasantry. By 1873, there were approximately fifty-thousand followers of Bakunin in Spain, who carried the conviction that the State's authority was based on power it had usurped from the Civil Society, and that in its place it was necessary to set up a self-governing civil sphere comprised of political Communes and economic co-operatives.[24]

In 1871, the bitter rivalry between Marx and Bakunin produced

---

[23] Kropotkin, 'Anarchist Communism', pp. 64–70.
[24] Gerald Brenan, 'Anarchism in Spain', pp. 369–73; Thomas, 'Anarchist Labour Federations, pp. 507–8.

a split within the First International. While the majority of European sections followed Marx, the Spanish remained faithful to Bakunin, consciously brandishing the banner of Anarchism rather than Marxism. The first anarchist groups were primarily comprised of printers, schoolteachers and students. They united in a general campaign to educate the peasantry, moving from village to village almost in the manner of itinerant friars. When trade unions were legalised in 1881 Anarchism spread to the cities, especially to Barcelona, where many Andalusian peasants migrated in search of steady employment. Both in the country and town the General Strike was vaunted as the most appropriate means for bringing down the existing social order. Many thought that violent and decisive action would rapidly demolish the State. Thus they made little effort to consolidate the resources that would be necessary for a protracted struggle of the kind that took place during the Civil War of 1936–39. When the Spanish unions united as the National Confederation of Labour (CNT) in 1911, there was no strike fund. In fact as late as 1936 there was only one paid trade union ófficial. The urban workers of the CNT drew inspiration from the French syndicalist idea of electing workers from individual factories to regional and national bodies which would negotiate co-operative solutions to problems of housing, food, health, etc. The rural anarchists, especially in strongholds like Andalusia, were committed to protecting the local way of life in small villages. This could only be accomplished by working together and resisting the intrusions of the State and big capital. Hatred of the forces of the State and capitalism became prevalent throughout Andalusia and sections of Barcelona. By 1927 the Spanish Anarchist Federation (FAI) welcomed into its ranks all those (even criminals) who opposed the bourgeois order. Indeed, the exploits of some of its most legendary members, such as Buenaventura Durruti, have contributed to Anarchism's reputation as a violent creed.[25]

Although the anarchists were the most powerful contingent in opposition to Franco's army at the time of the outbreak of civil war, they were often in conflict with the other factions of the republican cause. Dissent between anarchists, socialists and communists made it extremely difficult to establish local Communes on a stable foundation, to say nothing of the problems connected with co-ordinating activity between Communes. In total, more than one thousand collectives were formed during the civil war, ranging in

[25] Thomas, 'Anarchist Labour Federations in the Spanish Civil War', pp. 508–10.

size from less than one hundred people to several thousand. In the province of Aragon approximately three-quarters of the land was administered by co-operatives working in conjunction with local Communes. The most important decisions were made by the collaboration of the town Commune and a political committee comprised largely of CNT militants. For every ten or so workers a delegate was sent to the committee to relay information and receive guidance. Expropriating large estates and collectivisation of the small holdings of the peasantry placed all arable land in the hands of the community, while raw materials and tools also became common property. Though hiring labour was not allowed, those who had individual land holdings could continue to work independently if they so desired. Relations between individual proprietors and collective enterprises seemed to have varied from peaceful coexistence to direct confrontation. In the latter case the individual proprietors were usually forced into ceding their property to the community.[26]

David Miller reports that though varying methods of production and distribution were adopted, all of the collective enterprises made significant steps towards the communitarian anarchist goal of distribution according to need. In some cases this was achieved in the manner proposed by Guillaume and Kropotkin, that is, by placing all produced goods in a central warehouse and making them available upon request. It is easy to understand that, given civil war conditions, this degree of co-operation was possible almost exclusively with regard to basic necessities. Other goods had to be rationed, or purchased with allowances each family in the community received on the basis of the number of people they housed. In defiance of the old system, several towns actually decided to print their own currency to replace the peseta. Within such self-regulating communities medical care was free, while requests for the means of production were handled by the appropriate trade union delegate after being examined by the political committee. Moreover, Berkman's comments on laziness seem to have been borne out: under the new conditions of co-operative production there was surprisingly little in the way of attempting to benefit from the work of others without actually working oneself.[27]

It has also been maintained that, in addition to realising a limited form of Communitarian Anarchism, agricultural production during

[26] Miller, *Anarchism*, pp. 161–2; Peirats in Dolgoff, *The Anarchist Collectives*, pp. 112–20.
[27] Breitbart, 'The Integration of Community and Environment,' p. 100; Miller, *Anarchism*, pp. 161–2; Borkenau, *The Spanish Cockpit*, pp. 166–70; Leval, *Collectives in the Spanish Revolution*, Chapter 8.

the 1936–37 period actually increased.[28] This provided evidence for a cherished anarchist belief, namely that private property and the wage system of remuneration decrease the motivation to work. Apart from the obvious exception of piecework – in the few places that this barbaric practice could be forced on the workers – remuneration through wages suffers the obvious defect that reward is the same regardless of the level of output. What incentive was there for an agricultural worker to improve crop yields when such increases benefited the landlord, who was a despised figure in the first place? Obviously things were completely different when the worker was producing together with fellow workers to satisfy their common needs. On the one hand it is arguable that this sense of community was tremendously enhanced by the urgency created by the war. On the other hand it is undeniable that the war opened up new possibilities that may have contributed to a genuine social revolution. Sadly, the victory of the forces of reaction made any such revolution impossible.[29]

However great the difficulties of sustaining anarchist production and distribution in the countryside, these problems were even greater in the cities. There were generally two approaches to common ownership in the urban centres, determined by the attitude of the now expropriated owner. The owner was permitted to stay on and contribute whatever technical and managerial skills they could offer, while overall direction was provided by a CNT-led management committee. If the former owner left, the CNT would assume total control of the operation, as in the case of the Barcelona bus company. Apart from Alcoy and a few other cities, Barcelona was really the heart of the anarchist urban collectivisation programme. As can be imagined, however, the cities faced problems that the semi-autonomous agricultural communities did not have to deal with. Primary amongst these was co-ordination of different branches of industry. While small agricultural communities could attain self-sufficiency by pooling their foodstuffs and trading for what they needed, large-scale industry could not aspire to autonomy in any meaningful sense. Each branch had to rely on several others to maintain production, not all of which were in the same city. To repair buses metal workers conceivably needed tools for which they could offer nothing immediately usable (like food) in return. This raised the problem of money and credit. As we have seen, the

---

[28] Peirats, La CNT en la Revolucion Espanola, Vol. II, pp. 97–110; Thomas, 'Anarchist Agrarian Collectives', pp. 253–60.

[29] Bookchin, The Spanish Anarchists, pp. 308–13.

anarchist ideal society would have no money. While this was feasible in the countryside, the needs of large-scale industry and the rigours of war precluded any such experiment in the cities. At the outbreak of the war a Central Labour Bank and an Economic Council were created to help plan production, provide credit on favourable terms and facilitate transactions between co-operatives. However, many difficulties were encountered in supplying the various enterprises with the necessary tools and raw materials. As a result, a large number were forced to work at half speed or part time.[30]

An additional problem was that although there was a general commitment to collective production and distribution according to need, there was the obvious difficulty that some workers had saved more money than others, and that those workers with families had far greater needs than those that were single. While the Economic Council was responsible for resolving the tensions arising from this situation, it enjoyed only limited success. In response to growing inequalities, socialists and communists charged that some form of central authority was required to plan and co-ordinate production, and to redistribute income when necessary. Indeed, this raised what is still today an extremely important question: how can equality be ensured without relying on the State to redress the varying fortunes of different economic units? If for some anarchists the Proudhonian formula of reward according to performance was unacceptable, there remained the as yet unanswered question of how to ensure widespread redistribution without the State, that is, voluntary redistribution.[31]

Towards the end of October 1936, with Franco's troops approaching Madrid, the CNT in Barcelona was forced to engage in joint action with the socialist trade union federation (UGT), and to cease the confiscation of privately owned businesses. A rather stunning concession to traditional politics was made the next month when four CNT leaders became ministers in the socialist government of Largo Caballero. In order to attract foreign support and stem the fascist advance such measures were necessary. Collectivisation was slowly abandoned, and the popular militias were gradually assimilated into a traditional army structure, further demoralising anarchist militants. Spanish communists, aided by Moscow,

---

[30] Miller, *Anarchism*, pp. 164–5; Leval, *Collectives in the Spanish Revolution*, pp. 230–40.
[31] Miller, *Anarchism*, pp. 166–8; Joll, *The Anarchists*, pp. 236–56. George Orwell's novel *Homage to Catalonia* gives a convincing portrayal of Barcelona as both a place where the 'working class was in the saddle', as well as a city torn apart by the conflicting factions of the left.

embarked on a policy designed to replace the CNT committees with communist-controlled municipal governments. This state of internecine rivalry culminated in May 1937, when the predominantly communist police of Barcelona attacked the Telephone Exchange, under anarchist control. By now the defeat of the anarchists and the republican cause was imminent.[32]

Despite the eventual fall of the Spanish republic, the anarchist collectives have left an invaluable source of experiences for our understanding of the likely problems in a revolutionary situation, as well as the possibilites for radical change given propitious circumstances. In their short history the collectives and anarchist communities realised a remarkable degree of social solidarity, providing direct evidence for the claim that people do not need to be forced to work or respect each other when living with a profound sense of solidarity with their fellows. Under such conditions it is not unreasonable to expect that they will participate in community life and enjoy work to a far greater extent. Finally, as Miller argues, the Spanish experience proves that 'industrial democracy of a quite radical kind is not a pipedream, given the appropriate background conditions'.[33]

After the defeat of the republican cause in Spain, Anarchism entered a period of dormancy throughout Europe. Intellectuals and university students continued to be attracted to the doctrine, but there was no mass movement to give practical impetus to its radical rejection of the principles of both capitalism as an economic system and the State as the source of legitimate political authority. This quiescence came to an abrupt end when the foundations of capitalism and the State were dramatically called into question by the student protests which swept Europe and the United States in the 1960s.[34] These protests reached their apogee in March–June 1968, especially in France, when students occupied administrative build-

---

[32] Peirats, Los Anarquistas', pp. 293–306; Marshall, Demanding the Impossible, pp. 464–7.

[33] Miller, Anarchism, p. 167.

[34] Although this discussion will focus on France, radical protest movements inspired by anarchist ideas erupted throughout Europe. For the 1968 events during the 'hot autumn' in Italy, see Lumley, States of Emergency, Part III. For an analysis of events in Britain and Holland, see the articles by Stafford and Jong in Apter and Joll (eds), Anarchism Today.

ings in Bordeaux, Strasbourg, and the Sorbonne in Paris.[35]

There was a definite anarchist thread running through the student protests. Aside from a certain amount of support for Maoism, they rejected Bolshevism in all its forms. The protests aimed at the creation of a libertarian Socialism compatible with the newly emerging forms of contestation: Feminism, Ecologism, and other new social movements which were gaining momentum outside of and against the traditional party system.[36] The party system was severely criticised for channelling all dissent into the struggle for control of the State bureaucracy and the right to administer capitalism. To the rebelling students this was no less true of the French Communist Party (PCF) than it was of the Gaullists and the other parties. Indeed, the events vindicated this assessment: when on 13 May the students and workers united in a massive demonstration against Charles de Gaulle's government, the PCF tried to control the situation by calling for a coalition cabinet comprised of socialists and communists. However, this was not the aim of the students or workers, whose primary objective was self-management, not the rule of a bureaucracy now calling itself 'communist' or 'socialist'. This orientation had already been established in the preceding months. On Friday 22 March, after the arrest of six militants of the National Vietnam Committee, a group of students gathered to protest at Nanterre University in Paris, where they decided to occupy the administrative buildings. That evening, more than 150 students met in the staff common room and participated in heated debates on the nature of contemporary capitalism, imperialism and the French State. The results of these debates were summarised in a document that was then widely distributed to students and workers, while the coalition of students adopted the name of 'The 22 March Movement'. The movement was severely critical of the traditional institutions of the left, especially the PCF and CGT, and consciously avoided any authoritarian forms of organisation resembling a political party. Indeed, radical participatory democracy was the avowed goal of the student militants, for which they were castigated as

[35] The French historian Richard Gombin has questioned the content of the Anarchism of the participants in the French events of 1968, though he does concede that student coalitions such as the Movement of 22 March certainly drew on anarchist ideas in their demands for greater democracy in the French higher education system. See Gombin, 'The Ideology and Practice of Contestation, pp. 15–20.

[36] For an analysis of the links between the new social movements and Anarchism, see Bookchin, 'New Social Movements', pp. 259–74.

anarchists by the PCF leadership.[37]

From an anarchist perspective, the call for self-management and participatory structures in all areas of Civil Society gave 1968 its enduring significance. It was a socialist challenge to the PCF, the CGT, and other purportedly left-wing institutions which had become ossified and hierarchical. At a time when the PCF remained committed to the cult of the personality of its leader Georges Marchais, the students and workers were demanding control of their universities and workplaces. Where the PCF promised better hours and wages, the student assemblies and factory strike committees demanded the end of hierarchy in school and at work, and the abolition of degrading work altogether. Increased wages were less important than having a say in what was to be produced. In this regard the Communists simply failed to understand that the typical material concessions like more money and vacation time were secondary at best. Thus in 1968 French historian Richard Gombin remarked that the very forms of protest had changed, opening up new possibilities:

> Only the future can show whether the unions will be supplanted by new structures such as factory committees, or a French equivalent of the British shop stewards . . . it has been noticeable that the traditional framework has tended to disappear: the radical contestation of all aspects of power within the factory, the attempts at self-organization, even self-management, criticism of the very role of the unions, the unleashing of conflicts in whole sectors, are distinctive signs of a mode of action which may well be described as libertarian.[38]

What was being called into question was precisely the persistence of arbitrary authority and the cult of the personality – after all, why should anyone prefer to look at and listen to Marchais all the time instead of de Gaulle? Student leader Daniel Cohn-Bendit quipped that you make the revolution to enter the political arena yourself, not to watch the televised images of an ageing apparatchik. In this regard what was being demanded was real participation, not symbolic participation, which is all de Gaulle, Marchais, and their party machines could offer. The student militants and those workers that rejected the PCF and CGT demanded the abolition of what Guy Debord and the 'situationists' have called 'The Society of the

---

[37] See Daniel and Gabriel Cohn-Bendit's scathing assessment of the CGT and PCF during the May–June events in *Obsolete Communism*, pp. 145–69; Bookchin, *Post-Scarcity Anarchism*, pp. 249–62; Hamon and Rotman, *Generation* (I), pp. 448–52.

[38] Gombin, 'The Ideology and Practice of Contestation', p. 32.

Spectacle'.[39]

Debord and the situationists continued the work of the French philosopher Henri Lefebvre, who at the end of the 1950s developed a 'critique of daily life'. Lefebvre argued that the tremendous increase in our technical capacity to produce and consume had not opened up new possibilities for creativity and fulfilment. Instead, technical rationality invaded our daily lives and reduced the idea of emancipation to that of comfort, which was essentially passive and non-creative. Debord and the Situationist International (SI) took these ideas further, claiming that the bureaucratic domination made possible by technological advance had rendered modern industrial society more oppressive and exploitative than anything experienced during the period of free market capitalism and the liberal State of the nineteenth century. The post-World War II State operated with the benefit of sophisticated information systems and in accordance with the demands of international capitalism. This State had the capacity to manipulate and control all aspects of life. Under these conditions there was no genuine participation in public life, but rather staged events or 'spectacles', which people watched on television. Since the modern European State could finance its operations with revenues accrued from the Third World, it was no longer dependent on the surplus value of its own population. The perpetuation of State control required the passivity of the population, which was easily secured by convincing them that comfort would be guaranteed by the experts: economists, scientists, sociologists, psychologists and bureaucrats who administered society's physical and mental health.[40]

The situationists called for the re-appropriation of authentic individual experience. Debord, Raoul Vaneigem and other members of the SI drew on Marx's theory of commodity fetishism to construct a comprehensive critique of the reified social relations characteristic of modern capitalism. Advanced capitalism vitally depended on the majority's equation of happiness with comfort, which could be purchased in the form of so many trivial commodities. The commodification of social and political life would only be superseded when the masses consciously rejected the advertising and consumerism that saturated their daily existence, and united to participate in 'Situations', live happenings and encounters in which people confronted each other directly, rather

[39] Cohn-Bendit, Obsolete Communism, pp. 61–9; Bookchin, Post-Scarcity Anarchism, pp. 281–6.
[40] Lefebvre, Critique de la vie quotidienne (II), pp. 8–11; Debord, La societé du spectacle, p. 31.

than through a myriad of signs which reproduced sex, class, and racial hierarchies. Here the separation of art and life would be overcome. Politically, this meant breaking with party and union bureaucracies, for the more immediate contact provided by the workers' Council. For Debord, the Council

> is the place where the objective conditions of historical consciousness are united; where the realisation of direct and active communication is achieved, and where specialisation, hierarchy and separation end as existing conditions have been transformed into conditions of unity.[41]

Thus situationist anarchists were not opposed to organisation in principle. Indeed, they extolled the direct democracy of the Council as the paragon of undistorted and domination-free communication. They are thus the descendants of a revolutionary tradition that precedes World War I. That is, as far back as 1911 a group of theorists also argued that practical political and economic questions could be solved through the Council. Like the situationists, they emphasised the importance of cultural change and the need to revolutionise daily life. Indeed, the Council Communists argued that this was the chief virtue of the Council form of democracy. Chapter 3 will provide a full exposition of the ideas of Council communism.

Concluding remarks: a note on liberals, communitarians and anarchists

In a study of the historical evolution of liberalism, it has been observed that contemporary liberal theory can be characterised as a mixture of philosophical sophistication and political naivety.[42] Despite the veracity of this statement, the discussion between liberals and communitarians on the tension between individual liberty and the claims of community rages on in total silence of the anarchist contribution to the subject. There has been a tremendous outpouring of books and articles contrasting liberal conceptions of 'neutrality' with communitarian conceptions stressing the inseparability of the individual and their social milieu. The political naivety of both parties in this debate is striking, relying as they do on

---

[41] Debord, *La societé du spectacle*, pp. 97–8; see also the English translation of the introduction to the fourth Italian edition of Debord's book in *Italy: Autonomia, Post-Political Politics*, pp. 96–9; Vaneigem, *Traite de savoir-vivre*, pp. 15–18; Plant, *The Most Radical Gesture*, pp. 12–18, 90–1. Plant provides a fascinating account of the SI and its precursors.

[42] Bellamy, *Liberalism and Modern Society*, p. 217.

hypothetical situations which bear no remote relation to the political and economic realities of modern industrial societies. And yet
Anarchism's stress on co-operation and communal solidarity is
somehow ridiculed as naive![43]

Communitarians have correctly pointed out that such thought
experiments do little to illuminate the political reality of individuals
living in concrete historical situations, deriving their sense of meaning and justice from the communities in which they find themselves.
While such accounts are indeed a welcome relief from contemporary liberal abstraction, they do not go far enough in examining
what forces actually undermine communities, and how present-day
communities might re-assert their claims for autonomy. The point
that individual freedom is only realised in society with one's fellows
seems so obviously true, that we need hardly debate hypothetical
'Robinson Crusoe' arguments postulating possible other worlds.
What is interesting and important, however, is to investigate the
conditions under which communities can provide the participatory
and democratic culture in which individuals can flourish. Communitarian anarchists from Kropotkin to the present have correctly
observed that where communities are governed by external forces
such as the State or imported capital, political control is lost and
social inequality results. In such circumstances community
repeatedly breaks down, as different sections of the local population
are pitted against each other in the scramble for jobs. The level of
co-operation realised by agrarian and industrial collectives during
the Spanish Civil War suggests what is really at issue.

When talking about community we cannot forget that some
form of co-operative control of basic necessities is the precondition
of a community's ability to govern itself, that is, to function democratically. When the productive forces of a community or even an
entire country (the example of the Third World is immediately
relevant here) are controlled by private interests that have no basic
concern for the welfare of its members, all talk of community and
democracy is illusory. If the Spanish urban and rural Communes did
realise high levels of socio-economic equality and democratic participation, they did so by taking productive and political matters into
their own hands. It has been objected time and again that the
Spanish situation was unusual, isolated, and probably irretrievably

[43] For a good summary of these hypothetical situations see Kymlicka, *Contemporary
Political Philosophy*. On the extremely important link between Anarchism and
co-operation, see Michael Taylor, *The Possibility of Cooperation*, pp. 165–8, and
Hartley, 'Communitarian Anarchism'.

linked to a now bygone era of social solidarity. While this claim has been greatly overstated, it is certainly true that the Spanish anarchists did not have answers to fundamentally important questions, such as, how to redistribute resources without a strong central State, and how to co-ordinate activities between autarkic communities. These are undoubtedly serious flaws. Thus we are in the fortunate position of being able to learn from their successes and failures.

The Spanish experience was a practical alternative to both the syndicalist vision of centralised trade union control of the economy and Proudhon's version of Market Socialism based on competing mutualist firms. It was noted that if realised, Proudhon's model was likely to create major inequalities between successful and unsuccessful competitors. This inequality would, in turn, have been translated into differential political power, and we know that Proudhon was against any form of State to deal with such problems. Spanish practice marked a decisive break with Proudhon's ideas. It was instead an attempt to implement the Communitarian Anarchism advocated by Bakunin and Kropotkin, which in economic terms is based on small-scale agricultural and industrial production for local markets. Directly faced with the numerous problems encountered by this system during the course of the Civil War, socialists and communists pointed to what they considered the superiority of the Soviet economy. They argued that a Bolshevik-style vanguard was ideally suited for the direction of a centrally planned production and distribution system. This seemed to be the logical response to the problems of isolation and resource shortage suffered by individual autarkic communities. These problems were multiplied by the sabotage of Franco's army, which did indeed exploit the dispersal of anarchist forces and eventually defeat the Republic. The resulting legacy of acrimony between the forces of the Spanish left has abated to this day.[44]

If the isolation of the anarchist communities revealed itself as a tragic weakness during the war years, we know that the Bolshevik approach produced its own disasters. Thus if we do acknowledge the flaws of the anarchist approach, we must also resist the tendency to settle for a bureaucratic and centralist solution to the problem of economic democracy. The key to the creation of a socialist Civil Society depends on retaining the many positive aspects of the political and economic ideas of Communitarian Anarchism, while taking more concrete steps towards regional and national co-ordination. The possibilities for such action is explored in subsequent chapters.

[44] Marshall, *Demanding the Impossible*, pp. 466–8.

3

Council Communism

Like revolutionary syndicalists and anarchists, the Council communists fiercely contested the notion that Bolshevism was the only alternative to Social Democracy and the ideas of Bernstein and Kautsky. While Bernstein was censured for his views from diverse sections of the German and international labour movement, Kautsky continued to represent Marxist orthodoxy after the Bolsheviks came to power in 1917. Left-wing opposition to Kautsky began to take shape as far back as 1905 in Germany, however, and it is here that the origins of the Council communist vision are to be found.

The mass strike debate

The Jena Conference of the German Social Democratic Party (SPD) of 1905 took place amidst the great excitement caused by the revolutionary upheavals in Russia at this time. Not only did the Czarist regime seem to be on the point of collapse, but the Russian events also appeared to bear witness to a new form of political organisation, the workers' and soldiers' Soviet. The Soviet, or workers' Council, was foreshadowed in the Paris Commune of 1871, and was based on the same principles of radical democracy, popular participation, and accountability of power for which Marx had praised the communards. The participants of the Jena Conference celebrated the resurgence of this paradigmatic institution of direct democracy, and for the first time in the history of German Socialism openly criticised the reformist tendencies of the trade unions. Such criticism immediately raised questions about the State, revolution and the meaning of democracy which were seriously discussed for the first time as a result of Bernstein's challenge to Marxism at the turn of the century. One particular contribution to the debate was of decisive importance, namely Rosa Luxemburg's *The Mass Strike, the Party, and the Trade Unions*. Luxemburg combined a trenchant critique of the unions with a detailed account of how the SPD itself could only have a limited role in a truly mass revolutionary movement.[1]

Luxemburg was greatly impressed by the fact that such a relatively uneducated and inexperienced working class like the Russian proletariat was making revolutionary demands through the Soviets. At the same time the reputedly more sophisticated and class-conscious German proletariat was shackled by its own trade union and political party bureaucracy. While Luxemburg developed no detailed theory of Council democracy, she first advanced the premise that was to become a central tenet for all Council communists: the socialist revolution would come to fruition only when the masses created their own institutional forms in which they were no longer under the tutelage of intellectuals. That is, they had to learn the art of self-government by practising it themselves. The party and union, because of their hierarchical and bureaucratic structure, were not suited for this task. The party and union were historically important defensive institutions in the workers' struggle for justice within the economic system dominated by private property and individual interests. But the new epoch of class struggle was engendering new revolutionary organisational forms which raised serious doubts about the future role of the party and union bureaucracies.[2]

Luxemburg argued that the unions and party bureaucracies had become patrons of working-class officaldom, whose privileged members had an interest in maintaining the social order and the advantages of secure employment and relatively high wages it offered them. In opposition to the tendency of the union and party to act as a break on revolutionary activity, Luxemburg advocated the mass strike, which in essence was akin to the syndicalist General Strike. She was not opposed to political parties, however, and did agree that there was a continuing need for a certain amount of ideological guidance and party organisation. But she strongly opposed Kautsky's position which, she argued, encouraged the workers to believe that the road to revolution lay in a succession of political reforms. The Russian events of 1905 indicated that working-class spontaneity might overcome the reformist tendencies of the SPD. Hence the immediate task for German revolutionaries was to develop support for the mass strike and Council democracy.[3]

[1] Grünenberg, Introduction to *Die Massenstreikdebatte*, p. 30.
[2] Grünenberg, Introduction to *Die Massenstreikdebatte*, pp. 31–2.
[3] Luxemburg, *The Mass Strike*, pp. 47–8, 64–5; Gombin, *The Origins of Modern Leftism*, pp. 80–1.

The ensuing debate between Luxemburg and Kautsky was played out in the major SPD theoretical organ the *Neue Zeit* (New Age) in the years from 1905 until 1912. Luxemburg insisted on the revolutionary spontaneity of the masses to support her argument. Kautsky replied that in fact the Russian events of 1905 clearly demonstrated that without conscious organisation the masses could only protest against existing social conditions while remaining powerless to transform them. This exchange of positions had reached an impasse until the decisive intervention of the Dutch Marxist Anton Pannekoek in 1912. Pannekoek's *Marxist Theory and Revolutionary Tactics* was the first of several major theoretical contributions which placed him at the head of the European Council Communist movement in the years directly following World War I.[4]

Pannekoek first established contact with Kautsky in 1900, when he attended a conference directed by the German SPD leader in Amsterdam. Regular contact between them developed in the ensuing years, as Pannekoek wrote to Kautsky wishing to find out what Kautsky knew about the written correspondence between Marx and the philosopher Joseph Dietzgen (1828–88). Dietzgen formulated a detailed critique of Kant's epistemological system, and postulated the unity and interaction of the material world and our mental representations of it. For Dietzgen, any rigid separation between mind and matter was inimical to our understanding of actual mental processes. From here he went on to develop a critique of mechanical theories of materialism asserting the primacy of matter and the passive role of the intellect in organising sensory data. Pannekoek combined the scientific background he acquired as an astronomer with a close reading of Dietzgen. He thus arrived at an original approach to Marx's ideas on the relationship between philosophy and revolution. For Pannekoek, Marx had shed light on the crucial significance of the relations of production for social structure, while Dietzgen was more helpful in explaining the relation between material forces and our mental conceptions of social reality. All of Pannekoek's subsequent work stressed the spiritual component of the revolutionary movement, and the need for the proletariat to develop its own forms of philosophy, art and consciousness.[5]

Kautsky quickly perceived Pannekoek's talent as a theorist, and asked him to contribute articles to the *Neue Zeit*. Their initial relations were amicable, and through Kautsky Pannekoek was able to establish contacts with leading figures of German Socialism such as Franz

[4] Bock, *Syndikalismus und Linkskommunismus*, pp. 49–50.
[5] Gerber, *Anton Pannekoek*, pp. 12–19.

Mehring and August Bebel. At this time Pannekoek was in broad agreement with Kautsky on most issues in Marxist theory, though Pannekoek was already seeking to integrate Dietzgen's ideas on consciousness within a Marxist framework. In 1903 Pannekoek expressed his wish to move to Germany to work for the SPD's theoretical and educational school in Berlin. He took up the position in November 1906, though the next year the police used the pretext of his Dutch citizenship as a means of preventing him from teaching. The secretary of the SPD in Bremen, Wilhelm Pieck, was able to offer him a position in the local Party educational programme. Kautsky secured him a post as a book editor for the Neue Zeit, which enabled Pannekoek to continue to live in Germany.[6]

By 1911–12, Pannekoek's synthesis of Dietzgen and Marx began leading him to conclusions which were incompatible with Kautsky's defence of parliamentary democracy. Relations between them had already come under some strain in 1909 when Kautsky refused to defend the left-wing of the Dutch Social Democratic Party, the Tribunists, in which Pannekoek was a leading member. When the German government reneged on its commitment to increase the number of eligible voters in February 1910, a strike wave swept Germany. In response, Rosa Luxemburg wrote an article entitled 'What Next?' which the Neue Zeit would not publish. Kautsky used the incident to attack Luxemburg and defend the parliamentary strategy of the SPD, insisting that the Party's task was to organise for the Reichstag elections of 1913, not to become entangled in meaningless debates on the revolutionary capacities of the masses. Luxemburg turned to Pannekoek for support, which came in the form of a series of articles in the Bremen Citizen's Newspaper, in which Pannekoek emphasised the contradiction between the proletariat's evident desire to achieve its emancipation, and the inadequacy of the political party to realise this aspiration. In contrast to Kautsky's call for steady but gradual reform, Pannekoek argued that the working class was struggling to find new forms of organisational struggle to accelerate the revolutionary process. Indeed, for Pannekoek the Mass Strike debate was indicative of a situation in which the workers were unsatisfied with their present institutions, but unsure where new impetus for change might come from.[7]

In two articles published in the Neue Zeit in 1912, 'Mass Action and Revolution' and 'Marxist Theory and Revolutionary Tactics', Pannekoek expounded the premises of his subsequent ideas on

---

[6] Gerber, Anton Pannekoek, pp. 43–6.
[7] Gerber, Anton Pannekoek, pp. 67–74; Bock, Geschichte des Linken Radicalismus, pp. 76–8.

proletarian revolution. The crux of these articles was that the phenomenon of imperialism, marking a new phase in the political evolution of capitalism, required new forms of working-class resistance.
Without yet specifying exactly what these new forms would consist
of, he argued that as free market capitalism evolved towards monopoly capitalism, internal class struggles were displaced onto the
international arena in the form of imperial wars for new markets,
raw materials and cheap labour. This offensive by capital required
the active participation of the working class in its entirety, not only
those engaged in trade union and Party activity. The outbreak of
World War I in August 1914 signalled the utter failure of the international socialist movement to unite the working classes of all
countries against their respective capitalist oppressors. This dramatic
event confirmed Luxemburg and Pannekoek's belief that capitalism
was re-organising its political, social, and ideological superstructures
in accordance with the new requirements for capital accumulation.
Pannekoek would soon formulate his vision based on workers'
Councils as the appropriate response.[8]

Council Communism in Germany

The war acted as a catalyst for the break-up of the existing international socialist movement. In 1916 a group of Italian and Swiss
socialists called for a conference of all socialists remaining
intransigent in their opposition to the war. The conference, which
Lenin attended, was held in the Swiss mountain village of
Zimmerwald during 8–15 September. The 'Zimmerwald Left' movement was born, declaring itself committed to finding new ways of
furthering world revolution and avoiding the reformist mistakes of
the past. In January 1917 the formation of a new revolutionary Party
in Germany became particularly exigent with the expulsion of the
entire anti-war opposition from the ranks of the SPD. In the port city
of Bremen a left-wing opposition began to form, distinguishing itself
from both Rosa Luxemburg's Sparticists and the independent Social
Democrats (USPD). The 'Bremen Left', of which Pannekoek was a
member, declared that both the party and the trade union were
inappropriate forms of political and economic struggle in the face of
world war and imperialism. They argued that a new revolutionary
movement in Germany could base itself on the organisational
models used by the American syndicalist group, the International

[8] Pannekoek, 'Massenaktion und Revolution', pp. 264–94; 'Marxistische Theorie',
pp. 49–63.

Workers of the World (IWW). American sailors frequently called in to Bremen and discussed what was happening in the United States with German sailors. German radicals were familiar with the IWW from the Hamburg militant Fritz Wolffheim, who edited an IWW journal in America.[9]

In March 1917 Wolffheim proposed the creation of a new type of proletarian organisation combining the functions of the party and trade union. In the journal *Arbeiterpolitik* (*Workers' Politics*) he argued that the best way to combat the centralising tendencies of monopoly capitalism in its imperialist stage was with a federation of factory-level Councils elected by workers of all trades. At the same time, strikes broke out all over Germany. In April 1917 a workers' Council was formed in Leipzig, which assumed the task of co-ordinating the efforts of striking workers in different industries. In order to combat trade union opposition to such initiatives, a network of Factory Committees with workers of all trades was organised. These committees provided the basic structure for the workers' Councils which sprung up all over Germany in 1918.[10]

As Germany's chances of victory in the war became increasingly slim, militant workers throughout the country pressed for the immediate replacement of the existing SPD regime with a federation of Councils. In November 1918 in Kiel, over a hundred thousand workers' Councils formed and temporarily held power in the city. Similar developments in Bremen precipitated a headlong confrontation at the national level between the two dominant factions of the German workers' movement, with one calling for a National Assembly and the other calling for a *Räterrepublik*: (Council Republic). The SPD-led provisional government attempted to curb the power of the Councils by bringing them under Party control. In Bremen a Council Republic held power for three weeks, until the SPD minister for internal security, Noske, repudiated the authority of the Councils. On 3 February fighting broke out, resulting in considerable damage of property and casualties, after which the Councils were dissolved. In Munich a *Räterrepublik* was established in April 1918, which managed to hold power for three weeks against overt SPD aggression. The government went on to suppress Council movements in Munich, Kiel, Bremen, and Berlin. But there was no way to suppress the fact that Council Communism was born, with

[9] Gerber, *Anton Pannekoek*, pp. 110–11, 118–20.
[10] Wolffheim, 'Gewerkschaftsprobleme', pp. 92–5; Gerber, *Anton Pannekoek*, pp. 118–20.

its own methods of organisation and philosophy of working class self-government.[11]

The following year, in March 1919, the Communist Third International or Comintern, was founded in Moscow to consolidate the Bolshevik revolution and to co-ordinate the activities of the international communist movement. During the early months of its existence, communication with Western Europe was impeded by the blockade of the Soviet Union and the devastation of transport networks caused by the war. These problems necessitated the establishment of Western European bureaux of the Comintern in Berlin and Amsterdam. The Amsterdam office held its first public conference in 1920, with the express purpose of articulating the future orientation of communists in Western Europe. Although the conference was badly organised and disrupted by the police, the resulting manifesto emphasised the future importance of workers' Councils. The manifesto also contained severe criticisms of parliamentary Socialism and trade unionism.[12]

Meanwhile the Free German Workers' Union (FAUD), the General Workers' Union of Germany (AAUD) and other groups attempted to set up shopfloor organisations on the basis of the experiments in the Bremen and Hamburg factories during the years 1917–19. The FAUD in particular defended the idea of workers' unions, which, they insisted, were different from traditional unions. Indeed, by uniting all the workers in a given industry rather than protecting the sanctity of individual trades, these workers' unions challenged the existing hierarchy within the labour movement between unskilled, semi-skilled, and highly skilled workers. Only to the extent that such artificial distinctions could be overcome would it be possible for workers to think of themselves as members of a single class, rather than accepting the limitations on class unity imposed by capitalist control over the labour process. In this regard it was hoped that the workers' unions were an intermediate step towards Council control of production.[13]

In August 1919 the Bremen left called for a federation of workers' unions, which was to co-ordinate its efforts with the German Communist Party (KPD, formed in January 1918), and the Comintern. Their stated aim was the creation of a Council Republic

---

[11] Gerber, *Anton Pannekoek*, pp. 123–4; Linse *Gustav Landauer*, pp. 22–30; Beyer, *Die Revolution in Bayern*, p. 8.

[12] Gerber, *Anton Pannekoek*, pp. 132–3.

[13] Bock, *Syndikalismus und Linkskommunismus*, pp. 132–9, 353–5; Bauer, 'Die Sozialisierung', Vol. 2, p. 205.

in Germany as a preliminary step towards a worldwide federation of Councils. The basic unit of each Republic was to be a Council comprised of workers of various trades, so that each Council represented all of the various trades required in the production process. All of the Councils in a city were called upon to federate in local networks, which would in turn send representatives to regional and national-level producers' Councils. In an article in the Bremen-based *Der Kommunist*, Pannekoek argued that while the traditional trade unions were dominated by a privileged officialdom, the workers' unions represented a direct challenge to the wage system by negating trade-based pay differentials. However, the KPD, led by Paul Levi since the assassination of Luxemburg and Karl Liebknecht in January 1919, defended the role of the Party as the communist vanguard and leader of the revolution. Left-wing opponents of KPD politics agreed that what was severely lacking in Germany was a party that could increase workers' awareness of the revolutionary potential of the post-war situation across Europe by promoting Council activity as well as the cultural and theoretical dissemination of ideas. This desire to spread Council democracy as well as the recognition of the importance of the cultural and subjective factors in the revolution inspired the founding members of the German Communist Workers' Party (KAPD, formed in April 1920).[14]

The KAPD programme announced the decisive significance of developing proletarian consciousness, that is, subjective factors, for the success of the German revolution. The workers' Council was heralded as the primary institution for preparing the workers for self-government and autonomy from both Party officials and union bosses. The KAPD Party Programme of 1920 states:

> The factory committee is the economic precondition for the construction of a communist community. The political form of organisation for a communist community is the Council system. The Factory Committees defend the idea that all political power must be exercised by the Executive Committee of the Councils.[15]

KAPD member Otto Rühle (1874–1943) amplified these remarks by declaring that 'the revolution is no matter for the party'. In an article entitled 'The Councils' of 1921, Ruhle maintained that although it was in Russia that the workers' Councils made their first appearance, the Bolsheviks were now preventing the further development of the Council system in the Soviet Union. The Party had to assume a

14 Kool, *Die Linke*, p. 8; Fowkes, *Communism in Germany*, pp. 37–40.
15 'Programe der KAPD', in Kool, *Die Linke*, p. 324.

secondary role in order to allow the Councils to flourish once again.[16]

At the same time similar arguments for the Councils were being put forth by Otto Bauer, Max Adler and Karl Korsch. Like Rühle, Bauer argued that though the Council system had its first widespread success in the form of the Russian Soviets, the movement for workers' democracy in that country was being frustrated by the hegemony of the party. Bauer insisted that the radical participatory democracy of the kind practised in Russian and German factories and local communes was incompatible with the elitism of both parliamentary democracy and single party government. He asserted that the establishment of the Council form of democracy on a society-wide basis depended not only on the co-ordination of workers' with soldiers' and peasants' Councils, but depended also on the organisation of women's and consumer associations as well. Adler claimed that Marx's remarks on the Paris Commune being executive and legislative at the same time should guide the spread and development of the Council system. Council democracy demanded the participation of all sectors of society in both the formulation as well as the execution of the laws.[17]

In his 1919 pamphlet 'What is Socialisation?' Karl Korsch argued that attempts to bring production under the control of the community could only be accomplished in a system of workers' Councils acting in concert with consumers' councils. Korsch was aware of the enormous inequalities in wealth and power generated by the capitalist market. But he also understood that State ownership of the means of production gave workers no more control over the labour process than they had under private ownership. Hence Korsch recommended what he called the socialisation of production as an alternative to both State ownership and Syndicalism. He believed that the syndicalist solution of 'giving the mines to the miners' would encourage a sectarian attitude amongst workers which would lead them to pursue the interests of their branch of industry at the expense of the needs of the community as a whole. Refusing to accept the Bolshevik solution of subjecting producers to the will of the State, Korsch suggested a model of 'industrial autonomy' which would attempt to set up a network of producer and consumer Councils in Civil Society to steer a path between State planning and Syndicalism. In an extremely prescient manner he

[16] Rühle, 'Die Räte', in Kool, pp. 534–6; Mattick, 'Otto Rühle', pp. 12–13, 28–9.
[17] Bauer, 'Rätediktatur oder Democratie', Vol. 2, pp. 135, 151–5; Adler, *Democratie und Rätesystem*, pp. 28–38.

reasoned that the implicit neglect of consumer interests by both Bolsheviks and syndicalists could generate a strong movement for the re-introduction of private property which would threaten any socialist revolution.[18]

As the Council system gained wide support in Germany, Austria, Italy and Hungary, the Comintern intervened to stem the tide of what Lenin derided as 'left-wing communism'. The term was coined and made famous by Lenin's *Left-Wing Communism: an Infantile Disorder*, which reproached Pannekoek, the KAPD, and other 'deviations' from Bolshevik orthodoxy. In response Pannekoek hoped to reach a compromise with the Comintern in March 1920. In his long essay, *World Revolution and Communist Tactics*, Pannekoek argued that 'left communism' had a firm foundation in Marx's ideas on workers' democracy, and thus the Comintern could not simply dismiss the movement as some variety of Syndicalism.[19] *World Revolution* is an extremely important work in the anti-Bolshevik tradition of revolutionary Socialism, for it outlines the central themes of subsequent western Marxist theory from Antonio Gramsci to the Frankfurt School.

In *World Revolution* Pannekoek gives a coherent account of what had always been presented in a fragmentary form in his preceding writings. His initial interest in the importance of working-class consciousness was expanded into a sustained critique of both reformist trade unionism and vanguard elitism. Like Sorel, Pannekoek realised that a true revolution in social relations would never be the simple result of better working conditions either under bourgeois or Bolshevik hegemony. Within bourgeois society it was possible that despite Marx's predictions workers might eventually attain greater purchasing power and higher living standards. In the Soviet Union material security might also eventually be achieved, though within the unacceptable framework of unconditional submission to the Party leadership. In both cases Pannekoek linked the tendency to passively emulate with the related tendency to defer to authority. He conceded that the trade union and political Party had served indispensable functions in securing a stable existence for most workers within the bourgeois order. But their revolutionary capacity had also been limited by these institutions, which perpetuated the rift between leaders and masses which was also exploited by the Bolsheviks. Meanwhile, how could one be

---

[18] Korsch, *Was ist Sozialisierung?*, pp. 16–17; 'Die Sozialisierung', pp. 163–4.
[19] Smart, *Pannekoek*, pp. 37–8.

astonished at the betrayal of internationalism witnessed at the outbreak of World War I, when trade union leaders who had attained
high living standards began emulating bourgeois lifestyles and eventually identifying their interests with those of their respective
national bourgeois masters? The power of capitalism had penetrated working-class leaders at the spiritual and ideological level.
This would remain true as long as the proletariat relied on outdated institutions for its emancipation: the sharp authoritarian turn
of the Russian Revolution was conclusive proof. All of these considerations shaped Pannekoek's ardent defence of the Councils as
qualitatively new institutions in the history of political struggle.[20]

Pannekoek argued that world war and the scramble for colonies
in Africa and Asia made it abundantly clear that political struggle had
to be seen within a global context. Colonies provided the advanced
capitalist countries with cheap labour, raw materials and new
markets, all of which contributed to higher living standards in
Europe and the United States, as well as the formation of a labour
aristocracy whose interests were tied directly to bourgeois national
interests. As long as the majority of workers remained within the
confines of trade unions and parties in which deference to an over-
paid and essentially middle-class leadership was the norm, revolution was impossible. Pannekoek's praise for the workers' unions in
Bremen and workers' Councils in general stemmed from the tendency of the Council form of organisation to make workers think of
themselves as a class of producers. Traditional organisations left
workers as an agglomeration of wage-earners with different trades
and therefore different possibilities for promotion at one another's
expense.[21]

The fact that such bourgeois modes of thought and action had
penetrated into the heart of working-class institutions convinced
Pannekoek that new institutions and a spiritual revolution would
necessarily precede a truly socialist revolution. Anticipating themes
in Gramsci and the Frankfurt School, he argued further that the
spread of bourgeois ideas and culture throughout the capitalist-
dominated civil sphere highlighted an important difference
between pre-revolutionary Russia and the advanced industrial
societies of Western Europe and North America. As Luxemburg had
originally observed, the political, economic, and cultural gulf
between the Russian aristocracy and the mass of workers, peasants

---

[20] Pannekoek, 'Weltrevolution und kommunistische Taktik', pp. 130–1.
[21] Pannekoek, 'Weltrevolution und kommunistische Taktik', pp. 131–3; Mattick, 'La
     prospettiva', pp. 357–8.

and soldiers enhanced a militant consciousness that was already in evidence during the events of 1905. In Western Europe and North America, however, the clash between the ruling class and the rest of society was not nearly so direct, but mediated through a complex set of ideological and cultural practices via intellectuals of many diverse backgrounds:

> The intelligentsia – priests, teachers, literati, journalists, artists, politicians – form a numerous class, the function of which is to foster, develop and propagate bourgeois culture; it passes this on to the masses, and acts as a mediator between the hegemony of capital and the interests of the masses. The hegemony of capital is rooted in this group's intellectual leadership of the masses. For even though the oppressed masses have often rebelled against capital and its agencies, they have done so under the leadership of the intelligentsia.[22]

This situation signified that power relations in the parliamentary democracies of the West were far more complex than in Czarist Russia, and as a result, a different revolutionary strategy which took account of this complexity was also needed. The Bolshevik 'seizure' of power, while effective in Russia, was inadequate for those countries where bourgeois culture stressing possessive individualism and conspicuous consumption had penetrated the way most working people viewed the world. At the same time, the Bolsheviks were attempting to control the Comintern and model all of the member Communist Parties on their own hierarchical example. This was inimical to spreading a revolutionary class consciousness in the West: where power was complexly mediated and diffuse, the response had to be diffuse. The vanguard, by its very nature, centralised power and knowledge.[23]

Despite Pannekoek's overtures to the Third International, Lenin's *Infantile Communism* in April 1920 ensured that there was no further doubt about the Comintern's attitude towards workers' Councils and left Communism in general. Moreover, the future orientation of the international communist movement was also clear. The KAPD was expelled, Pannekoek was censured and other Parties and individuals who did not step into line came in for equally harsh treatment. Pannekoek responded to Lenin with an appendix to *World Revolution and Communist Tactics* which was included with subsequent editions of the book. He quite accurately predicted that far from becoming a rallying point for international Communism,

---

[22] Pannekoek, 'World Revolution', p. 105.
[23] Pannekoek, 'Anhang' to 'Weltrevolution und kommunistische Taktik', pp. 163–4. Pannekoek returned to these themes in his book *Lenin als Philosoph*, pp. 118–5.

the Comintern would become increasingly subjected to the vicis-
situdes of the internal politics of the Communist Party of the Soviet
Union (CPSU). Comintern policy was indeed dictated with the aim
of maintaining a stable atmosphere in which the Soviet Union could
build up its economic infrastructure on the basis of the Five Year
Plans. This policy received its consummation in 1924 with Stalin's
programme for creating 'Socialism in one country'. In the meantime,
the Kronstadt Soviet was brutally suppressed, the Workers' Opposition banned, and Soviets in the USSR dismantled. Pannekoek's
compatriot Hermann Gorter attempted in vain to change the course
of Comintern policy with his 'Open Letter to Comrade Lenin',
which denounced the Bolshevik dictatorship and defended the
conception of Communism as working-class self-government.
Rühle and other left communists defied Comintern orthodoxy and
called for a return to Lenin's own principles in *The State and Revolution*.
The closure of the Amsterdam Bureau of the Comintern seemed to
destroy the institutional base of anti-Bolshevik Communism, but in
fact this was not the case. In Vienna Georg Lukács helped found and
edit the journal *Kommunismus* (Communism), which continued Pannekoek's work by emphasising the vital importance of culture,
philosophy and consciousness for socialist revolution. In Italy a
group of young intellectuals in Turin had been passionately
defending the Council ideal since June 1919. Under the leadership of
Antonio Gramsci, the Turin militants gave Council Communism its
most sophisticated theoretical articulation.[24]

Gramsci and *L'Ordine Nuovo*

In Italy, large concentrations of workers flocked to the industrial
centres of Turin, Milan and Genoa from the turn of the century until
World War I. Many were poor peasants from the surrounding
countryside and the south, who quickly joined the Italian General
Confederation of Trade Unions, CGL, founded in 1906. Some of the
less conservative industrialists like Agnelli of the automobile manu-
facturer Fiat perceived that they stood to gain from a more flexible
bargaining structure with labour than was possible with the large and
powerful Italian union organisation. In order to settle wage and
other disputes without losing working time, a number of capitalist
firms consented to the formation of ad hoc committees operating

---

[24] Pannekoek, 'Anhang' to 'Weltrevolution und kommunistische Taktik', pp. 162–7;
Gorter, 'Offener Brief', pp. 410–95.

on the shopfloor which could settle disputes quickly. These committees were typically comprised of representatives from both management and the workforce. In pre-war times they normally existed only until the problem for which they had convened was solved; once this task was accomplished the committee frequently dissolved again. During the war they acted primarily as grievance committees.[25]

After the war the future role of these committees, or Internal Commissions (CI), as they were called, became an important issue. This was especially true for the more militant sections of the working class, such as those in the Federation of Italian Metal Workers (FIOM). By the summer of 1918 the CI had been recognised by management in many factories in Liguria, Lombardy and Piedmont. In Turin a group of young intellectuals at the university founded the journal L'Ordine Nuovo (The New Order) in May 1918 as a review of socialist culture, philosophy and aesthetics. From June 1919 L'Ordine Nuovo was centrally concerned with providing a rigorous theoretical and practical defence of the CI. The journal's founders, Antonio Gramsci, Angelo Tasca, Umberto Terracini, and Palmiro Togliatti, would all leave the Italian Socialist Party (PSI) to found the Communist Party of Italy (PCd'I, later PCI) in January 1921. The Factory Council movement and the related events leading up to this break were decisive in the political experience and future orientation of the most powerful Communist Party in the history of Western Europe.[26]

The driving intellectual force of the group was Antonio Gramsci, who achieved posthumous world renown for his Prison Notebooks, written during 1928–35 when he was incarcerated in a fascist jail.[27] Born in Sardinia in 1891, Gramsci arrived in Turin in 1911 to pursue a degree in linguistics. He joined the PSI and quickly became absorbed in revolutionary politics, writing for the socialist journals Avanti! (Forward!) and Il Grido del Popolo (The Cry of the People). By the time L'Ordine Nuovo was founded in May 1919, Gramsci had abandoned his studies to devote his entire life to politics. During the biennio rosso (two red years) of 1919–20, Gramsci argued that the political and economic inequalities stemming from Italy's unification in 1861

[25] Guarnieri, I consigli di fabbrica, pp. 11–12; Abrate, La Lotta sindacale, pp. 67–8.

[26] For a detailed history of the 'biennio rosso' of 1919–20 in Italy see Clark, Antonio Gramsci. For an in-depth look at Gramsci's Factory Council theory during the period see my Gramsci and the Theory of Industrial Democracy.

[27] For an analysis of Gramsci's intellectual development and the relation of the Factory Council writings to the Prison Notebooks, see Bellamy and Schecter, Gramsci and the Italian State.

could be overcome by completely reorganising the economy and polity of the country as a federation of workers' and peasants' Councils. In his June 1919 article in L'Ordine Nuovo, 'Workers' Democracy', Gramsci claimed that the basis of this radical reorganisation could be found in the CI, whose functions could be enlarged to those of full-fledged Factory Councils:

> Today the Internal Commissions limit the power of the capitalist in the factory and settle matters pertaining to workshop arbitration and discipline. Developed and enriched, tomorrow they must function as the organs of proletarian power capable of substituting the capitalist in his present useful functions of direction and administration.[28]

Like Pannekoek, Rühle and other Council communists, Gramsci argued that the evolution of free market capitalism to monopoly capitalism had fundamentally transformed the conditions of class struggle. Like them he seized upon the potential of the Soviets as a new form of political organisation which originated with the Paris Commune. This placed Gramsci in the same confrontational relationship with the existing institutions of the workers' movement. He was particularly critical of the tactics of both syndicalist and reformist wings of the Italian trade union movement. Advocates of Council democracy faced tremendous opposition from the reformists in particular, who correctly perceived that the Councils were capable of fulfilling all of the essential functions of the trade unions. While several prominent trade union leaders drafted various proposals suggesting how the emerging Councils could be directed by the CGL, Gramsci steadfastly maintained that the Council must remain separate from both the union and political party. He argued that since production was to be the basis of the new producers' State, the working class needed representative institutions on the shopfloor uniting workers of all trades in collective decisions.[29]

Gramsci rejected both syndicalist and anarchist conceptions of the revolution. These movements underestimated the need for organisation and discipline, and greatly overestimated the capacity of the trade union to provide such structure. He accepted Pannekoek's assertion that the new conditions of proletarian struggle necessitated new working-class institutions. But Gramsci extended his analysis further than Pannekoek to develop a theory of State which simultaneously refuted anarchist arguments against State authority, syndicalist celebration of the trade union, and vanguardist

[28] Gramsci, 'Democrazia operaia', ON, p. 11.
[29] Gramsci, 'La conquista dello Stato', ON, pp. 17–18.

insistence on the leading role of the Party. In July 1919 in the *Ordine Nuovo* article 'The Conquest of the State' he affirms that 'the State has always been the protagonist of history'.[30] He goes on to explain that in any State the dominant class exercises its control over production, which is grounded in some form of law or conception of citizens' rights. A capitalist society is organised on the basis of the right to private property and private control of the means of production. For Gramsci the separation between the private sphere of property ownership and the public sphere of parliamentary activity was encapsulated in the idea of the citizen, who in all of his or her activity accepts this separation of public and private as progressive. Thus even when a worker enters a trade union or political party and struggles to protect his or her rights, their action does not question the basic structural premise of bourgeois society. That is, that there should be a certain measure of equality in the public sphere of citizens, but that such equality is irrelevant in the private sphere of production:

> The revolutionary institutions (the political Party and professional trade union) are born in the sphere of political liberty, in the sphere of bourgeois democracy, as an affirmation and development of liberty and democracy in general, in a sphere in which the obtaining political relation is that between citizen and citizen: the revolutionary process is realised in the sphere of production, in the factory, where the obtaining relation is that between oppressor and oppressed, exploiter and exploited, where there is no liberty or democracy for the worker.[31]

In Gramsci's workers' democracy membership in the political community would not be based on the bourgeois notion of citizenship, but rather on one's role as a producer. Moreover, all producers would have equal rights and incomes, regardless of their particular trade or their level of technical skill. All non-producers, that is, either those who refused to work, or capitalists who sought to make money through speculation, would be excluded from power. For Gramsci it was clear that only the Factory Council could provide the foundation for a democratic Civil Society of equal producers. Unlike the political party, the Council was rooted in the workers' world of production. Unlike the trade union, it united all workers in a single industrial unit transcending craft differences. Let us thus look at Gramsci's arguments against the union and party in turn.

The trade union is inadequate for two principal reasons. In the

---

[30] Gramsci, 'La conquista dello Stato', ON, p. 14.
[31] Gramsci, 'Il consiglio di fabbrica', ON, p. 124.

first place, within a trade union workers are organised as wage-earners rather than producers. They are divided according to the various trades they practice, while it is precisely the role of the Council to transcend such differences. Gramsci accepted that as in any political community there would be conflicts between different members. Indeed, in any society the State must adjudicate between the interests of the different groups that compose it. However, conflicts between different groups of workers in the Council State would have a completely different character from the struggle between labour and capital. This followed from the fact that the underlying basis of conflict – private ownership of the means of production – has been removed. Throughout Europe capitalist production relations had resulted in widespread social cleavage, exploitation and poverty at home and had led to imperialist wars for colonies abroad. In the new order, by contrast, there would be widespread acceptance of the need to organise production peacefully according to a central plan taking account of the rights of all producers who participated in the decision-making process in the Councils.[32]

In the *Ordine Nuovo* article of November 1919, 'Syndicalism and the Councils' Gramsci explains that the traditional method of union organisation placed workers in separate groups on the basis of either the tool they used in their craft, like printers, or on the basis of the raw materials they worked with, as in the case of miners. This framework encouraged workers to think of themselves first and foremost as printers or miners rather than belonging to the same class of producers. Gramsci emphasised that the syndicalists were badly mistaken to put so much faith in the General Strike. True, workers did spontaneously unite in Italy in 1904 and 1917. But without some permanent organisational form like the Council, workers of distinct trades would retain distinct identities and conceive of their interests differently. By encouraging workers to cherish the sanctity of their individual trades, unions served to perpetuate the idea that some trades were more valuable than others or more difficult than others. Conceived in this way, labour continued to be bought and sold as a commodity, with some commodities acquiring greater exchange value than others. All of these factors helped maintain capitalist control of production – and thus the State.[33]

---

[32] Gramsci, 'Il consiglio di fabbrica', ON, p. 126–7.
[33] Gramsci, 'Sindacalismo e consigli', ON, p. 45.

In the Council State, however, labour would not be a commodity exchanged for the purpose of buying other commodities, but rather the essential purpose of every member of the community of producers:

> The Factory Council is the model of the proletarian State ... The Council is the most appropriate organ for the mutual education of workers and the development of the new social spirit that the proletariat has succeeded in drawing from the vibrant and fertile experience of collective labour. The solidarity which in the trade union was directed against capitalism, in suffering and sacrifice, becomes something positive and permanent in the Council. This solidarity is incarnated even in the most trivial moments of industrial production. It is captured in the joyous realisation of forming part of an organic whole, a homogeneous and compact system of productive labour which disinterestedly produces social wealth, affirms its sovereignty, and realises its power and ability to create history.[34]

Gramsci conceded that the unions would be indispensable in the future socialisation of the means of production, provided that production decisions were made by the Councils. But he argued that the union leaders of the CGL and the syndicalist USI had become a privileged caste of officials who were more concerned with maintaining their positions of power than with providing workers with technical training or providing them with a communist consciousness. It was thus impossible to expect union officialdom to discard its respect for bourgeois law. Labour law in a capitalist society was designed to facilitate agreements between the opposing sides of the class struggle which were acceptable to each. The premise for such agreement was that labour could demand only so much that was acceptable to capital, the implications of which were obvious. To the extent that union leaders attained privileged positions which removed them further and further from shopfloor realities, they became increasingly akin to an unaccountable executive capable of usurping the functions of the legislature. Like other Council communists Gramsci insisted that the Council form of organisation combined productive, legislative and executive functions, and thus could not be compared to the union or party.[35]

Similarly, in the manner of many councilists, Gramsci's ideas on the political party were far less clear than his assessment of trade unions. Like Korsch and Rühle, he regarded the Soviets as the most

---

[34] Gramsci, 'Sindacati e consigli', ON, p. 37.
[35] Gramsci, 'La conquista dello Stato', ON, pp. 17–18; 'I sindacati e la dittatura', pp. 41–2.

crucial factor in the Russian Revolution. Both associated political parties with parliamentary systems of government which separated the masses from power. The Russian case proved that the working class would no longer allow itself to be governed by a group of professional politicians. While the French Revolution had replaced one set of rulers with another, the Russians had fundamentally changed the relationship between the governers and the governed. At the PSI conference in Bologna in October 1919, the majority of Party members concluded that reformism had been tried and had failed, and that the Italians should emulate the Russian example with a proletarian government based on Soviets. Where did this leave the party? If Lenin's call for 'all power to the Soviets' was to be followed, the party, like the trade union, could only have a co-ordinating role in a society constituted as a federation of self-governing Councils. The revolutionary wing of the PSI was divided between those who backed L'Ordine Nuovo's call for a federation of Councils, on one hand, and the intransigent vanguardism of the Neopolitan leader Amadeo Bordiga, on the other. When it became clear during the course of the Factory Council movement of 1919–20 that Party leader G. M. Serrati would not be able to hold the PSI together, the debate between Gramsci and Bordiga took on immense significance for the future of revolutionary politics in Italy.[36]

In his defence of the Councils against Bordiga's exaltation of the vanguard Party, Gramsci insisted that the party and union were formed on the somewhat arbitrary individual decision to join or not join. Membership in these institutions was sustained by a contract which the worker could reject at any time by simply failing to renew their membership card. But in Gramsci's conception the workers' State, like the bourgeois State before it, could not be based on such contractual foundations. Every member of bourgeois society was born a citizen, with all that this status implied in terms of private property rights, market relations and the separation of the public and private spheres. Unlike voluntary associations such as the party and union, which the worker could contract out of at any time, nobody could voluntarily abandon their status as a citizen of the State. Gramsci maintained that the new order had to have a similar non-contractual basis – though with the fundamental difference that nobody could decline to participate in the State. Since the Council is a public institution, and all individuals worked at some level in the

---

[36] For the Bordiga–Gramsci debate in the years immediately before the formation of the PCI, see Spriano, Storia del Partito comunista italiano (I), pp. 37–77; De Felice, Serrati, Bordiga, Gramsci, pp. 180–3; Levrero, La formazione del PCI, pp. 44–5.

hierarchy of producers' Councils, there could be no distinction between worker and citizen in the new order:

> The Factory Council is a public institution, while the Party and the trade unions are private associations. The worker takes part in the Factory Council in his capacity as a producer, that is, by virtue of the universal character of production, in the same way that the citizen takes part in the parliamentary democratic State. The worker enters the Party and trade union on a voluntary basis, by signing a contract he can cancel at any moment: the Party and the union thus cannot, as voluntary and contractual institutions, be confused with the Council.[37]

Gramsci believed that it was possible to combine the mechanisms of recall on demand practised in the Paris Commune with a planned economy structured as a hierarchy of workers' and peasants' Councils. In his proposed model every factory is subdivided into departments, which are in turn comprised of work crews with workers of various trades and skills. The workers in each crew would elect a delegate from their ranks. This person could be recalled from the moment they lost the confidence of the members of their crew. The delegates of the various crews would come together to form a Factory Council. The Factory Council would in turn elect an Executive Committee. Each Executive Committee of a factory would then nominate a Political Secretary from its ranks. The body constituted by the Political Secretaries of the various Executive Committees in a city would form the Central Committee of Factory Councils for that urban district. The Central Committee would be staffed with various sub-committees, such as an Urban Commissariat charged with drawing up production plans, assessing the feasibility of proposals from individual work crews, and organising educational and cultural activities.[38]

Gramsci realised that this model would be opposed by the majority of trade union leaders, who naturally tended to regard the advent of the Council as the demise of the union. But he had confidence that with the support of a revolutionary party the Council system could be brought into existence in Italy in 1919-1920. It is arguable that this may have been true in the climate of instability and militance that immediately followed the war. But would such a Party be committed, in principle, to phasing itself out as the Councils

---

[37] Gramsci, 'Il programmma dell'Ordine Nuovo', ON, p. 150.
[38] Gramsci, 'Il movimento torinese dei consigli di fabbrica', ON, pp. 183-4. Pannekoek developed a similar model in Les Conseils Ouvrières, p. 127. An English version, Workers' Councils, was published in Melbourne in 1950 as a series of supplements to the monthly review The Southern Advocate for Workers' Councils.

took on an ever greater share of society's productive, political and educational functions? The Russian example suggested the contrary. In any case, support from both Serrati and Bordiga was weak, while disagreements on theory and strategy broke out within the *Ordine Nuovo* group itself. When the PSI refused to support the militant metal workers in the Turin General Strike in April 1920, the Factory Council movement foundered. Gramsci had demanded a 'renewal' of the PSI since January 1920, but in the aftermath of the April events in Turin he began to doubt the Party's long-term viability as a credible revolutionary organisation.[39]

In September 1920 strikes and factory occupations broke out across Italy. In Turin alone 185 metal-working factories were occupied, including the main vehicle producing plants. By mid-September representatives from different factories successfully managed to organise a complex network of exchange between various Turin factories. The direction of production was assumed by FIOM and the Chamber of Labour, while the local Factory Councils carried out distribution and exchange functions and attended to disciplinary matters. The Councils and 'Red Guards' defended the factories from possible government sabotage. Contrary to Gramsci's expectations, however, it was the unions, especially FIOM, which organised production rather than the Councils. The Councils had not been able to fulfil their imputed role of uniting workers of different trades and different levels of skill. Defections by technicians and other highly skilled workers hampered the production effort during the occupations.[40]

More important was the fact that military power remained firmly in control of the Italian State. That workers were electing their own delegates in the occupied factories did not alter this fact. Gramsci demanded the party to call for the formation of an urban Soviet for the purpose of defending the factories and eventually making an assault on State power. In practice, however, there was no practical means of achieving this goal as long as the vast majority of military power remained under army control. The Council strategy was based on the premise that political power ultimately issued from control of society's productive apparatus, so that once the workers controlled the factories State power would fall into their hands as well. Bordiga and Serrati were quick to point out that even if workers controlled factories in Turin, Milan and a few other industrial cities,

[39] Maione, *Il biennio rosso*, pp. 116–55; Williams, *Proletarian Order*, pp. 203–9.
[40] Clark, 'Factory Councils', Ph.D. thesis in the Department of History, University of Reading, 1966, pp. 253–4, 256–9.

there was no political leadership to co-ordinate the efforts of the isolated 'factory-republics'. In their eyes a disciplined vanguard was the only solution to this problem. They also reproached Gramsci for failing to distinguish between Factory Councils and Soviets. Marx and Lenin based their theories of workers' democracy on federated territorial units, while Gramsci maintained that such political Soviets could be set up only after the Councils had effectively secured control over production. This raised an extremely important point, since it was entirely conceivable that the interests of workers living in a district could clash with those working there, that is, over issues like air pollution and land waste. Gramsci did not adequately show how such adjudication could proceed within the framework of his proposed Council State. Larger questions remained about the feasibility of combining a planned economy executing top-level production decisions with any real measure of autonomy for local political Soviets. As we shall see in chapter 4, this point was of major concern for the Guild socialists.[41]

Towards the end of September 1920 Prime Minister Giovanni Giolitti simply waited until the Council movement ran out of momentum and its leaders were forced to come to the negotiating table with the State. In the ensuing negotiations it was stipulated that the trade unions would have a say in the overall direction of production. The Councils would continue to exist much as they had since the first CI made their appearance, that is, as disciplinary bodies taking up issues like dismissals and suspensions. Crucial matters concerning investment remained in the hands of the industrialists. This result was obviously far from Gramsci's conception of workers' control, convincing him that the PSI was henceforth a spent force in Italian revolutionary politics. He thus participated in the founding congress of the PCI under Bordiga's leadership in January 1921 in Leghorn. The presence of the *Ordine Nuovo* nucleus at the congress ensured that the statutes of the new party would contain support for Factory Councils and principles of workers' democracy in general. However, the overall tenor of the founding documents reflected Bordiga's preference for a highly centralised and hierarchical vanguard. The PCI thus joined the other Communist Parties of the Third International, which was by this time already censuring the work of Pannekoek, Rühle and other advocates of Council democracy. Gramsci would go on to work for the Comintern in Vienna and Moscow before assuming leadership of the PCI in 1924, when

[41] Gramsci, 'Lo strumento di Lavoro', ON, pp. 79–80; 'Programma d'azione della sezione socialista torinese', ON, pp. 393–4.

Moscow decided that Bordiga was no longer the man for the job. Bordiga firmly opposed the strategy of class alliances that the International advocated in this period, which would have necessitated close links with the PSI. These disputes allowed Gramsci to take over leadership of the Party until his imprisonment in November 1926. Two years later be began writing the *Prison Notebooks*, in which the emphasis on Councils of the *Ordine Nuovo* faded and the role of the Communist Party took on primary importance.[42]

Workers' Councils after the *Biennio Rosso*

During the 1920s, the prospects for revolution that looked so promising all across Europe in 1917–20 began to fade. Stalin succeeded Lenin at the head of the CPSU and continued the bolshevisation of all the member parties of the Comintern. The flourishing Council activity in Germany was repressed, and Council activity quickly came to an end in Italy following Mussolini's March on Rome in October 1922. Defenders of the Council ideal were faced with the alternative of either putting aside their views, as in Gramsci's case, or being excluded from Comintern activity, as in the case of Pannekoek and Korsch. Pannekoek temporarily returned to his astromomy studies in Holland. Revolutionary socialist opposition to Bolshevik control of the international communist movement slowly emerged, however, as small activist groups struggled to articulate a non-bureaucratic and non-statist vision of Communism. In 1930 the Group of International Communists (GIC) published a manifesto entitled *Basic Principles of Communist Production and Distribution*. The pamphlet was primarily the work of the German communist Jan Appel during the 1920s. Following Appel's arrival in Holland, the *Basic Principles* was revised and debated until it came out in book form in 1930. Appel insisted that despite the Bolshevik move to State-organised capitalism, the abolition of the capital–labour relationship and an end to the system of commodity production remained as essential prerequisites for the emancipation of labour. The USSR embarked on the authoritarian fulfilment of the Five Year Plans under quasi-Taylorian capitalist forms of management. This proved that the abolition of private property was merely one step along the road to a true socialisation of the means of production. In order to bring democracy to the world of labour it would be necessary to

---

[42] For the relations between Gramsci, Bordiga and the Comintern during 1921–26, see Bellamy and Schecter, *Gramsci and the Italian State*, chapter 3.

establish a system of Councils which would reward labour in relation to the number of hours expended in social, that is, collective
production. Eventually, the point would be reached where individual consumption came into equilibrium with social consumption.
This would signify a marked departure from capitalist patterns of
distribution, which were weighed almost exclusively in favour of
individual consumption.[43]

The GIC elaborated the concept of average social labour time,
which they hoped would be capable of measuring all categories of
production and distribution in communist society. The eventual
aim was to transform the production process from a drive for capital
accumulation into a system geared towards the satisfaction of
human needs. Pannekoek's ideas on Workers' Councils served as a
primary touchstone for the GIC, though it was not until 1929 that
formal ties were established. Pannekoek was asked to write an
introduction for the *Basic Principles*, and to contribute to the group's
work on educational and cultural issues. During the dark years of
Fascism's rise to power in Italy, Germany and Spain, Pannekoek
reiterated his initial observations on the need to find creative responses to the crisis of capitalism and its political degeneration
towards authoritarianism. The rise of Fascism, like the betrayal of
working-class internationalism in 1914, conclusively demonstrated
that the time-honoured institutions of the labour movement were
not adequate vehicles of resistance. In *Lenin as Philosopher*, *Workers'
Councils*, and the to date unpublished *Workers' Way to Freedom*, Pannekoek stayed true to the basic aim of his life's work: articulating a
revolutionary path between Social Democracy and Leninism.[44]

In his version of Council Communism, Pannekoek followed
Gramsci by arguing that the Councils would not simply replace the
former organisations of the workers' movement. Rather, the
Councils negated leader-oriented politics of all stripes which had
plagued the workers movement from its inception, and of which
Bolshevism was the most advanced symptom. Whereas Gramsci
looked for the germ cells of the new proletarian institutions in
existing shopfloor institutions like the Italian CI, Pannekoek argued
that the Councils would develop spontaneously, usually in connection with wildcat strikes. The orientation of the resulting strike
committees would be decisive in either propelling a Council movement forward or halting at reformist compromises. Like Gramsci,
Pannekoek argued that the mechanism of instant recall would

[43] Gerber, *Anton Pannekoek*, pp. 164–7; Appel, *Grundprinzipien*.
[44] Gerber, *Anton Pannekoek*, pp. 175–9.

ensure close collaboration and confidence between legislators and executors of community decisions. This collaboration would curb the tendency for leadership to distance itself from the masses and protect its interests through bureaucratic structures.[45]

In *Workers' Councils* Pannekoek provided a rich theoretical perspective on the possibilities of Council democracy, comparable in scope and detail only to Gramsci's *Ordine Nuovo* writings. As in Gramsci's model, Pannekoek's Councils would be elected by individual work crews, which would be subject to the same conditions of recall on demand. Where Gramsci envisaged a pyramidal structure of Councils presiding over a planned economy, however, Pannekoek was willing to concede far greater power to local and regional Councils. It was not clear this could be achieved without reintroducing some form of market between Councils. He may have envisaged some form of direct exchange of produced goods without the use of money, as some anarchists have proposed. In any case, the Councils would be primarily responsible for carrying out the decisions made by shopfloor workers. Pannekoek stressed that if the Councils were taken over by technical experts, the system would revert into a sham parliamentary democracy reproducing all of the problems of unaccountability that the Councils were supposed to combat. It was imperative that *all* played an active role. But until that time experts could only have a supervisory function. They were to contribute to bringing various work crews and factory delegates together for discussion, but in no circumstances were they to usurp the political basis of Council democracy: all power to the shopfloor workers.[46]

Pannekoek went on to sketch how the local Factory Councils might be federated into a diverse though co-operating network of regional and national Councils. Central Councils would be formed at the national level to co-ordinate production decisions, though their power would also be restricted by the recall on demand mechanism. These central Councils would be assigned the task of collecting and disseminating information to workers, who would then be in a

[45] Pannekoek, *Les Conseils ouvrières*, pp. 127–8. Gramsci, 'I gruppi comunisti', ON, pp. 142–3. It is worth noting that like Gramsci and many other councilists, Pannekoek's position on the party was unclear. At times he accepted the party as a necessity, at times he condemned it as necessarily rigid and bureaucratic. Unlike Gramsci, who remained within the ambit of international Communism and subsequently achieved great fame, Pannekoek found himself increasingly marginalised despite his highly original contributions to Marxist theory. See Gerber, *Anton Pannekoek*, pp. 182–3. Gerber's book is the best English book on the Dutch theorist.

[46] Pannekoek, *Les Conseils ouvrières*, pp. 76–7; Gramsci, 'L'unita proletaria', ON, p. 100.

position to meaningfully participate in the decision and voting process. The central Councils were also charged with the task of maintaining horizontal ties between different factories in the same industry, and steering co-operation between the distribution of raw materials to factories that needed them. A parallel and more decentralised network of Consumer Councils would also be set up. Like Korsch, Pannekoek saw the dangers of a production system geared entirely towards producers' needs. The aim was rather to co-ordinate production and consumption, as well as technical and non-technical knowledge, so that society could progress as a harmonious totality with no further need of managers and experts:

> In the domain of production itself, each enterprise must not only carefully organise its particular field of activity, but must also create horizontal links with similar enterprises, and vertical links with those enterprises that supply them with raw materials or that use their products. In this relationship of mutual dependence and co-ordination between enterprises, and in their links with other branches of production, the Councils, who discuss and decide, englobe ever greater spheres of activity, extending all the way to the central organisation of the totality of production. At the same time, the organisation of the consumption and distribution of all necessary goods will require their own Councils of delegates, which will have a more local or regional character.[47]

Pannekoek hoped that this structure of democratic self-management would not only increase productivity, but engender a spiritual revolution amongst all workers that would completely change the nature of social existence.

But Pannekoek's vision, like Gramsci's, was more rooted in the traditional assumptions of capitalist development than either of them realised in their Council writings. Like Lenin, Gramsci was prepared to apply the 'positive' aspects of Taylorism, i.e., extensive division of labour and firm discipline, to obtain maximum productivity. The 'rationalisation' of production and the exaltation of the work ethic all became unequivocally positive values for the worker when he or she was working for their own State. Long hours and repetitive tasks thus ceased to be a problem. In marked contrast to the ecological socialists and anarchists we will look at in chapter 6, Pannekoek and Gramsci were ready to accept the neutrality of technology. The productive apparatus bequeathed by capitalism and shaped by capitalist production relations was to be appropriated and wielded in the interests of the working class via the Council system.

[47] Pannekoek, *Les Conseils ouvrières*, p. 127; Gerber, *Anton Pannekoek*, pp. 183–4.

But what would happen when democratically self-managed firms polluted the air in a given community? Pannekoek and the young Gramsci tended to reduce human interests to producer interests in their Council writings. Thus the Council system they envisaged would reduce political questions to technical problems.[48]

Concluding remarks: the endurance of Council democracy

Post-World War II developments have shown that various forms of Council democracy often emerge in instances of political crisis, especially when existing institutions are unable to satisfy popular demand for participation on a mass scale. This was notably the case in Eastern Europe, where Councils have had an enormous impact in the re-assertion of Civil Society against an authoritarian State. Contrary to the expectations of the earlier generation of Council communists like Pannekoek and Gramsci, the question of the workplace was often merely one issue among other general matters concerning human rights and freedom of expression. This development is of the utmost theoretical and practical significance, and has thus been the subject of an enormous exegetical and often polemical investigation. There is unfortunately only limited space here to discuss the role of Councils in a renascent Civil Society. Nonetheless, it is important for us to note the broad contours of this phenomenon.

In October 1956 in Hungary a demonstration against Soviet interference in Poland's internal politics was organised by a group of students and intellectuals called the PETOEFI circle. The demonstration was initially banned, then at the last moment permitted by the government of Imrye Nagy. In a show of solidarity there ensued a mass walk-out by factory workers and white-collar workers, many of whom formed worker Committees to express their views on the Russian military presence in Poland and Hungary. In the city of Miskole a Council was elected consisting of delegates from the various factories in the city holding a variety of political viewpoints. A General Strike was planned, which was to affect all sectors except transport, electric energy and health. On 25 October several delegates of the Miskole Council travelled to Budapest to confer with similarly formed Councils in the capital. A joint statement was issued demanding: (1) the immediate withdrawal of Soviet troops from the two countries; (2) the formation of a new government in Hungary;

[48] Schecter, *Gramsci and the Theory of Industrial Democracy*, pp. 166–72.

(3) recognition of the right to strike; (4) amnesty for all arrested in anti-government demonstrations.[49]

The resolution of the Miskole Council called for international working class solidarity, and refusal to submit to any form of subordination to the military strategies of the USSR. The Council continued to provisionally support the Nagy government, but rather than complying with the government's request to down arms and return to work, the Miskole Council organised the formation of workers' militias, an extension of the General Strike, and the formation of a network of committees and groups which in effect constituted a local government challenging the authority of the State. On 26 October, radio Miskole made an appeal to the workers of all the surrounding cities to take similar measures, and to co-ordinate their efforts into a single powerful movement. Thus in Gyoer and Pecs similar Councils sprung into existence, co-ordinating economic activity with political and military functions. Meanwhile the Nagy government vacillated, at times pleading with the Councils and at times threatening them with severe punishment. Finally Soviet tanks rolled into the capital and other cities of agitation, dismantling Councils and disarming militias, and replacing Nagy with their own man, Janos Kadar.[50]

Though the Soviet troops were able to put down the Hungarian Councils in October–November 1956, they could not extinguish the spirit that animated them. Councils of workers, intellectuals, and community groups played an important role in the Prague Spring of 1968, when Warsaw Pact troops were once more employed to smash the forces of Democratic Socialism. Again, however, the Council ideal re-emerged. At its 1981 congress, the Solidarity movement in Poland called for the transfer of economic power from the Communist Party to a democratically elected Council system. Once martial law was lifted, Solidarity continued to press for its programme of self-management not only in the economy, but in the fields of education, culture and communication. Moreover, while intent on protecting individual rights, the movement aimed at the creation of greater openness and dialogue between workers' groups like KOR and other groups in Civil Society like students, peasants and members of the Catholic Church. The important role of workers' and community Councils was also a notable feature of the revolutions of 1989 in Eastern Europe. The proliferation of groups

[49] Lefort, 'L'Insurrection Hongroise', pp. 86–90.
[50] Lefort, 'L'Insurrection Hongroise', p. 112. For similar developments in Poland, see Chaulieu, 'La voie polonaise', pp. 70–3.

like New Forum, Bundnis 90, and Democracy Now in East Germany leads us to the conclusion that the rich history of the Council ideal from Rosa Luxemburg to the present day is not over. Indeed, there is an urgent need for empirical and theoretical research to grasp the implications of the 'velvet revolutions' for current and future practice. Such research would be usefully directed at examining the role of the Councils within broad social movements aiming at the constitution of an increasingly autonomous and self-managed Civil Society.[51]

---

[51] Pelcynski, 'Solidarity', pp. 365, 375–7; Mason, 'Solidarity as a New Social Movement', pp. 50–4; Arato, 'Civil Society', pp. 46–7, and Arato's 'Empire vs. Civil Society', pp. 23–4; Schulz, 'Neues Forum' in Enbergs, Schulz and Wielgohs, Von der Illegalität, pp. 11–104, and Hampel, 'Das Wahlbündnis', pp. 307–41.

4

Guild Socialism

In 1918 Bertrand Russell succinctly summed up the case for Guild Socialism:

> Marxian Socialism, I fear, would give far too much power to the State, while Syndicalism, which aims at abolishing the State would, I believe, find itself forced to reconstruct a central authority in order to put an end to the rivalries of different groups of producers. The best practicable system, to my mind, is that of Guild Socialism, which concedes what is valid both in the claims of the State socialists and in the syndicalist fear of the State, by adopting a system of federalism among trades for reasons similar to those which are recommending federalism among nations.[1]

In that same year, in *Labour in the Commonwealth*, G. D. H. Cole, the leading theoretician of Guild Socialism, asked what is still today our central question: why in a democracy are the many nominally supreme but actually powerless? Cole provided a detailed and cogent answer to this question, which we will look at below. Let us first have a look at the origins and development of the Guild socialist idea.[2]

The forerunners: Ruskin, Morris and the *New Age*

It has been noted that Guild Socialism has been among the few revolutionary political ideas to have seized the imagination of theorists in English-speaking countries in the twentieth century. Its continued relevance for our purposes lies in the sustained effort of the Guild socialists to construct a non-authoritarian vision of Socialism. The spiritual and practical roots of the movement can be traced to a certain confluence of ideas between early British Socialism and the romanticism of Thomas Carlyle, John Ruskin and

---

[1] Russell, *Roads to Freedom*, p. 177.
[2] Cole, *Labour in the Commonwealth*, p. 35.

William Morris, on the one hand, and the producers' co-operative movement, on the other. The former group of social critics focused their attention on the alienating consequences of the division of labour, increased specialisation and fragmentation of individual experience. They stressed the importance of returning to small artisanal production and the right of all members of society to find joy and self-expression in work. This concern with overcoming alienating work was combined in the writings of the Guild socialists with an attempt to chart a course between Syndicalism and State Socialism, both of which they considered to be fundamentally flawed. As the quotation from Bertrand Russell indicates, it was feared that Syndicalism in practice would result in the tyranny of the producers over the general needs of the community, while State Socialism would extend technocratic planning until the workforce was deprived of its right to organise work creatively on a day to day basis.[3]

Ruskin and Morris impressed later Guild socialists with the insight that economic theory had direct implications for the conduct of human life in society, and thus could in no way be freed from moral theory. Ruskin in particular saw the need for a moral critique of modern working conditions in the face of the supposed objectivity of both Marxists and liberals. The economist of 'homo oeconomicus' fame did little to conceal the assumption that what the *selfish* person did is what the *rational* person should do. The so-called 'laws' of supply and demand took little account of the conditions governing the supply of labour and the circumstances which created the demand for a given product. The imperative to buy in the cheapest market and sell in the most expensive required turning a blind eye to the conditions which made one market cheap and the other dear. Similarly, to speak about labour in terms of it being 'cheap' or 'dear' was to willingly ignore how fundamental labour was in the reproduction of the human species. For Ruskin, labour was the process of human self-creation, not something which could be bought or sold – all other things could be measured in terms of labour, but labour itself was priceless.[4]

William Morris added an imaginative dimension to Ruskin's moral critique of capitalism and industrial production. Morris first developed an antipathy towards capitalism from reading Thomas Carlyle. Carlyle charged capitalism with reducing all human values to

[3] Richards, 'Introduction' to Cole, *Guild Socialism Re-Stated*, pp. v–vi; Anthony, *John Ruskin's Labour*, pp. 190–1; Glass, *The Responsible Society*, pp. 6–8.
[4] Anthony, *John Ruskin's Labour*, p. 149.

the cash nexus. In *Past and Present* he cited the questions of work and wages as the largest of the age. However it was Ruskin who had the greatest impact on Morris. By the time Morris arrived in Oxford to study, Ruskin's *Modern Painters* and *The Seven Lamps of Architecture* had already been published. But it was *The Stones of Venice* which inspired Morris's vision of a self-governing society of creative individuals. Like Carlyle, Ruskin expressed the belief that the labour process had to be creative, joining the worker's moral and intellectual power to his or her physical strength. When comparing medieval art and society with nineteenth-century art and society, Ruskin noted a striking decline in intellectual and physical harmony. For Ruskin the most portentous aspect of this decline was the increasingly prevalent separation of mental and manual labour. Reading Carlyle and Ruskin pushed Morris to ask what exactly was the nature of the nebulous concept of 'progress'. How was it possible that there had been progress when one compared the artistry of the great cathedrals with modern architectural disasters? How could there be talk of progress when one compared the rise of an impoverished and unskilled proletariat with the artisans and craftsmen of the Middle Ages? In his *News from Nowhere*, which had a profound impact on the young Cole upon his arrival in Oxford, Morris adumbrated what a more modern version of medieval harmony might look like. He hoped for a revolution in European society bringing a return to standards of excellence in work and restoring a sense of harmony between humankind and nature.[5]

The ideas of Carlyle, Ruskin and Morris were immensely influential on the group of architects, artists and intellectuals who contributed to the journal the *New Age* between 1907 and 1920. Those who sought left-wing alternatives to Labour Party orthodoxy on art, history and politics looked to the *New Age* with high hopes of radicalising British political culture. Prior to the publication of the *New Statesman* in 1913, no other English journal could boast of such a diverse range of contributors, which included Hilaire Belloc, Ramiro de Maeztu, and Ezra Pound. The editor of the *New Age* was A. R. Orage, a gifted propagandist and synthesiser of other people's ideas. He came to the *New Age* during a period in which large-scale dissatisfaction with the Labour Party made a new Party seem desirable and possible. The journal was first published in 1904, at which time Ramsay MacDonald and soon after G. K. Chesterton were contributors. Orage's personal discovery of Nietzsche forced him to

[5] Thompson, *William Morris*, pp. 65–6; Redmond, 'Introduction' to Morris, *News from Nowhere*, pp. xix–xxix.

re-think his initially Fabian ideas. He found himself increasingly estranged from the Webbs's brand of technocratic Socialism, and gravitating towards what can be characterised as left-Nietzscheanism. He came to the conclusion that rather than a technical problem, Socialism had to be considered as a kind of political 'revaluation of values'. In the case of Orage, this implied an ethical and spiritual rejection of capitalism and its corresponding conceptions of science and progress. In the issue of 3 October 1907 Orage declared that:

> The world for the socialist is an everlasting becoming, a perpetual process of generation and regeneration, a continual mounting of life up the ladder of becoming. Hence it follows that the socialist has illimitable vistas for the future of man . . . If he is satisfied for the moment with demanding the political and economic rights of man, it is only as a step towards the other more lofty demands.[6]

These ideas helped form a common ground for socialists such as A. J. Penty and S. G. Hobson who were dissatisfied with both the Labour Party and the Fabians. Orage and Penty met in Leeds as members of a Theosophical Society. Penty trained as an architect, and while seeking to broaden his cultural horizons he read Ruskin, Morris and the ethical and aesthetic codes of the Middle Ages. In 1902 he came to London and began work on *The Restoration of the Gild System*, which was the first systematic statement of Guild socialist principles. Orage recognised the importance of Penty's book, and thereafter fashioned the *New Age* as the theoretical journal of the Guild socialist movement. Inspired by Ruskin and Morris, Orage, Penty and Hobson embarked on detailed historical and theoretical analysis of the evolution of capitalism and industrial production, arguing that the abolition of the wage system was the precondition for the emancipation of labour.[7]

In a series of *New Age* articles collected in 1914 as *National Guilds*, Hobson postulated that the practice of selling labour as a commodity like any other was incompatible with the essential role of labour in any creative individual's life. To this extent both existing trade unions and advocates of State Socialism had not grasped the essential point: reward for labour had to be dissociated from all considerations of profitability. Demands for higher wages and shorter hours were distractions from the basic goal of restoring joy and self-creation to the labour process. Such a restoration entailed

---

[6] Orage, quoted in Frank Mathews, 'The Ideology of Becoming', p. 159; Steele, *Alfred Orage*, pp. 228–9.
[7] Mathews, 'The Ideology of Becoming', pp. 149–52.

accepting that the need to experiment, innovate, and combine new and used techniques would at times retard production in ways incompatible with plan or market driven systems. But this was the worthwhile price to pay for restoring the dignity of the medieval craftsman that had been usurped by the capitalists, and which would be just as perniciously frustrated by proposed models of collectivism. Reminiscent of Wolffheim and Pannekoek's call for the formation of industrial unions to overcome the divisions caused by the multiplication of craft unions, Hobson defined the Guild as the amalgamation 'into a single fellowship' of all those employed in any given industry.[8] Such an amalgamation did not necessarily preclude certain subdivisions, provided that they remained firmly within the scope of the parent Guild: steel, coal, etc. Within the Guild all decisions would be made democratically, and all material benefits distributed equally. Thus for Hobson:

> The fundamental distinction between Guild Control and private capitalism is that, whereas the latter merely buys labour as a commodity, at a price (known as wages) which will yield the maximum rent and interest, the Guilds co-operatively apply the human energy of their members, render themselves and their members independent of capitalist charges, and distribute the proceeds of their members' labour amongst their members without regard to rent or interest.[9]

As in Germany and Italy, various plans for worker control of industry were proposed in the years immediately following the end of World War I. Workers returning from the front who had risked their lives for the nation were unwilling to return to the previous authoritarian system of industrial relations, in which capitalist control of the labour process was accepted as the unconditional prerogative of the owners of the means of production. Government-sponsored initiatives such as the Whitley Report called on the major industrialists to adopt some form of worker participation in decision making, however anodyne it might be. The Whitley reforms were greeted with optimism by the majority of trade union leaders, while Penty, Hobson and the New Age group regarded such halfway measures as unacceptable compromises with the wage system. The latter were much more favourably impressed by the militancy displayed during this period by the Shop Steward movement.[10]

   Shop Stewards were union representatives who, unlike the union bureaucracy, usually worked on the shopfloor. Moreover,

---

[8] Hobson, National Guilds, p. 132.
[9] Hobson, National Guilds, p. 146.
[10] Hobson, National Guilds and the State, pp. viii–ix; Penty, Old Worlds for New, pp. 58–9.

these militants often had close contacts with workers and union leaders of various trades, thus providing unity to the working class that was being eroded by task specialisation and increasing fragmentation of the labour process. In *National Guilds and the State* (1920) Hobson argued that the qualitative increase in Shop Steward militance after the war opened up new possibilities for the establishment of a labour-managed economy. The most positive evidence for such a possibility were recent Shop Steward demands for the amalgamation of industrial unions into large federations capable of directing the entire labour process. They hoped to make the workshop the basic unit of industrial democracy by cutting across craft lines. Hobson believed that the workshop unit was a potent source of worker spontaneity and direct democracy which could assert its autonomy at any moment. In this respect it was a great advantage over a craft union, whose actions were slow and filtered through an elaborate chain of command. But the workshop unit by itself was too isolated to really challenge capitalist control of the labour process. The Guild socialist movement thus sought to frame the direct democracy afforded by workshop units within the structure of national-level production units.[11]

Hobson argued further that only when industry was controlled by Guilds could the wage system be abolished, and only then could the State play its true role as the pre-eminent cultural and spiritual institution of the nation. He thus shared the Hegelian belief that the State is the ideal institution for fostering the community of language and cultural history that shape the identity of a nation, while rejecting the Hegelian illusion that the State could play such a role when Civil Society was riven by economic conflict and inequality. Yet he did not attempt to reformulate Marx's basic position, that is, to bring production under the jurisdiction of the community organised politically. Rather, he maintained that a democratically controlled civil sphere was the precondition of a communitarian (as opposed to an authoritarian) State, without thereby proposing to reconcile economic and political activity in a higher dialectical unity. Marxism, as a specific form of collectivist Socialism, had made the mistake of merging the economic and political aspects of human existence. A true democracy would in fact separate these processes of social reproduction, as Hegel had argued. However, one could not ignore the crucial link between the democratisation of economic life, on the one hand, and the real possibility for the

---

[11] Hobson, *National Guilds and the State*, pp. 217–18.

genuine expression of the interests of the community, on the other. This had been the great shortcoming of the *Philosophy of Right* which Marx had noted. Though he correctly diagnosed the problem, Marx prescribed the wrong solution. Hobson summed up his position thus: 'The logic of this is plainly that citizenship means pursuit of the spiritual, whilst Guildmanship is the application of social principles to the material.'[12]

Hobson thus insisted that in conjunction with the self-government in industry realised by the Guilds, all areas of the State would be democratised in Guild socialist society. Wages would be abolished, thus giving all members of the working populatuion a fixed income and a say in the management of their work. In this way the fear, greed and envy that destroyed creativity in all fields of human endeavour under capitalism would vanish. Such arrangements would allow teachers and other workers serving the community to really concentrate on the vital task of education, rather than continually struggling with precarious conditions of employment, intolerably low wages and excessive hours. When the teaching profession acquired the status of a self-governing Guild within the ambit of the State, it could perform its true role of pedogogy and transmit spiritual and cultural values to successive generations. This was equally true of all those fields serving the public, such as health and justice.[13]

Penty had already called for the abolition of the wage system in his *Restoration of the Gild System*, which he completed in 1906. He intentionally adopted the term 'Gild' to emphasise the need to adapt what was still vital in the social structure of the Middle Ages to conditions prevailing in modern Britain. In his later work of 1917, *Old Worlds for New*, he explained that Guildsmen of the past had correctly understood that a currency, when unregulated, lent itself to manipulation for profit. This prevented money from playing its legitimate role as a medium of exchange. To guard against this they fixed prices, thus rejecting the logic of the market. Their goal was to maintain high standards of quality, provide thorough training in the practice of a trade, regulate the size of individual workshops, the number of workers and the quantity of goods produced. While in the context of the Middle Ages such practices could only be sustained by the protection of jobs through exclusion, Penty

[12] Hobson, *National Guilds and the State*, p. 293.
[13] Hobson, *National Guilds and the State*, pp. 302–25.

optimistically assumed that a modern Guild structure would provide an apprenticeship and fixed wage for all, while finding a place
for women and the young as well.[14]

Drawing on Kropotkin's *Mutual Aid*, Penty stressed that in the
past society was divided into groups of producers who co-operated
and co-ordinated their productive efforts through the local Commune. The Guild, like Pelloutier's *Bourses du Travail*, was an association
of producers in a given industry, but also a centre of mutual aid,
education, and social interaction. The Guild provided assistance to
the sick and unfortunate, regulated wages and working hours, fixed
prices and working standards, and arranged the training of new
apprenticeships and the number of workers that could be employed
in a workshop. Penty advocated a return to such decentralised forms
of control to restore democracy to limited spheres of human activity
like the workshop where it could be meaningfully practised. Such
reconquest of local autonomy was a central pillar in Penty's argument for the eventual abolition of the wage system and a return to
creative work:

> Unless a man can work leisurely, it is impossible for him to put his best
> thought into his work, and unless a man is protected from the competi-
> tion of unscrupulous rivals, who undercut him in price and jerry their
> work in unseen parts, it is impossible for him to remain a conscientious
> producer.[15]

Penty argued that while the abolition of the wage system was the
long-term goal of the modern Guild socialist movement, the most
immediate objective was combatting the effects of modern industrial production techniques, which continually substituted
machinery for human labour power. The result was the steady
decline of any sense of personal responsibility for one's work, and
an erosion of personal relationships in and outside the workshop.
Penty reiterated Carlyle's condemnation of the intrusion of the cash
nexus into personal relations. Yet the modern age admittedly had
brought certain benefits to industries like transport and communication which would be preserved in a revitalised Guild system. In such
industries economy of scale provided efficient service to the consumer that was foolish to ignore. But in most other fields of production, and wherever possible, Guild socialists of the *New Age* proposed
a return to small-scale production, lengthy apprenticeships, and

---

[14] Penty, *The Restoration of the Gild System*. See also Penty, *Old Worlds for New*, pp. 11–12,
46–8.
[15] Penty, *Old Worlds for New*, p. 48.

personalised relationships in the workshop and local community. Penty recalled that Ruskin had spent most of his life trying to convince his readers that political economy was above all a moral exercise, and that the ostensible benefits of Adam Smith's pin maker – lower expense and greater output – were far outweighed by the tremendous degradation of the lives of the producers that such changes had caused.[16]

Along with Orage, Hobson and other *New Age* contributors, Penty proposed to fuse all trade unions connected with a given industry into large national bodies. After recruiting all the workers in a trade, including the unskilled, to become members, these bodies would organise themselves as labour monopolies which would be powerful enough to refuse to sell labour as a commodity. They would be in the position to demand from the owners of capital an equal say in the direction and control of industry. In the event that the capitalists should perceive that such a step was in the inexorable direction of their own demise and refuse, a General Strike would be declared. Penty in particular was convinced that the amalgamated unions could assume control of industry without capitalist interference. With the intelligent public on the side of the workforce, the State would be forced to compensate the owners, and then henceforth let the Guilds assume control over production. In return for a national charter guaranteeing a monopoly in production matters and a pledge of non-interference from the State, the Guilds would undertake a range of responsibilities, from maintaining high standards and sufficient output to attending to the diverse economic and social needs of its members.[17]

Through the *New Age* the ideas of Orage, Hobson and Penty shaped public opinion in the years immediately before and following World War I, and also had a decisive influence on the leading English social theorist of the period – perhaps of this century – G. D. H. Cole.

Cole and Guild socialism

Like Penty and several other Guild socialists, Cole admired certain aspects of medieval social and political life. His initial positive evaluation of the former Guild system is evident in his introduction to the English translation of Georges Renaud's *Guilds in the Middle Ages*. What particularly inspired Cole was his belief that the Guild was a private

[16] Penty, *Old Worlds for New*, pp. 76–82, 115.
[17] Penty, *Old Worlds for New*, pp. 50–1.

institution to the extent that it managed its own affairs without political interference, yet public insofar as it held itself responsible to the needs of the community in which it produced. For Cole this dual nature of private and public existence represented key elements for a model democratic society in which the activity of production was not regarded as the combined effort of private individuals in pursuit of personal gain, but rather the process by which the community as a whole satisfied its essential needs. Cole reiterated Penty's argument that producer accountability to the community would engender a demand for high quality, which, in turn, was best realised in small-scale and artisanal production. As we shall see, Cole believed that with a return to small-scale production and the right institutional arrangements, the communal spirit of the past could be given new life, and in the process modern society would be radically demo-cratised.[18]

The young Cole's most immediate points of reference were the Fabian tradition of collectivist Socialism, represented by Sidney and Beatrice Webb, and French Revolutionary Syndicalism. The Webbs descended from a long line of Enlightenment thinkers who argued that industrial technology combined with the expert planning of socialist technicians would result in maximum productive efficiency and a just distribution of social wealth. Thus the Webbs sought to articulate a twentieth-century socialist version of the ideas of Auguste Comte and Henri de St Simon. These ideas found their most complete expression in the Webbs's *For a Socialist Commonwealth of Great Britain* (1920). Cole had equally strong roots in the revolutionary romantic tradition of Ruskin and Morris, however, which soon led him to break with the bureaucratic and elitist underpinnings of Fabian thought. In this respect he was more attracted to Revolutionary Syndicalism, with its stress on industrial democracy and the autonomy of the producers. But if Collectivism was bureaucratic and elitist, Syndicalism did not adequately grasp the necessity of the co-operative relationship between the State and industry which was the subject of continual debate in the pages of the *New Age*. In 1913 Cole received a double first in Classical Moderations and Literae Humaniores at Baillol College, Oxford. He was awarded a 7-year Fellowship at Magdalen College, Oxford, where in 1913 he wrote *The World of Labour*. By the age of 24 Cole had already fashioned an original

---

[18] Richards, Introduction to *Guild Socialism Re-Stated*, pp. xiv–xv; Cole, *Guild Socialism Re-Stated*, pp. 43–6.

synthesis of Fabian, syndicalist and *New Age* ideas which addressed the major themes of his subsequent work.[19]

What was absent in Gramsci's *Ordine Nuovo* writings and only barely sketched in those of Bauer and Pannekoek – the importance of the consumer – was given full exposition in Cole's work. In the *World of Labour* he stated his position clearly:

> It is, on the face of it, improbable that either producer or consumer ought to have absolute control; it is unlikely that either the State or the unions should take the place of the exploiter entirely; for then either the State would be in a place to exploit the worker, or the worker would be in a position to exploit the community – just as the capitalist exploits both at the present. The solution must surely lie in some sort of division of functions, allowing both producer and consumer a say in the control of what is, after all, supremely important to both.[20]

Cole's stress on the importance of representing consumer interests with the same vigour as producers' interests led to an important innovation in socialist political thought: a non-anarchist attack on the principle of State sovereignty, on the one hand, and the related theories of functional representation and political pluralism, on the other. Let us look at these notions in turn.

Cole developed his ideas on sovereignty and democracy while grappling with Rousseau's *Social Contract*, which he translated into English. Combining his knowledge of medieval society with what he took to be erroneous interpretations of the Frenchman's thought, he arrived at the conclusion that the State was merely one social institution among many in which the individual in a democratic society participated and had rights and interests. Any attempt to privilege the State over other spheres of action - such as production and consumption – in which each individual had a vital interest was an injustice to the complexity of social life and the richness of social action. He went further to argue that the notion of the individual as citizen, when unqualified by the corollary roles of the individual as mother, friend, student, consumer, etc. was a mere abstraction. Thus one could not represent the individual in his or her capacity as citizen in a body called Parliament and thereby maintain that their interests were thus accounted for. Each facet of social existence required a forum for expression and representation, and none had absolute priority over the others.[21]

[19] Carpenter, *G. D. H. Cole*, pp. 16–17.
[20] Cole, *The World of Labour*, p. 352.
[21] Cole, *Self-Government in Industry*, p. 260; *Social Theory*, pp. 75–6.

This was the essence of Cole's notion of functional representation, which was first sketched in *The World of Labour*, and further developed in *Self-Government in Industry* (1917) and *Social Theory* (1920). However, it was in *Guild Socialism Re-Stated* (1920) that he provided the most complete statement of the principles of Guild Socialism, and it is this book which will be the most important text for our discussion of his social theory. At the most basic level, Cole shared Marx's belief that the strict accountability of political representatives was an important element of a socialist politics. But Cole gave this imperative a particular functional interpretation in *Guild Socialism Re-Stated*:

> The essentials of democratic representation positively stated are, first, that the represented shall have free choice of, constant contact with, and constant control over, his representative. The second is that he should be called upon, not to choose someone to represent him as a man or as a citizen in all the aspects of citizenship, but only to choose someone to represent his point of view in relation to some particular purpose or group of purposes, in other words, some particular function.[22]

What would this entail in practice? Cole's theory can be broken down into the functional categories: (1) production; (2) consumption, which is in turn sub-divided according to its various forms, that is, personal, household and collective; (3) political functions, which consisted primarily in co-ordinating production and consumption related interests at different territorial levels. In marked departure from the English social contract theorists in the tradition of Hobbes and Locke, Cole regarded the State as a national-level association that had to share power and authority with regional and local associations of consumer interests understood in the widest sense. Let us look first at Cole's proposals for the organisation of production, before moving on to his ideas on consumption and the role of politics in co-ordinating the two in Guild socialist society.[23]

Cole's view of trade unions was somewhat contradictory, for on the one hand he was quite conscious of their limitations within a capitalist system, and on the other hand he placed great hope in the possibility that the unions might themselves take the initiative to amalgamate into industrial Guilds. Like Gramsci and Pannekoek, he did not hesitate to point out that, for the most part, trade unions had limited their activity to resisting capitalist prerogatives. Within the private enterprise system they had little power to make their own

[22] Cole, *Guild Socialism Re-Stated*, pp. 32–3.
[23] Cole, *Guild Socialism Re-Stated*, pp. 29–31.

positive contribution to the organisation of production. The result was often a stalemate between the forces of capital and the forces of labour, with disastrous consequences for production as a whole. For Cole the division of the trade union movement on a craft basis was its crucial limitation. Like Orage, Hobson, and Penty, Cole hoped to reduce the approximately 1,100 existing unions to some 20 industrial unions as the precondition of an eventual Guild-managed economy. He approved of Penty's proposal to use the collective contract to force the government to buy out private production interests and then turn them over to the Guilds. Cole referred to this transition strategy as 'encroaching control', which would ensure continuity between the 'before and after' stages of the revolution.[24]

Cole accepted that large-scale industry would continue to be the norm in those industries where it was clearly the most efficient way to carry on production, for example, in mining and on the railways. But wherever possible he urged a return to small-scale production. The return to the ethic of the craftsman was of course a Guild socialist tenet and an intrinsic part of their argument that higher-quality goods would result from such a restoration of the old workshop. Equally important for Cole, however, was that industrial democracy could only be practised where there was constant contact and accountability between workers and managers on the shopfloor. Here Cole criticised both Fabian and Bolshevik plans to reduce the working class to executors of plans formulated by technical experts removed from shopfloor realities. Rather than seeking to impose an authoritarian blueprint, Cole had faith that experimentation and innovation would result in a variety of compatible forms of industrial democracy:

> Just as factory autonomy is vital in order to keep the Guild System alive and vigorous, the existence of varying democratic types of factories in independence of the National Guilds may also be a means of valuable experiment and fruitful initiative of individual minds. In insistently refusing to carry their theory to its last logical conclusion, the Guildsmen are true to their love of freedom and social enterprise.[25]

While he expected some vestiges of previous internecine trade union competition to persist at the outset, Cole envisaged an eventual transition to a system of equal remuneration for all. His concern to safeguard consumer interests entailed the provision of some form of market, though not that usually associated with the competition

---

[24] Cole, *Guild Socialism Re-Stated*, pp. 19–20.
[25] Cole, *Guild Socialism Re-Stated*, p. 65.

of private firms offering various commodities. It was thus necessary
to devise measures in the event that one Guild produced below cost,
while for unspecified reasons others were constrained to produce at
cost or perhaps above cost. Cole hoped that in general competition
between Guilds would exist at the level of quality rather than price.
Nonetheless, institutional measures were needed to restore equality
of incomes between Guilds. He hoped to achieve this by co-ordinating producer interests with consumer interests through the political intermediary of the Commune, to which we will turn shortly.[26]

Cole's endeavour to combat the notion of State sovereignty by
elevating consumption to the same level as the productive and
political aspects of human endeavour created tensions within the
Guild socialist movement which were never resolved. Penty,
Hobson and several other contributors to the *New Age* decried Cole's
evident desire to sully the State with material concerns. Cole replied
that the State could only fulfil its positive functions once: (1) production was no longer to be left to the arbitrary will of competing
capitalists; and, equally important, (2) an adequate solution was
found to the eventual problem of holding producer interests
accountable to the broader interests of the community. While he
framed his proposed solution in terms of empowering consumers'
associations, we shall see that Cole understood the activity of consumption in a very broad sense. He supplemented his concern for
the consumer by arguing for the widest possible representation of
interests in Civil Society as a corollary of his attack on State
sovereignty. The attack on the State was rooted in his conviction that
the individual could not be represented 'in general'; moreover, this
implied that democracy could not be realised at the level of the State.
Rather, democracy was realised by harmonising the different
spheres in which individuals had vital interests, that is, by harmonising conflicting partial wills rather than stiffling such interests in the
name of the general will. This was only possible if there were
appropriate public spaces for communication between producers,
consumers and the State.[27]

In *Guild Socialism Re-Stated* Cole divided consumption into two
main categories. Personal consumption included individual
preferences in the routine purchasing of food, clothes, etc. To
ensure high quality and responsiveness to consumer preference
without relying on the usual mechanisms of price and market
demand, Cole advocated the establishment of Co-operative

---

[26] Cole, *Guild Socialism Re-Stated*, pp. 71–3; Carpenter, G. D. H. *Cole*, pp. 59–64.
[27] Cole, *Guild Socialism Re-Stated*, pp. 87–8.

Societies. Mass consumption of such goods as water and electricity were to be regulated by a separate body which he called the Collective Utilities Councils. Cole believed that these Councils would inherit some of the functions previously assigned to local authorities. The practice of planned obsolescence showed that a market dominated by the exchange of privately owned commodities normally resulted in the unfair distribution of primary goods and encouraged bad craftsmanship. What was needed instead was a relation of democratic participation and dialogue between producers and consumers which could revive the co-operative spirit of the medieval communities:

> It is clear, that the normal conduct of each industry and service is placed in the hands of the Guild, and that the best chance for the consumers of securing really efficient, because willing and communally inspired, service is to leave the producer as far as possible to manage his affairs . . . The relation of the consumer and his representatives is essentially complementary, therefore, and not antagonistic: the real reason for consumers' representation is that the 'consuming' point of view requires to be definitely expressed, in order that articulate demand may cooperate with and direct the course of organised supply.[28]

Some of the thinkers we considered in the last chapter, such as Karl Korsch, recognised the need for the representation of consumer interests. But Cole was able to develop this insight much further to include the entire range of other activities in Civil Society as well. While he envisaged joint consultation and constant dialogue between the Guilds and consumers' organisations at the local, regional and national level, he also proposed citizen associations 'for the fulfilment of spiritual, mental, and other non-economic needs and desires'. To this end he supported the establishment of Civic Guilds, and stressed their importance in the vital areas of health and education.[29] The Civic Guilds in health and education played an important role in his theory of the self-governing community. In the educational sphere he argued that the principle of self-government would eventually result in students exercising an ever greater control over their school life, that is, forming associations and taking disciplinary matters into their own hands. The principle of self-management would rapidly extend to include criticism of the school curriculum and teachers, as well as the authority to propose new

---

[28] Cole, *Guild Socialism Re-Stated*, p. 88; Carpenter, *G. D. H. Cole*, pp. 64–6.
[29] Cole, *Guild Socialism Re-Stated*, pp. 90–7.

forms of study and criteria of evaluation. Such an educational background stressing democratic decision making, constant participation and strict accountability of authority were, in fact, the preconditions for the system of self-management that every student
would be called upon to practise later in his or her working life in the
Guilds. Cole believed that the desire to participate was either
fostered or stifled at an early age, producing character traits in the
individual which would determine future reactions to authority in
the workplace. Thus the democratisation of the workplace was
inseparable from the democratisation of both the educational
system and all other areas of socio-political life where the exercise of
power affected the constitution of individual subjects. Again we see
Cole deconstructing the citizen into his or her various constitutive
identities, and trying to find the appropriate institutions to promote
individual diversity and choice.[30]

In addition to Health and Education Guilds 'to express the civic
point of view', Cole's Guild socialist society would also have Cultural
Councils. Here members of the community would meet to discuss
their views on music, drama, painting and sculpture. Like all other
Councils, Cultural Councils would exist at the local, regional, and
national level to support funding for the arts, encourage artistic
experimentation, and to ensure interaction between artists and the
community in general. Cole regarded such cultural activity as having
a vital role in stimulating individual development and transmitting
values of openness and tolerance for diverse forms of expression
and modes of thought. The ability to think, criticise and create were
ends in themselves, but of course they would also contribute to
resurrecting the individual genius that the Guild socialists saw in the
figures of Ruskin and Morris.[31]

Though Cole discussed the necessity of Civic Guilds in health,
education and all the other areas of competence normally reserved
for government ministries, he also envisaged a specifically political
institution to unite all the Guilds. He called this the Commune,
which, he claimed, could not be compared with the existing State.
The Commune co-ordinated the activities of an essentially democratic and pluralist Civil Society, while the modern State had the task
of somehow preventing the various competing private interests of
capitalist society from tearing the entire social fabric asunder.
Despite this fundamental difference the Commune did have the last

---

[30] Cole, *Guild Socialism Re-Stated*, pp. 108–16; Patemen, *Participation and Democratic Theory*,
     pp. 38–41.
[31] Cole, *Guild Socialism Re-Stated*, pp. 115–6; Wright, *G. D. H. Cole*, pp. 42–3.

word in settling economic and other kinds of conflicts in Cole's scheme, which to some extent ran contrary to his own arguments on the untenability of State sovereignty. Communes were the territorial equivalents of the functional representation secured in the Guilds. In Guild socialist society the Communes would exist at the level of the smallest country hamlet and extend to the regional and national levels, culminating in the National Commune to replace the existing State apparatus. Representatives of the Producers' Guilds, Consumers' Guilds, Civic Guilds and regional Communes would meet in the National Commune.[32]

To illustrate Cole's view of politics and his vision of a society based on participation and dialogue, let us look for a moment at an example of his alternative to both planned and market driven economies. In agriculture he did not propose what we would typically consider a market, but rather a negotiated price between the Transport Guild (sometimes also referred to as the Distributive Guild), basing its estimate on the price to be paid to the Agricultural Guild, and on its own cost of distribution. The Transport Guild would then submit a proposed price to the Co-Operative Society in charge of protecting consumer interests in the region. If the Transport and Co-operative Guilds came to an agreement, the agreed price would become the actual selling price. If there were disagreements the matter would go to the appropriate-level Commune, which would attempt to bring the various parties to an acceptable compromise price. In general, resources would also be allocated by way of constant dialogue between affected participants. Each Guild would propose a budget illustrating its estimated needs in terms of goods and services required for immediate use; such budgets would be drawn up on the basis of inter-Guild consultation. The resulting budget proposals would be presented to the relevant Consumer and Civic Councils. These in turn would have the right to criticise and seek amendments, and, reciprocally, to propose alternatives which they could suggest to the Producers' Guilds. Following such communications, all budgets would go to the Commune for final approval. At the national level the Finance Committee of the National Commune would bring the various budgets into harmony with the yearly estimated national production targets. After any final changes the budget would come to the plenary session of the National Commune. But Cole emphasised that the bulk of these compromises between producer, consumer, and citizen would for

[32] Cole, *Guild Socialism Re-Stated*, pp. 117–37.

the most part be settled in the Guilds, Councils, and Regional Communes rather than at the level of the National Commune. While the National Commune would necessarily be involved in the adjudication of producer and consumer interests (departing from Hobson's proposals), it would not have even a fraction of its present authority to intervene in all aspects of producers' and consumers' lives.[33]

With the vision of Guild Socialist society enunciated in *Guild Socialism Re-Stated*, Cole thus sketched his political and economic alternative to private ownership of the means of production existing in constant tension with the Leviathan State. Industrial Guilds, Co-operative Councils, Collective Utilities Councils, Health and Education Councils and Cultural Councils would meet at the local, regional, and national level, thus substituting the authority of the general will with a series of colliding and communicating partial wills. In departure from the syndicalist tones of *The World of Labour* and *Self-Government in Industry*, Cole had made a number of significant concessions to the importance of planning in *Guild Socialism Re-Stated*. He hoped that in exchange for recanting on some of the libertarian themes of his earlier work, he had outlined the possibility for the political participation for all those not directly involved in production, that is, consumers of all kinds, students, lovers of the arts, etc. The final result would be the realisation of the greatest imaginable degree of pluralism and transparency.[34] By the time of the failure of the General Strike in England in 1926, Cole conceded that he had perhaps placed too much hope in the ability of the unions to amalgamate in producers' Guilds. Moreover, the intensity of civic participation required to make the whole system work at all of its levels could not be realised within the framework of a society that continued to be dominated by the economic, political and ideological power of hierarchy and elitism. Together, these factors spelled the eventual demise of the Guild socialist movement. The world recession of 1929 once again placed the labour movement on the defensive until the arrival of the Atlee government in 1945.[35]

Despite the collapse of Guild Socialism, many of Cole's ideas remain relevant to the task of reconstructing a socialist alternative today. We thus conclude this chapter with a brief comparison

---

[33] Cole, *Guild Socialism Re-Stated*, pp. 141–7.
[34] Hirst, *Introduction to The Pluralist Theory of the State*, p. 28.
[35] Cole, *Guild Socialism Re-Stated*, pp. 191–5; Carpenter, *G. D. H. Cole*, pp. 105–10; Wright, *G. D. H. Cole and Socialist Democracy*, pp. 61–8; Houseman, *G. D. H. Cole*, p. 65.

between Cole and Marx on the concept of Civil Society as a preliminary discussion to our final conclusion.

Concluding remarks: Marx and Cole on Civil Society

In the Introduction it was noted that it was originally Hegel who
grasped the significance of the emergence of modern Civil Society as
a sphere of social action and economic activity distinct from both the
family and the State. Marx was quite forthright in his praise of Hegel's
depiction of Civil Society as the site of social struggle between
classes, characterised by the attendant ills of poverty, alienated
labour, and above all, the reign of private property and private
interests. Hegel viewed the rise of a large mass of exploited workers
with great alarm, for he saw the obvious divisions and tensions that
inevitably followed. While Marx praised Hegel for recognising the
importance of the distinctness of the modern civil sphere, he condemned Hegel's ultimately metaphysical argument that the centrifugal tendencies of Civil Society were overcome by the essential
social unity realised in the institutions of the modern State. Marx's
early work attempted to theorise the possibility of creating the
conditions for the unity of individual experience at the level of
worker, citizen and legislator.[36] In his political writings on the Paris
Commune and on the State in general, Marx argued that contrary to
Hegel's assertions, individual freedom and social harmony were not
to be found in the State. As a concentration of alienated political
power the State was an inappropriate vehicle for popular democratic
politics. Rather, the State had to be dismantled while legitimate
authority was vested in democratically constituted bodies at the
local level like the Commune. Thus, as we saw in the Introduction,
the chief legacy of the Paris Commune was Marx's now famous
remark that 'one thing was proved by the Commune, viz., that the
working class cannot simply lay hold of the ready-made State
machinery and wield it for its own purposes'.[37]

In the Introduction we touched upon one of the major problems inherent in Marx's plans to re-unify State and Civil Society,
namely, the political consequences of the total command planning.
Equally important is Marx's reduction of Civil Society to what he
calls its anatomy, that is, political economy. While his early works
such as the *Critique of Hegel's Philosophy of Right* and *On the Jewish Question*

---

[36] Marx, *Critique of Hegel's Philosophy of Right*, MECW, Vol. 3, p. 119; Arato, 'A
Reconstruction', p. 308.
[37] See p. 8 below, and MESW in 1 Vol., p. 32.

raise the possibility of a general emancipation from all forms of domination, Marx's later concentration on the dynamics of political economy steered him away from issues of former concern such as alienation, communication and community. By contrast, as he matured, these became increasingly central concerns for Cole. Marx's insistence on the necessity of the planned economy to rescue humanity from the aleatory clash of private interests barely concealed his assumption that the elimination of private property would eliminate the real basis of social conflict – and with it the State. This position does not take into account the range of interests individuals have in addition to those rooted in the politico-economic reality of social classes. Cole's great contribution to socialist theory was to rescue the complexity of Civil Society from economic reductionism by stressing the equally important interests people have as consumers, patients, students, members of communities, etc. In this respect he avoided the shortcomings of both Hegel and Marx. Like Hegel he saw the complexity of Civil Society and refused to reduce its dynamism to the site of class struggle. But at the same time he refused to believe that the State could function democratically while the institutions of Civil Society were left to function according to the logic of private interest, commodity fetishism and unaccoubtable power. Rather than seeking some transcendent solution to the State/Civil Society problem, however, he called for the *democratisation of both spheres*, recognising that a certain division would always be necessary and indeed, desirable.

Hegel was certainly correct to argue that the interests deriving from private property and what in the *Philosophy of Right* he called the 'system of needs' are but one aspect of interaction in the civil sphere. The administration of justice, the police and the corporation had to be carefully taken into consideration in addition to the system of needs in order to grasp the dynamic tension between private and public interests. Hegel's ideas on the administration of justice reveal an attempt to formulate a theory of social action regarding the individual as more than a private person seeking to protect purely material interests. For Hegel the civil sphere was indeed dominated by private interests and exploitation, yet there were also civil institutions with a dual public/private character which prepared the individual for the fully public-political life in the State. The corporation, as one such institution, was to some extent guided by ethical principles (*Sittlichkeit* in the Hegelian system) which found their full realisation only in the State:

> Under modern political conditions, the citizens have only a restricted

> share in the public business of the State, yet it is essential to provide men
> – ethical entities – with work of a public character over and above their
> private business. This work of a public character, *which the modern State
> does not always provide*, is found in the Corporation (my emphasis).[38]

On the one hand, Hegel's corporation is organised with the aim of
furthering private interests. On the other hand, individuals working
in corporate bodies rely on certain norms and shared understandings to attain collective goals, much in the spirit of Cole's notion of
colliding and compromising partial wills. Thus it was false to portray
the civil sphere as a conglomeration of isolated individuals in constant conflict with one another. Hegel's corporation, like Cole's
Guilds, Co-operative Councils, Civic Councils and local Communes
had its own system of freedom and authority, functioning according
to the rules of dialogue and accountability of power. Cole, however,
who unlike Hegel made no secret of his normative purposes, placed
far more stress on spreading norms of dialogue and understanding
as the precondition of a democratically functioning National Commune. While Marx insisted on reducing the complexity of Civil
Society to its 'anatomy', Hegel gives us a far richer picture stressing
the importance of the public rights of private individuals, civil law,
corporate identity, and the role of public opinion in influencing
debates in the legislature. Nonetheless, Cole goes considerably
further than both Hegel and Marx by outlining a thorough democratisation of the production process, and the possibilities for consumer representation. Cole's consistent attack on State sovereignty
is inseparable from his theory of socialist pluralism, while for Hegel
the State provided the ultimate reconciliation of conflicting
interests.[39]

Hegel was undoubtedly correct in emphasising that it is not only
economic forces, but the totality of sentiments, practices and beliefs
which shape social relations and our view of politics and our fellows
in general. Cole took this insight further by arguing that these
elements of *Sittlichkeit* could be modified by providing the individual
with new institutions to re-structure daily existence. He hoped that it
would thus be possible to transform a person's experience from

---

[38] Hegel, the *Philosophy of Right*, addition to Paragraph 255, p. 278; Cohen, *Class and Civil Society*, pp. 23–4, pp. 76–7; Black, *Guilds and Civil Society*, pp. 207–8; Bobbio, *Studi hegeliani*, pp. 148–57.

[39] Thus Arato notes that there is a tension between Hegel's defence of a multi-layered and pluralistic Civil Society and the etatistic strain in his thought. Cole by contrast, was unabashedly socialist and pluralist in both his methodology and conclusions. See Arato, 'A Reconstruction', pp. 316–17.

wage-earner to that of producer and integral member of a community, rather than a passive observer of its laws. Cole's social theory is fully informed by Marx's remark that 'Political emancipation was at the same time the emancipation of civil society from politics, from its even having a semblance of a general content' (see p. 6 above). With the industrial Guilds, Co-operative Councils, Collective Utilities Councils, Cultural Councils, Health Councils and Communes, Cole hoped to restore Civil Society with its political content. He deconstructed ideologically charged terms such as 'politics' and the 'State' into our concrete experiences as workers, patients, students, parents, citizens, consumers and friends. An immediate challenge for contemporary and future socialist theory is to make better use of this rich patrimony of ideas.

5

Market Socialism, self-management and the case for workers' co-ops

In the previous chapter we saw how the Guild socialists were concerned to safeguard producer autonomy from both the State and the tyranny of private interests. In the writings of G. D. H. Cole this implied a role for a modified market to facilitate direct exchange of goods between producers. It became clear that the particular kind of market advocated by Cole was highly unusual, featuring a negotiated price and a continual dialogue between producers, distributors and consumers. Cole intended that producer autonomy be reconciled with high standards of craftmanship reminiscent of the Guild era, as well as full producer responsibility to the interests of the local community. But trade union scepticism, the depression of the 1930s and general confinement of Guild socialist ideas to intellectual circles spelled the eventual failure of Guild Socialism as a political movement.

The post-World War II world was not long in existence, however, before the demand for non-statist Socialism was once again heard – this time in Yugoslavia. This chapter will examine the Yugoslav experiment in self-management and the origins of contemporary Market Socialism in post-war Europe. It will conclude with an assessment of the current theoretical debates on the feasibility of combining a market economy with socialist ideals of participation and accountability of power. There is a great deal at stake here, since the role of the market has always been a highly contested issue amongst socialists of every persuasion. Recent market socialists have made bold claims suggesting that the market is not only compatible but actually indispensable for Socialism. In contrast to Cole's fairly complex conception of a mediated form of market, David Miller has declared his intention to equip the theory of Market Socialism with 'a full-blooded unapologetic commitment to a market economy'.[1]

Market Socialism in Yugoslavia

The ideal of Socialism as self-government in the economy as well as in the polity long precedes the Yugoslav break with central planning. It will be recalled from the introduction that in the Paris Commune Marx had seen the possibility of smashing the State by democratising it, that is, by dismantling the central State apparatus and dispersing political power to a federation of de-centralised Communes. These organs of local democracy would then manage the affairs of 'even the smallest country hamlet'. For Marx this seemed to be the pre-condition for any genuine self-government of the producers. But we also saw how this highly participatory and de-centralised vision was impossible to reconcile with a centrally planned economy which would necessarily come under the control of a socialist officialdom. In fact, this is what happened in the former USSR and State socialist countries of Eastern Europe. Rather than withering away, the State continually expanded its role as it sought to control all of society's economic functions. Thus the Bolsheviks, presiding over the State and the economy, deprived the Soviets and other bodies of local power of any real authority. By 1927 the Five Year Plans could be implemented without 'interference' from shopfloor workers in the various regions of the country. It was soon apparent that such centralisation of economic power, along with the political mono-poly of power held by the Communist Party, was not in any way compatible with the self-government of the producers. Groups like the Workers' Opposition demanded greater producer autonomy through the empowerment of trade unions and workers' Councils. These attempts proved futile. As Leninism was succeeded by Stalinism, any attempt to question the centralised model of political economy was rejected as counter-revolutionary.[2]

Though the Workers' Opposition had raised important objections to Bolshevik tyranny which also figured prominently in the writings of syndicalists, anarchists, Council communists and Guild socialists, it was not until 1948 in Yugoslavia that an alternative conception of Socialism was given a chance to function on a large

[1] Miller, *Market, State and Community*, p. vi. See also Holmström, *Industrial Democracy in Italy.* Holmström says: 'The Market is not incompatible with socialism but essential to it' (p. 157).
[2] Nove, *The Economics of Feasible Socialism*, pp. 10–15, pp. 77–8.

scale. It was here that the market, traditionally associated with capitalism, was seen as an alternative to the State as a means of allocating resources. This constituted a step further than Guild socialist proposals for a negotiated price between the parties affected in an economic transaction. Yugoslav theoreticians claimed that the introduction of the market would not only lead to increased production, but would have the equally important effect of democratising the country by diffusing political power. Stalinism was castigated as a tyrannical and bureaucratic deviation from Marx, while the Yugoslavs defended their reforms as a return to Marxist humanism. Right until the disintegration of the country in 1991, the Yugoslav leadership claimed to be returning to the spirit of the young Marx and the Marx of the Paris Commune writings, that is, rejuvenating the doctrine rather than departing from it.[3]

At the outset it should be noted that the advent of Market Socialism in Yugoslavia was to a large extent a historical accident. When World War II drew to a close the Yugoslav Communist Party (subsequently re-named the Yugoslav League of Communists) took control of the country, suppressed all opposition parties, established a monopoly on the media and generally eliminated freedom of expression. In this way they were simply following the Bolshevik model of the dictatorship of the proletariat. In fact, Yugoslavia was initially one of the Soviet Union's most loyal satellite countries. Led by Josip Broz Tito, Yugoslavia supported Stalin on all major issues of foreign policy, economic collectivisation and the subordination of Civil Society to the State. But by 1948 Yugoslavia was denounced by the USSR and expelled from the international organisation of communist economies, the Cominform, as a country that had betrayed the principles of Socialism. How did this come about, and what were the results?[4]

The first Constitution of the Federal Republic of Yugoslavia of 31 January 1946 called for State ownership of all major sectors of industrial production, with the corresponding demand that all major decisions on the setting up and closing of enterprises be taken by the government. Production targets and distribution were under tight control by the League. At this stage it was thought that the concentration of all resources and the confiscation of private wealth was

---

[3] For the sources of Yugoslav theory and the stated aims of self-management see Kardelj, *Democracy and Socialism*, pp. 7–10; Zukin, *Beyond Marx and Tito*, pp. 50–4; Drulovic, *Self-Management on Trial*, pp. 199–202; Smidovnik, 'Disfunctions', pp. 27–9.

[4] Lydall, *Yugoslavia in Crisis*, pp. 1–2.

necessary in order to put the war-ravaged country back on its feet
and gain some measure of political stability for the future. Thus
planned distribution and rigidly controlled prices were deemed
indispensable.[5]

However, in keeping with the country's agricultural traditions,
the Yugoslavs sought to resume small-scale agricultural production,
for which they drew heavy censure from Stalin and the Cominform.
It was made clear that such measures would only encourage 'petit
bourgeois' and 'typically peasant' attitudes towards land and work
which would retard Stalinist models of industrialisation and collectivisation. The Yugoslavs initially sought to fall in line with
Cominform policy, but it soon became apparent that such policy
was ill-suited to the needs and realities of the country. Tensions
between Stalin and Tito going back to the fight against Fascism were
exacerbated. But the Yugoslav leader remained steadfast in his belief
that his country had to chart an independent course based on its
own abilities and needs. The inevitable result was the ostracising of
Yugoslavia and the imposition of economic sanctions which, before
long, amounted to a total blockade forcing the country to look to
other parts of the globe for trading partners. Throughout the period
1946–48 Tito adamantly opposed Soviet-style collectivisation and
Stalin's notion of a single road to Socialism. Polemics were
exchanged until 1950, when Tito announced that Yugoslavia would
henceforth embark on a new path of development based on the
slogan, 'the factories to the workers'. This was the start of a highly
original and influential experiment in socialist self-management.[6]

In November 1949, Djuro Slaj, the President of the Yugoslav
trade union Confederation, and Boris Kidric, a government official
responsible for economic policy, sent out a notice to 215 large
enterprises, detailing plans for the establishment of Workers'
Councils in those firms. These Councils were given the task of
drafting enterprise-level production targets, including proposals for
raising productivity and efficiency. Councils were to be elected by all
employees working in an enterprise by means of a secret ballot. The
Council had in turn to elect a director, with the stipulation that
workers could vote to remove Council members before the expiry
of their mandate if two-thirds decided he or she was not doing an
adequate job.[7]

The self-governing enterprise became the basic unit of all

[5] Drulovic, Self-Management on Trial, pp. 37–9.
[6] Drulovic, Self-Management on Trial, pp. 40–2; Lydall, Yugoslavia in Crisis, p. 2.
[7] Drulovic, Self-Management on Trial, pp. 43–4.

economic activity. Other corporate bodies such as local Communes, banks, or self-employed craftsmen were granted similar status. The 1965 law on enterprise formation and activity clearly stated that:

> By freely combining their work in the basis of social assets and self-management, the working people in an enterprise organize and constantly expand production, trade, or other economic activities, so as to satisfy their individual and collective interests and the general interests of society.

The Basic Law governing enterprise functions contained 299 articles, along with legislation regulating employment relations, the election of Workers' Councils and management structures, and the distribution of enterprise assets. What was formerly the exclusive domain of the State was henceforth, in principle, a matter for shopfloor workers and the managements they elected and dismissed. These groups of workers would trade their products with other similarly organised firms via the market. The aim was to achieve both democracy in the workplace and economic efficiency.[8]

In theory, all workers in an enterprise, whether they be manual workers, technicians or managers, were meant to enjoy the same rights. Each self-managed enterprise was instructed by the law to determine its own basic rules and regulations, provided that this underlying equality of all members was not infringed. In all enterprises with more than 70 workers an elected Workers' Council, comprised of somewhere between 15 to 100 people depending on the size of the firm, would hold 1-year terms. During the course of these terms the Council would legislate on all policy issues, such as how much of revenue to apportion between investment and consumption. Disciplinary matters were also dealt with. Yugoslav law specified that Council members could not run for a second consecutive term, but could run again subsequently. The Council elected a Management Board each year, entrusting it with authority on issues ranging from investment to housing and social services for workers. The Management Board, in consultation with the Workers' Council, would in turn elect an Executive Director for a 4-year renewable term.[9]

Where such upper management had previously been appointed by the relevant planning ministry, self-management called for new procedures. Thus Executive Directors were chosen as

---

[8] Vanek, 'The Worker Managed Enterprise', p. 257.

[9] Vanek, 'The Worker Managed Enterprise', p. 258; Zukin, *Beyond Tito and Marx*, pp. 258–9.

follows: in accordance with individual enterprise regulations, the post was publicly announced and advertised by the Council, which then appointed a committee to evaluate applications. Committees were made up of Council members and local Commune members in equal proportion, who would narrow the field of candidates down to six people. The list was sent to the Workers' Council for approval, which then selected its top choice or asked the committee to reconvene to select a new group of prospective Executive Directors. Once elected, the Executive Director was in charge of all current business, including the implementation of decisions made by the Workers' Council and its sub committees. Following traditions of radical democracy established in the Paris Commune, the Executive Director could be recalled on demand if a majority on the Council found his or her management incompetent.[10]

Jan Vanek, a scholar of Yugoslav self-managed enterprises, reports that in large firms it was not uncommon for there to be self-management bodies at individual levels of production and administration. In such enterprises, mid-level directors were appointed by Workers' Councils without outside intervention. In a very large enterprise one might have had several dozen self-management bodies of various descriptions working in conjunction with sub-committees in charge of different aspects of production and distibution. Autonomy and co-operation were important goals in all such firms. Vanek thus concludes that in Yugoslavia the usual model of the single enterprise was replaced by the far more flexible ideal of an 'autonomous organisation of associated labour'. Writing in an optimistic vein that may strike us today as somewhat naive, in 1975 Vanek assessed the Yugoslav situation thus:

> All this amounts to an immensely complex decision-making process for which it is difficult to find an analogy or a precedent. According to most accepted management theories, it should paralyse all decisions, all action. Yet this conclusion is obviously incompatible with Yugoslav experience. There have certainly been cases where internal conflicts led to delays or inefficiency but, on the whole, there are few examples of actual paralysis of decision making within an enterprise. On the contrary, there are few examples of collectivities as active and action-minded as the average Yugoslav firm . . . New Projects, big or small, are collectively pursued in all areas, especially investment, training, and social development.[11]

---

[10] Vanek, 'The Worker Managed Enterprise', pp. 258–9.
[11] Vanek, 'The Worker Managed Enterprise', pp. 260.

Vanek goes on to stress that contrary to many people's association of democracy with inefficiency and slowness in the decision-making process, the Yugoslav market socialist economy embodied the advantages of not having to seek the approval of directing planning boards located in distant capitals. Moreover, since all the workers in a firm bore the consequences of economic success or failure, there was little incentive to prolong disputes between management and shopfloor workers. Such conflicts are a chronic problem in both privately owned and nationalised industries. At the same time, enterprise capital was collectively controlled, which ensured that decisions would reflect the interests of at least the majority of employees working in a firm. This system of collectively owned capital, or *social property*, as it was called, had an enormous impact on subsequent self-management ventures outside of Yugoslavia. From its inception, a worker-controlled enterprise disposed of a certain amount of capital in the form of assets and means of production, which were either acquired independently or conferred by the State. This capital was intended to help the enterprise begin its commercial activities; it was available for use but was not owned by the enterprise. This meant that assets could not be liquidated to buy private retirement homes or other benefits that did not contribute to society's productive needs. It was considered vitally important that there be constitutional measures against property speculation and other instances of private usurpation of socially controlled wealth. Thus in the 1959 Constitution of the Socialist Federal Republic of Yugoslavia we read that:

> Socially-owned means of production, being the common, inalienable basis of social labour and social reproduction, shall exclusively serve as a basis for the performance of work aimed at the satisfaction of the personal and common needs and interests of the working people and at the development of the economic foundations of socialist society and socialist relations of self-management . . . Since no one has the right of ownership over social means of production, nobody – not socio-political communities, nor organizations of associated labour, nor groups of citizens, nor individuals – may appropriate on any legal-property grounds the product of social labour or manage and dispose of the social means of production of labour, or arbitrarily determine conditions for distribution.[12]

Enterprises getting under way in one of the six regions that made up Yugoslavia often received their initial capital from a voluntary

---

[12] Quoted from 'The Constitution of the Socialist Federal Republic of Yugoslavia' (1959), now in Vanek, *Self-Management*, p. 71.

association of individuals pooling their resources, or from the Fund for Regional Development. From this moment on, however, authority was legally vested in the Workers' Council and the Executive Director. Each enterprise was legally registered according to its chief economic activity, though it was permitted to engage in related subsidiary activities in other markets. For instance, an industrial enterprise might list transport and marketing activities as secondary operations generating new commercial possibilities. Since all enterprises had an interest in diversifying their operations for competitive market strength, it was frequently the case that they would not limit themselves to manufacturing or transport, even if they began as manufacturing or transport firms.[13]

To a large extent, self-managed enterprises in Yugoslavia faced similar problems to those confronting private firms in a capitalist economy, that is, raising initial capital and reaching sufficiently high levels of profitability necessary to pay off debts and to hire new workers. Yugoslav firms had the advantage of public investment agencies like the Fund for Regional Development. Alternatively, prospective founders could publicly approach banks for their initial capital. Any public social organisation or group of citizens could found an enterprise, provided that they could secure the necessary capital. The Yugoslav banking system ran into a number of difficulties, however, often operating at a loss. This obviously curtailed investment. In this respect Yugoslav banks were far less successful than the Basque Casa Laboral Popular (CLP), which we shall examine in the next section.[14]

Since capital was socially controlled by the workers of an enterprise and could not be arbitrarily sold or transferred without the approval of the Workers' Council, there were few rules concerning the voluntary shutting down of operations. This is not surprising, since the workers of a firm had little to gain from such a move unless assured of jobs in another self-managed enterprise. If it became clear that an enterprise would not be able to meet its financial obligations, that is, repaying loans, finding sufficient investment, or paying its workers adequately, there were some provisions for closure, all of which were designed to find new sources of employment for the displaced workers. The creditor of an enterprise could call for the appointment of a Public Receiver to remunerate the workforce and take over the functions of the Workers' Council and the Executive Director. Such manoeuvres could be and at times were contested by

[13] Vanek, 'The Worker Managed Enterprise', pp. 266–77.
[14] Lydall, *Yugoslavia in Crisis*, pp. 14–15.

workers of the affected enterprise if they felt they were being exploited. In terms of workers' rights, this certainly represented an impressive advance over the condition of most workers elsewhere. A compromise between the contending forces might be found if the local Commune was ready to asssume responsibility for the enterprise until it managed to reverse its losses. Enterprises were legally required to inform the Commune of any likely financial problems of this kind.[15]

However, closure provisions became increasingly necessary as bankruptcy became more frequent. After two decades of economic growth, the system began to falter. Most importantly, the market, which was thought to be the key to economic efficiency, had actually exacerbated inequalities between the Yugoslav regions. This imbalance seemed to bear out the thesis that the market tends to produce winners and losers, leaving the latter with increasingly little bargaining power. This was an important discovery in the Yugoslav context, however, where workers had far greater protection than in most private enterprise systems. At the same time, participation levels at the workplace began to drop, which was unacceptable if the principle of self-management was to be taken seriously. In response, a number of counter-measures were taken. The Constitution of 1959 was updated in 1974, followed by the Law of Associated Labour in 1976. These changes were intended to extend the principles of participatory democracy and de-centralisation, and yet at the same time to introduce a greater element of planning into the economy. But tensions between successful firms on the one hand and constantly struggling firms on the other continued apace. Meanwhile, ethnic tensions between the country's various nationalities were getting worse. The final result, as we know, was the end of the Yugoslav search for self-management and the tragic precipitation of the country into civil war.[16]

In fact, however, even before the civil war many of the problems in the system continually plagued the Yugoslav experiment. In opposition to the highly optimistic assessments of people like Jan Vanek and Edward Kardelj, western observers cast a far more critical eye on Yugoslav developments. On the one hand, it cannot be denied that the system did achieve high levels of economic growth and embarrassed the orthodox communist world. On the other hand, it appears to be the case that the market economy gave further

[15] Vanek, 'The Worker Managed Enterprise', pp. 269–70.
[16] Lydall, *Yugoslavia in Crisis*, pp. 111–12; Mastnak, 'From the New Social Movements', pp. 59–61.

impetus to existing regional disparities in wealth and power. This created enormous problems for the local and regional Communes. In contrast to the more limited service-oriented role of local government in private enterprise systems, the Yugoslav Commune had an important role in local economic planning. In this task the Commune had to consider the objectives of both the federal government as well as the investment strategies of local enterprises. This active role for the Commune seemed to be the logical result of the move from central planning to a market economy. In practice, however, the politico-economic system was impaired by the competition between political and business elites. The market economy provided material incentives for enterprise chiefs to seek suppliers and customers throughout the country and even abroad. At the same time, the Commune was eager to protect employment within the region and to stimulate local industry. This tension became so acute that Communes began levelling heavy taxes on goods exported outside of the region, which prompted management bodies and Executive Directors to clamour for more market and less planning. To make things worse, many of these arguments were carried out by enterprise managements, Commune officials, and federal government officials without due regard for the Workers' Councils, thus making a mockery of the claim that it was a self-management system at all.[17]

The question as to whether self-management was real or ideological has also been raised by empirical studies documenting large-scale absenteeism and apathy by shopfloor workers who, in theory, were the key to the self-management system. The Workers' Councils and their sub-committees tended to be dominated by highly skilled technicians who could either do without the Councils, or present the Councils with highly complex proposals which the average worker would have to accept on faith. Once again, the discrepancy between the self-management ideal and Yugoslav reality was stark. Caught in the middle of these conflicts – between enterprise freedom and Commune authority, between elites and ordinary workers and citizens, between successful enterprises in wealthy regions and their less fortunate counterparts elsewhere, etc. – was the League of Communists. The League had made self-management the official ideology of Yugoslav society, but then found its own position weakened by the workings of the system in practice. This ideology stressed democratic participation at the same

[17] Nove, *The Economics of Feasible Socialism*, pp. 137–40; Comisso, *Workers' Control under Plan and Market*, pp. 46–8; Selucky, *Marxism, Socialism and Freedom*, pp. 113–14.

time that it made direct appeal to the material interests of the population. In time, however, emphasis continued to shift towards economic prosperity. To the extent that this prosperity did come, it was highly uneven and created demands for governmemt intervention. Those who were doing well out of the system denounced any moves for more planning or attempts by the League to re-assert its authority. The less successful enterprises decried what they considered the prevalence of capitalism over socialism. By the late 1980s and early 1900s, as new social movements came to the fore in Civil Society, the League saw its prestige weakened further. Environmental groups and youth movements that criticised the model of growth underpinning the Yugoslav market economy came in for heavy criticism from the League, who exhorted a return to the principles of self-management. By the time the regime collapsed in 1992, self-management looked like a hollow version of the original vision that had inspired Tito and his followers in the late 1940s.[18]

Such events would seem to point to a fairly negative assessment of Yugoslav Market Socialism, and lead us to question the validity of the premises underlying the model itself. Yet this must first be weighed against the very successful performance of workers' co-ops in Italy and, especially, in Spain. Our final assessment of market socialism would be incomplete without an examination of these developments.

The case for workers' co-ops

In *The Case for Workers' Co-ops* Robert Oakeshott provides us with a detailed empirical analysis of self-managed co-ops in France, Italy and Spain. Referring to the Mondragon co-ops in the Basque region of Spain, he makes the case for worker self-management thus:

> A Mondragon sector, though it might well take some sting out of the class war, would be working for its own interests and not for either traditional capitalism or for the state sector; it would be a genuine third alternative. Assuming it was anything like as successful as it is in the Basque country there would be a queue of workers – from both capitalist and nationalized undertakings – applying to join.[19]

How do workers' co-ops function and how might they offer a 'genuine third alternative' to Social Democracy and State Socialism? This section will take these to be the central questions

---

[18] Mastnak, 'From the New Social Movements', pp. 53–4.
[19] Oakeshott, *The Case for Workers' Co-ops* (second edition), p. 248.

concerning the political significance of the co-op movement. The movement has been described as a practical example of Market Socialism aiming to combine the democratic and participatory goals of self-management with the efficiency and responsiveness of the market. It is thus essential for our purposes to briefly look at how co-ops have fared in countries where they have gained a measure of popular support. Since co-ops can flourish in such diverse climates as Tito's Yugoslavia, Franco's Spain and in France and Italy as well, Oakeshott's claim must be taken seriously.[20]

First, how do workers' co-ops function? To a large extent this can be illustrated by comparing them to both State-controlled and privately owned companies. If the State owns an enterprise's assets, it may seek to promote political goals like equality, but the chain of command leading from the shopfloor upwards to the State effectively cuts the workers of the enterprise off from any genuine possibilities for self-management. Even if, as initially occured under the Soviet Five Year Plans, increases in productivity are registered, the workers must either be persuaded or coerced to produce for the State. The physical and psychological distance between enterprise workers and State planners has been continually cited as a reason for the poor economic performance of planned economies and their unresponsiveness to consumer preferences. In private companies the owners of capital can quite simply make use of their assets as they like, regardless of the interests of the workers they employ. Employees must follow orders, while managers are hired to ensure that this compliance is attained with the minimum possible conflict. Shareholders who have a stake in a privately owned company tend to have little knowledge or interest in the way they are managed, and are much more likely to be concerned with the rise or decline in value of their stock.[21]

Whether State- or privately owned, the underlying assumption is that whoever controls the means of production – the State or private capitalists – has the right to organise work and determine all major questions on wages and investment. Workers' Councils within planned economies and trade unions within capitalism may contest the prerogative to some extent, but power ultimately remains in either State or private hands. This is even true when enterprises in a capitalist private enterprise system are nationalised.

---

[20] Holmström, *Industrial Democracy in Italy*, pp. 18–19; Vanek, *General Theory of Labour-Managed Market Economies*, pp. 4–5.

[21] Holmström, *Industrial Democracy in Italy*, p. 46; Horvat, *The Political Economy of Socialism*, pp. 65–70.

Indeed, this has largely contributed to the waning of enthusiasm for nationalisation as a strategy for the left. The rather simple principle that governs co-op practice is that the right to organise production derives from investing one's labour – not capital – in an enterprise. This principle informed Yugoslav practice, and was subsequently adopted by workers' co-ops elsewhere. However, echoing the Guild socialist critique of Syndicalism, it has been suggested that such control of a community's vital resources might be potentially dangerous. In cases involving the water supply, etc., some form of shared control between the workers of an enterprise and the representatives of the community is certainly desirable.[22]

In 1975 Jaroslav Vanek listed 12 conditions for the successful functioning of workers' co-ops within a self-managed economy. Two points are of particular relevance: (1) the rules regulating who can join a co-op and under what conditions of entry and (2) the rules governing the creation of self-managed firms and their subsequent strategies for securing adequate investment. On this second point Vanek points out that:

> It is imperative to establish a shelter organization or institution on the national level (which can be decentralized according to need), whose express function would be to fund and promote the self-managed sector of the economy. More specifically, this agency would be charged with the supervision but not control of the capital market, the promotion and expansion of new firms or sectors according to national plans, the co-ordination and spreading of information regarding alternative investment projects, technical and other assistance to new groups desiring to form self-managing firms, and supervision designed to secure in the long run the equalization of income per worker.[23]

Perhaps the most significant instance of such a shelter institution has been the Basque CLP, as we shall see. In other situations, however, some such institution has been equally indispensable. In France, the movement for workers' co-ops gathered force in the mid-1970s in the wake of 'L'affaire LIP'. The workers at a watch-making factory in eastern France refused to accept management plans to close down, and decided instead to take over production themselves. The LIP episode was the first of several instances in which workers

---

[22] Holmström, *Industrial Democracy in Italy*, pp. 10–11; Horvat, 'An Industrial Model', pp. 127–8.

[23] Vanek, 'Introduction' to Vanek *Self-management*, p. 35. Perhaps of equal importance are points 11 and 12, which stress that self-management is more than a set of economic premises, but rather an entire philosophy of education and politics which aims at advancing our understanding of democracy beyond the terms offered by concepts like Socialism, Communism and capitalism (p. 36).

attempted to rescue sinking private companies by converting them into self-managed co-operatives. By 1975, the Workers' Co-operatives Production Society: (SCOP), began receiving appeals from workers in failing industries who sought a co-operative solution as an alternative to plant closure. Further impetus for French co-ops came quickly after the Mitterrand government's first unsuccessful experiments with nationalisation in 1981–82, which did not result in the much hoped for upswing of the French economy. Moreover, a significant number of young French engineers and managers were attracted to co-ops. They anticipated greater potential for creative work than would have been possible in either the private or State sectors of the economy.[24]

Like the members of the Rochdale consumer co-ops in England, French co-ops do not oblige their workers to be members of the co-operative they work in. Thus control is linked to shares and membership, not work alone. This has raised the question of the optimal roles for outside members – members of a co-op who do not actually work there, and non-member workers – that is, workers of a co-op who are not actually members. There were initial fears that co-ops might either be bought up by outsiders, or that members would hire non-members to do the hardest jobs for less pay. In general, however, most French co-ops insist that not less than two-thirds of the management must be comprised of worker members. In addition, in the event that a co-operative shuts down, remaining assets are not distributed among the members but passed on to other co-ops. This forestalls the risk of being bought out by external forces. There are also provisions in French co-op law to ensure the most equal possible distribution of wealth between members and non-members. The question of non-member workers came to the fore in the mid-1970s, as both the number of temporary and non-member workers rose to alarmingly high levels in the building sector and other sectors where seasonal work was common. One of SCOP's principal aims thereafter became safeguarding the income of non-members in the short term, and reducing the number of such workers in the long term.[25]

French co-ops can raise capital from three main sources: the Central Bank of Co-operative Credit, the French Bank of Co-operative Credit (BFCC) and joint stock banks. Unsurprisingly, the joint stock banks are reluctant to lend money to firms whose

[24] Oakeshott, The Case for Workers' Co-ops, pp. 120–1; Demoustier, Les Cooperatives de Production, pp. 5–7; Thornley, Workers' Co-operatives, p. 135.
[25] Oakeshott, The Case for Workers' Co-ops, pp. 141–3.

management can be dismissed by owner-workers! This leaves the majority of French co-ops dependent on the Caisse Centrale and the BFCC. In cases where a co-op has very limited resources but is judged to have good potential, SCOP has a fund from which it can offer help. If SCOP funds manage to get the firm on its feet, the co-op may then have some positive response from the Caisse Centrale. Like most banks, the Caisse Centrale and the BFCC will assess the risk involved when they loan money to co-ops. However, there is an important difference, in that they will advise co-ops on how to outline the best possible plans for future production and investment decisions, so that their case may eventually find favour with potential lenders. Moreover, the Caisse Centrale and the BFCC do support the case for workers' co-ops and are thus prepared to take greater risks on their behalf than the average joint stock bank.[26]

While the French Socialist Party and the other parties of the left have encouraged the growth and development of worker co-ops at various times, in Italy co-ops have been actively supported by political parties since the last century. The Italian Socialist Party (PSI) was formed in 1892, and quickly lent its support to the League of Co-operatives and Mutuals (the Lega), which was set up the following year. In 1919 a Catholic section of the Lega broke away to form an independent Confederation, and a second split followed in 1945 with the birth of the General Association of Italian Co-operatives. Since 1945 the co-operative sector of the Italian economy has experienced steady growth and expansion into new areas of economic life. Meanwhile, Italian co-ops have taken on an overtly political character: the Lega enjoys the support of the parties of the left, including the former Communists (now the PDS), the PSI and the Republicans; the Confederation is supported by Christian Democracy, while the Social Democrats and Republicans support the General Association. But since the end of the 1960s these ties have loosened, as the three co-op groups have attempted to forge stronger ties with one another to widen their base of political support.[27]

The co-operative sector of the Italian economy is so large, that co-ops dominate industry in parts of central and northern Italy, and account for 10 per cent of production nationally in the building industry. As such they offer us a picture of the successes that co-ops can have within predominantly capitalist economies. The Italian co-ops also illustrate the severe limitations on co-ops as primary

[26] Thornley, *Workers' Co-ops*, pp. 143–4.
[27] Thornley, *Workers' Co-ops*, pp. 152–3.

vehicles for a more general democratisation of Civil Society. It has become clear that while a co-operative sector of the economy is certainly necessary for the democratic organisation of work and the widest possible dissemination of ideas, the co-op movement leaves larger political questions unanswered. Many of the problems that we have already discussed in relation to the effects of the market in Yugoslavia also arise in other contexts such as Italy and Spain. Let us look at these difficulties for a moment.

In Italy co-ops have a history dating back to the 1880s, a time when they were also making their first appearances in England and France. Two factors in particular have contributed to their continued growth in the post-World War II world: (1) the access to affordable credit, which all co-ops are entitled to under Italian law; and (2) the co-ordination of efforts between the Lega and the CGIL, Italy's large left-wing trade union confederation. Indeed, contrary to practice elsewhere, Italian unions have played an important role in co-op affairs both in terms of converting collapsing privately owned firms into co-ops, and in defending workers' rights within the self-managed firm. However, commercial viability in the competitive world of the 1980s and 1990s has forced Italian co-ops to evolve considerably. First, the spread of new technology outside of the co-operative sector has forced co-ops to change their own production systems, which traditionally relied heavily on the specialised skills of master craftsmen ('artigiani'). To an increasing extent, these workers are being replaced by computer-driven production systems. Second, in a highly consumer-oriented society like contemporary Italy, advertising and marketing have become a vital part of successful commercial enterprise. As a result, co-ops have been forced to set up marketing departments with a totally different set of personnel than those working on the shopfloor, and often in an urban location distant from the point of production. These marketing specialists usually come from very different social backgrounds than the shopfloor workers, who, for the most part, they rarely see at all. This has substantially decreased enterprise solidarity, which, in turn, has prompted managers, technicians and marketing personnel to demand greater pay differentials and prerogatives in the firm's decision-making processes.[28]

As in Yugoslavia, it has been found that in Italian co-ops managers and technicians tend to enlarge their sphere of power and influence at the expense of the authority of the Workers' Council.

[28] Oakeshott, The Case for Workers' Co-ops, pp. 160–1; Holmström, Industrial Democracy in Italy, pp. 52–3.

This has become an urgent problem in the larger Italian firms, which, over time, may develop hierarchical management structures that do not differ significantly from private firms. When attempting to survive in a sea of capitalist enterprises, however, the logic of the market often demands such discipline. Mark Holmström presents the issue this way:

> In principle everyone sees the need to put the market first. In practice this goes against the grain and the tradition of a producer co-op, the pride in fine work, the respect for technical skill. Now the specialized knowledge that counts is not engineering skill or production technology . . . What counts now is marketing skill, a nose for new opportunities and the ability to make useful contacts: things to be learned through wide-ranging experience of the capitalist world.[29]

Obviously such developments would have horrified William Morris and the Guild socialists. But there seems to be a wide degree of consensus that this is the price of success for co-ops working within predominantly capitalist economies.[30] Problems arising from the implementation of new technology jeopardising the craftsperson, increased division of labour, the growing importance of marketing and increasing demand for pay differentials are hardly accidental: they show that self-managed firms are constrained to adopt strategies of capital accumulation and to accept the logic of continual expansion and growth. In Italy this has led to the formation of mergers to achieve economies of scale, product diversification for the sake of profits, and other similar measures to keep enterprises afloat.[31]

Perhaps even more serious for the future of Italian co-ops is the spread of the competitive ethos necessary for market transactions. This has undermined the very thing that initially made Italian co-ops look like the harbingers of a 'genuine third alternative': the feeling of community that pervaded regions like Emilia Romagna where co-ops flourished. In the uncertain political and economic climate immediately following the end of World War II, Emilian workers

[29] Holmström, Industrial Democracy in Italy, p. 68. Thornley remarks that former Lega chief S. F. Carpanelli's view is that the co-op movement did not create the capitalist system, but has no choice but to work within it. She writes: 'As businesses which are competing in this system, co-operatives are primarily a sector of the economy and not a force for building socialism.' See Thornley, Workers' Co-operatives, p. 158. For Carpanelli's and other views on the Italian movement, see Carpanelli, L'autogestione nell'industria.

[30] Oakeshott actually sees such developments as positive signs that co-ops are finally shedding their 'cloth cap' image. See Oakeshott, The Case for Workers' Co-ops, p. 162.

[31] Mellor, Hannah, and Stirling, Workers' Co-operatives in Theory and Practice, pp. 148–9; Holmström, Industrial Democracy in Italy, pp. 75–7.

joined together in a spirit of solidarity and community which gave co-ops their strength. Nazario Galassi reports that co-ops were not merely a means of attaining a certain measure of economic security, but were at the centre of human relationships, even to the point of adding a spiritual dimension to social interaction. But by the 1970s it became necessary to either accumulate capital and expand operations or go out of business. At this point co-ops all over the country were forced to produce for foreign markets and bring in white-collar managers from outside the community instead of hiring local working-class people. This has drastically changed the nature of co-operative production relations. Sooner rather than later Italian co-ops will have to decide whether they wish to work in close contact with the people of the communities in which they are located. If they decide to do this, it will mean returning to the practice of hiring local people, producing for local markets, and generally limiting their operations to the kinds of small-scale activities in which democracy and daily contact between members is once again possible. This will require a political and ideological commitment to resist the pressure to constantly expand operations and find new markets. However, such a redefining of priorities will not necessarily mean a return to parochialism, as we shall see in the conclusion to this book.[32]

The Mondragon co-ops in the Basque region of Spain provide a good example of how the spirit of community and solidarity can insulate co-ops from the above-cited problems in the Italian movement. The Mondragon co-ops employ approximately 21,000 workers, all of whom are members. They contribute to the production of goods as diverse as machine tools, refrigerators, gas cookers, as well as furniture and building materials. Co-op members have decided that all co-ops which exceed 500 workers should be split up into constituent organisations, with the notable exception of the founding co-op ULGOR, which employs some 2,700 workers.[33]

In the Mondragon case, what began as a pragmatic attempt to find jobs was transformed into a socio-economic experiment with much wider implications than anyone had imagined. The initial impetus was defiant Basque nationalism in the face of Franco's determination to curb all signs of Basque independence after the Republican defeat in the Spanish Civil War. A radical priest in the

---

[32] Nazario Galassi, *La cooperazione imolese*, p. 169; Holmström, *Industrial Democracy in Italy*, pp. 123–4, and p. 139.

[33] Holmström, *Industrial Democracy in Italy*, p. 7.

town of Mondragon called Father Arizmendiarrieta founded a technical school after his release from prison in an attempt to alleviate economic hardship in the area. In 1956, graduates of the school set up ULGOR, an engineering co-op. The ULGOR success inspired a number of similar ventures offering a range of services, from research and development to social security. One co-op in particular, a bank, gathered savings to create employment by investing money in local co-ops. This bank, the Bank of People's Labour, quickly assumed a dynamic role, providing consultancy, market research, and feasibility studies on proposals for new co-ops.[34]

The CLP classifies and assesses industrial co-ops by dividing them into five main sectors: (1) founding and forging; (2) capital goods and machine tools; (3) intermediate goods and component parts; (4) consumer goods; (5) building materials. Oakeshott notes that the CLP has been remarkably successful in mobilising the savings of the public for the purpose of local investment. This success would not be possible without the discipline of the co-ops themselves, which have agreed to return 90 per cent of their profit for re-investment rather than consumption. Mondragon co-ops also help solve the perennial problem of co-ops – financing – by insisting on large capital contributions from all new member workers.[35]

New workers must become members after a six-month probation period, and, as stated, they must contribute a substantial sum on joining. This sum amounts to roughly one year's pay. If the worker is unable to contribute this sum initially, he or she must pay what they can on joining, and then make up the rest in instalments. The difference in pay between shopfloor workers and managers is approximately 3.5 to 1, which means that managers and technicians in the Mondragon co-ops agree to work for considerably less money than their private-sector counterparts. As fixed by Mondragon law, co-op profits are not immediately divided amongst workers, but rather are credited to their share accounts. This sum is then indexed against inflation, and eventually collected in full by the worker when he or she reaches retirement age. In cases where workers decide they want to leave earlier, their share will depend on the reasons given for wanting to leave. In general, however, we can see that Mondragon law provides far more structure to co-op practice than

---

[34] Holmström, Industrial Democracy in Italy, pp. 7–8. The CLP was founded in 1959 as a credit co-op. It was designed to provide financial, technical and social assistance to those co-ops associated with the bank as well as to individuals. For a detailed analysis of its functioning, see Thomas and Logan, Mondragon, pp. 76–7.

[35] Oakeshott, The Case for Workers' Co-ops, pp. 178–85; Mellor, Hannah and Stirling, Workers' Co-ops in Theory and Practice, p. 63.

Yugoslav law had done previously. Where Yugoslav co-ops were allowed to determine their own formulae for finding the balance between investment and consumption, Mondragon co-ops must comply with fairly fixed regulations. This structuring implies a certain amount of planning in the Mondragon system that is not found in the other countries we have looked at.[36]

With the ground rules clearly defined at the outset and the CLP as a reliable source of finance, co-ops in Mondragon have been remarkably successful in terms of providing long-term growth and stable employment to co-op members. Within individual firms the self-management body with final say on internal matters is the General Assembly of All Members. This body elects a management committee from its ranks, the Junta Rectora. The Junta Rectora, in its turn, appoints the firms's chief executive, also known as the general manager. These provisions are set out in detail in the ULGOR statutes, which are highly representative of Mondragon practice as a whole. There are eight separate statutes: (1) provisions to ensure democratic self-government with all authority stemming from the base; (2) provisions to promote efficiency; (3) provisions to promote solidarity between management and the shopfloor; (4) provisions on initial capital contributions by all worker members; (5) provisions on job security and work discipline; (6) provisions on solidarity between co-ops to foster co-ordination between them; (7) provisions on solidarity between both the local community and non co-op workers and firms in the district; (8) provisions to ensure that co-ops remain committed to increasing jobs.[37]

A Social Council has been created to foster communication between the shopfloor and the democratically accountable management. Its members are elected by the different divisions of a given co-op. The Council performs the role of a trade union in an Italian co-op, that is, protecting workers' interests on health, safety and pay issues. Referring to the eight provisions and the Social Council, Oakeshott describes the general picture thus:

> Their rationale can perhaps best be understood as an attempt to harmonize various sets and pairs of interests: of the individual worker member and the co-op as a whole of capital and labour; of the co-op

---

[36] On this very important point see Thomas and Logan, *Mondragon*, chapter 4; Holmström, *Industrial Democracy in Italy*, pp. 7–8.

[37] Oakeshott, *The Case for Workers' Co-ops*, pp. 186–7, and p. 204. Oakeshott notes that there is a slight complication in all this, due to the formation in 1966 of the ULARCO federation of co-ops next to the ULGOR co-ops within the umbrella of

and the local community in which it works; of those who already work in co-operatives and of that potentially unlimited number still outside who, according to the Mondragon philosophy, must be given the chance of eventual membership by an unremitting open door policy of job expansion. Taken together these arrangements are an extra-ordinarily subtle and imaginative exercise in social engineering which make all other attempts at industrial structure building – whether by the Webbs or Ernest Bader or the Rochdale pioneers – look like artefacts of Stone Age workshops.[38]

Be this as it may, the most subtle and imaginative social engineering in the world could not compensate for the foundation of social solidarity and strong sense of community that underpins the co-operative economy and militates against the exploitative and divisive forces of market competition. This is a fundamentally important point, for as the picture elsewhere shows, without structures and traditions of a solidaristic Civil Society operating in the background, market forces will tend to create virtually insuperable problems for workers' co-ops. These problems will obviously centre on the perennial question of obtaining initial investment and credit, but will also include wider issues, such as the temptation to leave the co-operative sector for the private sector, where the salaries are almost always higher. Mondragon managers and technicians continue to make the political decision to forego such rewards in order to keep the co-operative economy functioning. Indispensable, in this context, are Basque traditions of local democracy and regional autonomy, Basque music and drinking clubs, and the sense of identity enforced by the still widespread use of the Basque language. It must be emphasised that these features of Basque society preceded the Mondragon experiment, and make such vitally important institutions as the CLP possible.[39]

The success of the Mondragon economy has in turn enforced established traditions of solidarity. By providing jobs and security, workers committed to the co-operative ideology have been able to stay local and build their lives in the Mondragon community. In the infrequent cases where enterprises have not been successful, the laid off workers have generally managed to find employment with other co-ops. While looking for new work, they are entitled to 80 per cent

Mondragon co-ops. However, he adds, the ULGOR arrangements are still representative of Mondragon practice as a whole, and continues to constitue a good general model.

[38] Oakeshott, The Case for Workers' Co-ops, p. 190.
[39] Oakeshott, The Case for Workers' Co-ops, pp. 168–9; Thomas, The Spanish Civil War, pp. 86–90; Fraser, Blood of Spain, p. 536.

of their normal income until full-time employment resumes, a figure which exceeds the provisions of most welfare States. Again, the combination of economic success in conjunction with traditional forms of solidarity make such extensive welfare provision possible. Indeed, with CLP support unemployed workers who join new co-operative ventures are not expected to turn a profit for at least two years.[40]

The political culture which sustains Mondragon, similar in many ways to the post-war communist culture of Emilia Romagna, provides the soil in which producer and consumer co-ops can flourish. It is a culture forged through common experiences and struggle over a long period of time. Its network of social clubs, support groups, and neighbourhood associations constitutes the kind of Civil Society in which a democratised economic system can work for the benefit of the whole community. A strong sense of independence and co-operative values are needed to sustain this kind of Civil Society against attempts at bureaucratisation by the State. Moreover, such consciousness is also necessary to ensure that the centrifugal forces of the market can be contained within their proper limits. Thus it would clearly be wrong to attribute the solidaristic characteristics of the Mondragon system to the existence of the market. As we have seen, the market is often praised for its efficiency in allocating resources, but the market will also produce results that are not compatible with the socialist values of participation and accountability. The key point is this: without the network of social institutions in which it is embedded in the Basque region, the market would have the same effects as it has had in Yugoslavia and elsewhere: regional inequality, class exploitation and political inequality.[41] Recent theoretical work on Market Socialism has made strong claims on behalf of the market's ability to allocate resources efficiently and to protect consumer interests, but what we already know about markets is that they generate vast disparities in wealth, power and life-chances. In the conclusion of this chapter I would like to address this point in relation to recent market socialist theory.

Concluding remarks: the theory of Market Socialism

The collapse of the Soviet Union and the transition to predominantly market economies throughout eastern Europe has prompted an almost universal cry for the free market as a remedy for the

[40] Oakeshott, *The Case for Workers' Co-ops*, pp. 206–9.
[41] Bradley and Gelb, *Co-operation at Work*, pp. 64–9.

problems of bureaucratisation and tyranny that did indeed characterise the countries of 'existing Socialism'. This demand for the market even managed to find resonance amongst some socialists before the Soviet collapse. Notable, in this context, was Alec Nove's argument for Market Socialism as 'feasible Socialism' in 1983. But the debate on Market Socialism actually has a longer history. In the 1920s the Austrian school of economics led by Ludwig Von Mises launched an attack at the version of a socialist market economy proposed by Oskar Lange. Anticipating the work of Vanek, Lange argued that a socialist society could exist with consumer choice and freedom of occupation, that is, markets for consumer goods and labour, but no market for capital goods. A central planning board would control capital and fix initial prices, which would remain within State control but subsequently fluctuate according to supply and demand. The task that Lange did not himself complete, but bequeathed to his market socialist successors, was to answer such questions as: who establishes new firms in Market Socialism? How do new firms secure investment as they grow, and according to what criteria? How large should firms be? These became pressing questions for market socialists in the 1970s and 1980s, as the planned economies foundered and the industrial democracies struggled with unemployment, inflation and persistent sociopolitical inequality.[42]

The publication of Nove's book had the general effect of giving wide currency to the idea that Market Socialism would offer efficiency and consumer choice, on the one hand, and satisfy socialist criteria of just distribution and equality, on the other. With the one-party planned economies in such widespread disrepute, Market Socialism was upheld as the last remaining 'feasible' alternative to State Socialism and the various social democratic variants of capitalism. Yet Nove's work acknowledges that the market brings with it its own set of problems, and that it would be unwise to regard it as some kind of political and economic panacea. David Miller has recently adopted a more unequivocal defence of the market in his *Market, State and Community*. Miller cites four primary market socialist goals: (1) economic efficiency; (2) checking the power of the State; (3) protection of worker autonomy; (4) more equal distribution of primary income. Briefly stated, the model retains the market as a means of resource allocation, while self-managed enterprises lease

---

[42] Richter, 'A Socialist Market Economy', pp. 186–9, and p. 196.

capital from the State and public investment bodies. Once established, however, enterprises choose their own strategies for product development, production methods, prices and marketing techniques. Once the competition between worker-controlled firms results in the usual balance of winners and losers, the State steps in to redistribute wealth according to need, and to ensure that no one starts the next round of competition with unfair advantages.[43]

Yet it is unclear how there will be political support for such redistributive measures in light of the overall thrust of the argument, which is heavily weighted towards sanctioning economic success. From what we know about the political economy of market societies, successful groups in the economic struggle will be well placed to protect their advantages both politically and socially. Thus what appears to be the most recent innovation in political theory actually takes us back to ideas of Marx and Hegel in our introduction. Miller confidently predicts that individuals can associate for the purposes of 'full-blooded' competition in their lives as producers, though somehow they miraculously espouse communitarian values once they leave the workplace. As we noted earlier, Marx remarked that Hegel was correct to perceive that the State/Civil Society division was the hallmark of modernity, but that Hegel was wrong to argue that the problems of Civil Society were resolved in the modern State. Miller's semi-Hegelian view is even more strange in light of his own accurate assessment of the market as an institution:

> The market has a structure and a logic, and it pays to go along with them . . .
> The market favours those with conceptions of the good which are centred on the private enjoyment of commodities, or which have non-commodity elements which run with the logic of the market – for instance, those who enjoy competitive success for its own sake as well as for the income it brings. It penalizes those whose conceptions require behaviour that cuts against that logic – for instance, those wanting to pursue time-consuming projects outside the market, *or to sustain co-operative relationships* (my emphases).[44]

Neither Nove, Miller or any market socialists have convincingly shown how this kind of market can be reconciled with socialist positions on equality, democracy and participation. Perhaps part of the market socialist problem is that it has conceded far too much ground to the resurgent liberalism of the 1980s, which championed

---

[43] Miller, *Market, State and Community*, pp. 9–10; see also Miller's article 'Why Markets?', pp. 45–8.

[44] Miller, *Market, State and Community*, pp. 93–4.

the market as the precondition of political liberty from the authoritarian State. Thus market socialists did not really question the extent to which the market is efficient in terms of resource allocation, production incentives and relaying information on supply and demand.[45] On the one hand it has been recognised that after a period of initial growth, command central planning develops rigid bureaucratic political and economic structures that stifle economic productivity. On the other hand, however, it is also mistaken not to distinguish between various forms and extents of planning, and to assume that planning is inherently incompatible with shopfloor initiatives, consumer interests and wider community interests. This point was clearly illustrated by Cole, and it is borne out by the economic planning role assumed by the CLP in Mondragon. We will return to this vitally important point in our conclusion. But I would not want to make the same mistake by placing all market socialists together in the same category. Indeed, a market socialist has recently argued that market socialists will have to face the negative consequences of market competition, such as waste, lack of co-ordination between producers, and the tendency of the logic of the market to invade areas of social life where it is not appropriate. But if these points are to be incorporated into a new and more theoretically coherent model, it will no longer be within the framework of Market Socialism.[46]

---

[45] That in fact the market is not efficient in these matters has been cogently argued by O'Neill in 'Markets, Socialism and Information', pp. 206–10. See also O'Neill's 'Exploitation and Workers' Co-operatives', p. 234.

[46] Thus Frank Roosevelt concedes that 'With resources often idle at the same time as there are unfulfilled human needs, a market economy can be said to be both irrational and wasteful.' See Roosevelt, 'Marx and Markets', p. 515.

6

Green and post-industrial Socialism

In the March 1983 West German elections, an ecological Party won enough votes to obtain parliamentary representation: albeit with only 5.6 per cent of the vote and 27 seats, Die Grünen (The Greens) had arrived. Though they secured just slightly more votes than the minimum needed to gain seats in the former West German parliament, the political impact of their arrival had immediate repercussions throughout Europe. The German movement was emulated across the continent, and also became a model for opposition groups within the former satellite countries of the USSR, especially East Germany. Ecological politics had already started to gain momentum because of the widespread dissatisfaction with the traditional parties and politics of the left that was the hallmark of the protests of 1968. Indeed, this dissatisfaction was registered in various circles even before 1968, as we shall see in a moment. This chapter examines the origins, development and proposals of the socialist wing of the Green movement, and the closely associated movement for a new kind of post-industrial socialist politics. We shall investigate the response of Green Socialism to the central questions asked by all of the theorists and movements discussed in this book, that is, to what extent can the economic institutions of Civil Society be democratised, and what kind of political authority is necessary to ensure this democratisation?[1]

Origins and aims of Green and post-industrial Socialism

The term post-industrial society was invented by the Guild socialist A. J. Penty, who denounced industrial societies as alienating, ugly and un-democratic. As we saw in chapter 4 when looking at the ideas

[1] Goodin, *Green Political Theory*, p. 11; Williams, *Sources of Hope*, p. 212. For an excellent summary of the various strands of Green Socialism see Martell, *Ecology and Society*, chapter 3.

of the New Age group, Penty demanded a drastic reduction of large-scale industry and the end of the Leviathan State. In their place he envisaged a return to artisanal production and the revival of the medieval Commune. Penty followed Ruskin and Morris in arguing that small-scale production and communal politics would lead to a more just society in which all members participated equally. Since nobody would be dependent on people outside of the local community for their livelihood, production could once again be restored to the scale necessary to assume a collective dimension; it could then be performed in small groups in the interests of everyone living within the walls of the Commune. This would restore creativity to work at the same time that it returned control of community life to the community itself.[2]

The theme of restoring creativity to work was taken up in the 1930s and 1940s by Herbert Marcuse and other social theorists of the Frankfurt School. Their writings went beyond the Guild socialist paean to the dignity of creative labour to call into question the very notion of the human individual as essentially *homo faber* (a practical, tool-making being). That is, while retaining many aspects of Marx's social theory, they also criticised the Hegelian-Marxist view that humans are primarily working beings that create themselves through their labour on the external world. Marcuse, in particular, saw that in certain respects Marx had appropriated the ideas of some of his intellectual opponents without actually transcending them, as Marx claimed to have done. Marx moved beyond Adam Smith and John Locke in demanding that the product of labour be returned to the worker. But apart from the occasional fleeting remark, Marx did not adequately specify in what ways the modern industrial process should itself be abolished or even modified. At times he called for the working-class appropriation of the existing capitalist production system, which could hardly be mistaken for a model of self-fulfilling work.[3]

Marcuse countered with the idea that it was through the instinctual forces of eros and playful activity – not work – that true freedom was to be realised. The discipline required to work either individually, in small teams, or in a large industrial system, presupposed the renunciation of instinctual pleasure and the indefinite postponement of desire. While Freud argued that such renunciation was the basis of any society, Marcuse linked such repression with economic scarcity, which he claimed was no longer a problem in

[2] Penty, *Old Worlds for New*, pp. 44–8.
[3] Heller, *The Theory of Need in Marx*, p. 108; Habermas, *Erkenntnis und Interesse*, p. 58.

highly developed societies. The possibility for the liberation of eros and play was made possible by the growth of the forces of production, which opened up the possibility of an unprecedented amount of free time. However, the majority of the working classes had always been taught that freedom could only come from having more, bigger, and 'better' goods. As Marx had predicted, capitalism had created the conditions for its own demise. However, people had to be shown that the objective conditions (material scarcity) for the necessity of a 40-hour work week no longer existed. The task was henceforth to allow technology to assume whatever productive functions were still necessary in terms of providing basic goods and services, in order to allow all of us to bridge the gap between work and play. As we shall see, these themes became central for a number of important Green socialist theorists like Andre Gorz and Rudolf Bahro.[4]

Despite the prescient analyses of Marcuse, Frankfurt School theorists like Theodore Adorno and Max Horkheimer were for the most part unable to influence the non-academic sectors of industrial societies. With the notable exception of Jurgen Habermas, their works are fraught with a deep strain of pessimism about the possibilities for substantial social change. Moreover, their abstract language and preoccupation with theory effectively cut them off from any significant communication with a potential mass movement. Nonetheless, several themes of Frankfurt School discourse would later be re-explored by Green theorists and activists. These include the critique of *homo faber*, mass culture and consumerism. Such issues were not specifically linked with environmental degradation until the early 1960s. The publication of Rachel Carson's *Silent Spring* (1962), Paul Ehrlich's *The Population Bomb* (1968) and Garrett Hardin's *Tragedy of the Commons* (1968) marked the first wave of Green writers that attracted the attention of a wide and highly alarmed readership. A second wave followed with the publication of the Club of Rome's *The Limits of Growth* (1972), the 'Blueprint for Survival' in the *Ecologist* (1972) and the more recent Brundtland Report entitled *Our Common Future* (1987). These books stressed that our industrial system and accompanying attitudes towards nature were rapidly contributing to the destruction of the planet. Long-term prospects for survival were thus poor unless we resolved to change our attitudes and behaviour.[5]

[4] Eckersley, *Environmentalism and Political Theory*, p. 89; Marcuse, *Counterrevolution and Revolt*, pp. 63–4; Schmidt, 'Existential-Ontologie', pp. 44–9.
[5] Vincent, *Modern Political Ideologies*, p. 211.

Before moving on to specifically Green socialist proposals to avoid the impending environmental catastrophe, we must briefly summarise what all Greens are opposed to. An appropriate starting point is the Green oposition to a view of nature common to liberals, Marxists, market socialists, and social democrats, namely, that the natural world exists for the sole purpose of human exploitation. The aforementioned groups all trace their materialist philosophy of nature to Francis Bacon's view that by observing the natural world we can separate it into its constituent parts. In so doing we can reduce the natural world to its fundamental units, which we can then fully understand as mathematical quantities. Since mathematics is a creation of human beings, mathematically understood entities can in turn be manipulated for human purposes. Manipulation, domination and exploitation of the natural world thus appear as benign ways of satisfying human desires, which, like the oceans and the skies, appear relatively limitless. Such logic leads to the conclusion that the greater our desire, the greater the necessity for our subordination of nature for the realisation of that desire, which in turn leads to our greater happiness. This endless spiral of new needs and their satisfaction has led to a demand for ever greater quantities of material goods and comforts, which become the basis of our existence and fulfilment. Whether of the political left or right, nearly all politicians in post-war Europe have worked within the framework established by this unequivocal commitment to the expansion of the productive forces. Political debates have generally centred on the distribution of the resulting products – not the quality of what was being consumed or the kind of workday that was needed to produce them.[6]

In the long term this position has proven devastating for the European left. In order to achieve election, socialist and communist politicians promised their working-class electorates that the fruits of the national industrial output would only be redistributed justly if they continued to vote socialist or communist. However, this position rested on two fundamental assumptions that in historical terms had an extremely limited period of validity: (1) steady and increasing economic growth; (2) the virtual inexhaustibility of the earth and our natural resources. In the aftermath of World War II and the massive influx of Marshall Plan aid from the United States, European economies experienced tremendous levels of growth which, at least until the early 1970s, seemed destined to continue indefinitely. During

---

[6] Pepper, *Communes and the Green Vision*, pp. 8–9.

this period the most industrialised countries of Western Europe invited unskilled workers from Southern Europe and the Third World to come to their countries and earn better wages than they could at home. It became commonplace to assume that growing economies could be taxed in order to provide a higher standard of living for workers and their families. The Welfare State came into existence across Europe, with the apparent capacity to guarantee all citizens basic levels of education, health care and income. The fortunes of left parties became inseparably linked to the growth model of future development, since they had made defence of the Welfare State and income redistribution the essential bases of their electoral politics. This position became increasingly difficult with the oil crises and recessions of the 1970s: instead of steady economic growth, inflation and unemployment became persistent economic and political problems. Keynesian techniques which proved effective in the past registered very limited and highly unpredictable successes. At this point the representatives of private capital made the logical claim that in times of low growth government spending had to be sharply curtailed, the money supply controlled, and welfare services cut back. By the end of the 1970s and into the 1980s and 1990s, right-wing governments came into power in England, Germany and France. Meanwhile Socialist parties have been thrown increasingly on the defensive in Spain and elsewhere. The parties of the institutional left, which had gone along with the growth model for so long, had no other choice but to accept austerity measures. Depending on the country in question, socialists and communists might temporarily adopt defiant positions, but on the whole the left had no alternative model of economic organisation. Left parties had to discipline the working class with threats of impending chaos and promises of an imminent return to growth in the future. The trade unions, who had defended working class interests within the logic of the growth/redistribution framework, were also highly discredited.[7]

The year 1968 marked a watershed in disaffection with the traditional left's complicity in the politics of growth. Socialist and communist parties lost members to extreme left parties and New Social Movements based on peace, feminist, gay, environmental and other issues that had been neglected in the gold rush for greater material prosperity. Throughout Europe (and in France in particular – see chapter 2), it became increasingly clear that the 'good old days'

[7] Laqueur, *Europe in Our Time*, pp. 435–40.

were not coming back, and any temporary improvement in the economic situation of the advanced industrial countries was only going to come as a result of further exploitation of the environment at home and the Third World abroad. To an increasing number of political militants this was no longer an acceptable option. Moreover, it became clear that the extent of environmental ruin already perpetrated required a drastic change in our ideas about industry, economic growth and the unlimited expansion of the productive forces. In the 1979 English elections the Ecology Party, led by Jonathan Porritt, put together a six-point Green Manifesto which captures the spirit of Green proposals in England, Germany and elsewhere. The Manifesto called for: (1) the re-orientation of the economy towards renewable and recyclable resources; (2) a move away from the boom and bust characteristic of the capitalist business cycle towards a stable economy capable of providing all citizens with basic levels of material comfort; (3) a move towards economic self-sufficiency, especially with regard to food and energy; (4) a more decentralised political system encouraging much higher levels of participation; (5) a move away from the short-term view typical of market transactions towards some form of decentralised planning; (6) a move away from materialism and consumerism in an attempt to see the human individual as a more complex being than *homo faber*, with creative and emotional needs that were not best satisfied by existing political and economic institutions. The manifesto concluded by affirming that:

> If there is an answer, then it lies in our own hands, working together in our own communities. We need the kind of political system that lets us all get stuck in, fully committed, fully involved in the decisions that concern us. Either we go on as before, indifferently supporting policies that in the long term will quite literally cost us the Earth. Or we consider the real alternative, of an ecological, sustainable future – even though at the moment it may seem an alternative fraught with difficulties.[8]

This view challenged both the role of existing political parties as mediators between State and Civil Society, and the growth-centred post-World War II consensus. While all Greens have made trenchant criticisms of this consensus, many limited their critique to the damaging environmental consequences of the industrial system and the shallowness of our consumerist culture. By contrast, Green socialists have attempted to analyse the economic and political roots of the environmental crisis, and to formulate a distinctly socialist

[8] Kemp and Wall, *A Green Manifesto*, pp. 26–7.

response. It is to these theorists that we now turn. Green socialists are divided between those who favour some kind of 'Eco-State' that would have a major role in protecting the environment, on the one hand, and those that call for a proliferation of largely autarchic and self-governing Communes, on the other. We will look first at the eco-statists.

The Green socialist vision (i): the Eco-State

It has been observed by Robyn Eckersley that the ecological movement is divided between anthropocentric and ecocentric wings rather than the left and right wings of conventional political discourse.[9] That is, there are those who still believe that nature can be justifiably harnessed for human purposes, and others who argue that the natural world should enjoy rights and privileges equal (if not superior) to the human world. An equally fundamental division exists within the camp of Green socialists between those who retain an important role for some kind of ecologically enlightened State, on the one hand, and those who believe that virtually all authority should be devolved to decentralised and quasi-autonomous Communes. Eco-State theorists argue that the Commune vision, appealing as it might be ideologically, does not offer answers to fundamentally important questions such as how to co-ordinate the political and economic activities of different Communes. Further, it is one thing to argue that 'small is beautiful' or some such slogan, but it is also true that small communities can simply displace problems of authoritarianism and environmental negligence to a local level, without in any way coming close to solving them. Hence the urgent need for the supervisory role of a greater institution with environmental expertise and the authority to enforce rules on pollution, production and consumption.[10]

However, if the eco-statists are wary of the problems of potentially authoritarian and isolated Communes, their more sophisticated representatives are also fully cognisant of the dangers of entrusting too much authority to the State. Indeed, they concede that the disastrous environmental record of the State socialist countries proves that not just any State will suffice to avoid the ecological precipice towards which we are hurtling. Their argument, then, is that somewhere between the parochialism of the Commune and the negligence of the socialist and social democratic States, there

[9] Eckersley, *Environmentalism and Political Theory*, p. 8.
[10] Goodin, *Green Political Theory*, p. 176; Vincent, *Modern Political Ideologies*, pp. 220–34.

exists the potential for a new ecologically oriented politics. At the centre of this vision is the Eco-State.[11]

Boris Frankel insists on the Eco-State not only to redistribute wealth and protect the environment, but to play a decisive role in the construction of a revitalised public sphere. He cautions against any reduction of politics to political parties and coercive bureaucracies. Eco-socialists that oppose the Commune to the State typically ignore how individual Communes are to co-ordinate their political and economic activities with other Communes. Frankel thus insists on the distinction between the exercise of class power within State institutions, on the one hand, and the role of the State in organising socio-economic and cultural practices, on the other. The former should be minimised by making State institutions as democratic and accountable as possible. The latter should be accepted as necessary for the reproduction of life in society.[12]

Eco-State socialists concede that if the socialist State proved to be an environmental nightmare, the record of social democratic States has been little better. This has largely been due to the fact that these States are predominantly financed by private enterprise, which operates according to the incentives of individual capitalist interests competing within a competitive market. As we saw in chapter 5, competitive markets can be relied on to produce winners and losers. The winners, in class terms, are well-positioned to translate their victories into considerable wealth and power. Moreover, market economies consistently resist democratic control. If we take the example of a local population that works for a private firm, we can assume that within the logic of a market economy the firm will have immediate incentives to substitute human labour with automation whenever this will result in savings in the firm's expenditure. It may well be the case that the local population depends vitally on that industry for its livelihood and can vote in political leaders committed to protecting their work and way of life. But the fact remains that labour power displaced by the introduction of automation will find new employment only if the firm finds new and expanded markets. As Martin Ryle observes, when the mechanisms of growth and accumulation falter as typically happens in a recession, entire production sectors and regional economies are jeopardised. Immediate profits are valued over long-term growth in the more basic sense of human potential. In such cases society's most precious

---

[11] Ryle, *Ecology and Socialism*, pp. 24–5; Frankel, *The Post-Industrial Utopians*, pp. 202–4.
[12] Frankel, *The Post-Industrial Utopians*, pp. 201–6.

resources – human energy and creativity – are being misused to the great detriment of future generations.[13]

The same pernicious relationship holds between competitive market incentives and environmental ruin. Inherent in the logic of market exchange is the current need for profit and expansion as well as unpredictability of the future. Thus it makes sense to ignore the future in favour of available returns on present investment. To an entrepreneur having to respond immediately to market cues, it matters little if in fifty years time essential ecological resources that he or she needs at the moment will no longer be available for future generations. That is, market logic and incentives are extremely short sighted, which in environmental terms is perilous. The price mechanism and the cycles of supply and demand may induce private firms to shed labour and devastate the lives of an entire community, but they will not respond to probable future scarcity that will not affect them. Moreover, if problems of ruin and waste become immediately pressing, the market may again offer its own short-sighted solution: why not hire someone to store the waste you can no longer hide? Third World countries who need the money may do it, and in the meantime you can get government off your back. What's the harm if the country becomes dependent upon your business and ruins its air and water in the process?![14]

Social democratic (and of course more right-wing) governments depend largely on the profits of private and nationalised industries to finance the non-profitable sectors of their economy, such as defence, health, education, environmental protection, etc. From the Green socialist perspective this is a dangerous situation. Within a national context it means that there will be money and research for environmental problems only to the extent that there are constantly new markets, growth and profits. However, it is precisely the logic of a productive system based on these incentives that has nearly brought us to the brink of ecological catastrophe. Moreover, the aims of industry will often clash with those of public environmental regulation. Industry will regard expenditure on safe waste disposal and related issues as a drain on resources that would much more profitably be invested in labour-saving techniques. Thus there will be a constant struggle between industry and government. But given government's ultimate dependence on industry for the financing of its own operations, it is not difficult to see that industry

---

[13] Ryle, *Ecology and Socialism*, pp. 44–5.
[14] Ryle, *Ecology and Socialism*, pp. 46–7; Ophuls, *Ecology and the Politics of Scarcity*, pp. 168–9; Weale, *The New Politics of Pollution*, pp. 75–6.

will find ways to make its interests prevail within the existing political economy, which is driven by the imperatives of unrelenting growth and market competition.[15]

The Eco-State contention is that this situation is based on a political consensus which is now in the process of erosion for two fundamental reasons. First, increasing numbers of people from all social classes are beginning to realise that the present industrial system is placing an intolerable strain on the planet, and that, quite simply, we must all change in order to survive. Extremely important in this connection is Albert Weale's argument that the State cannot be neutral with respect to all competing conceptions of the good when some conceptions threaten the continued existence of society itself. That is, the liberal notion of absolute neutrality makes some sense in a context where competing conceptions can flourish together. That is obviously not the case when some people's conception of the good threatens the earth, air and water that the rest rely on to live.[16] Secondly, it is argued that more and more people feel that the current industrial system requires that we spend most of our adult lives working in jobs that are not satisfying. Given our current level of technological sophistication, it should be possible to work less and engage in many varied social activities if we agree to consume less and destroy less. This position has been forcefully defended by Andre Gorz.

Gorz began his career as a sociologist and political activist as a relatively orthodox Marxist, who subsequently evolved in an eco-socialist direction. His work became well known to the English speaking public with the publication in 1982 of *Farewell to the Working Class*, which laid the groundwork for his future theses on ecology. The thread uniting this work with his more recent writings is the idea that whatever one may wish to argue about the validity of Marx's philosophical ideas, State Socialism was the living legacy of Marxism. From quite an early stage in its history State Socialism ceased to be a truly revolutionary doctrine, since it undertook to complete the work of liberalism and capitalism rather than transcend them. Rather than abolishing the division of labour, State Socialism made it more pervasive with the aim of out-producing capitalism. Rather than ending alienation, State Socialism exacerbated it by subjugating all aspects of social life to the State. Instead of reversing the liberal

---

[15] Ryle, *Ecology and Socialism*, pp. 52–4, 75–6.
[16] Weale, *The New Politics of Pollution*, pp. 150–2.

tendency to regard the natural world as an object for human manipulation, State Socialism elevated unfettered industrialism to a quasi-
religious status. Rather than countering the tendency of liberal
democracies to reduce the human individual to *homo faber* and
narrow the good life to commercial success, State Socialism absurdly
fetishised the working class and the importance of work in general.
The end result was a despotic State that did even manage to rival
what was good about liberal capitalist regimes.[17]

For revolutionaires in the West, this meant that it was equally
absurd to glorify the working class as the revolutionary subject of
socialist transformation. To begin with, most workers were now
integrated into capitalist society through mass education and consumerism anyway. But beyond this oft-repeated assertion, most
work, even when well paid, was unfulfilling. Moreover, no amount
of money could compensate for the amount of time that working life
robbed from the vast majority of working people – whatever their
position in the social structure. The revolution could thus no longer
focus on attaining bourgeois lifestyles for progressively larger
segments of the working class in return for 40 years of 40-hour work
weeks. Gorz addresses a similar point to the liberal wing of the
women's movement: should work be the focal point of our identity
and perception of success or failure, when so much of work is really
about producing goods that very few people really need? If not,
how might we reformulate our ideas about equality?[18]

Thus while arguing for radical change, Gorz maintains that the
working class alone will not be the agent of this change, nor will
change be centred on demands for greater upward mobility and
more incentives to work. Gorz maintains that because of
technological advances we have the opportunity to work less,
develop the many-sidedness of our personalities, and in the process
respect the limits of the natural environment. The first imperative in
this quest will be to contain the logic of the market and market
exchange to a well defined sphere that does not encroach on the
prerogatives of politics, culture, justice, the mass media, etc. At the
same time, we must not renounce our commitment to making the
work we continue to do more enjoyable and ecologically safe. In
Capitalisme, Socialisme, Écologie, Gorz puts the point thus:

[17] Gorz, *Farewell to the Working Class*, pp. 66–74.
[18] Gorz, *Métamporphoses du travail*, pp. 201–5. This has been published in English with
the title *Critique of Economic Reason*. A very powerful book that anticipates a number
of Gorz's insights and which has had a profound impact on contemporary social
theory is Laclau and Mouffe, *Hegemony and Socialist Strategy*, p. 169.

The ecological restructuring of society requires that economic rationality be subordinate to an eco-social rationality. This subordination is incompatible with the capitalist paradigm based on profit maximisation. It is also incompatible with a market economy that compels competing enterprises to continually reshuffle and vary their products, to continually create new needs, and to suggest that the satisfaction of these needs resides in the greatest possible consumption, thus preventing the self-realisation and 'free-time' which would lead to the auto-limitation of our needs.[19]

Accordingly, Gorz demands both a reduction in the working week and a Guranteed Minimum Income (GMI). He argues that technological innovation and automation within the capitalist market economy has created a situation in which there is increasingly less work for people. However, because of the prerogatives of the people who control the means of production and exchange, those who do not work are laid off with iniquitously low income supplements from the government, while those who continue to work must labour as before – if not harder – to maintain the cycle of growth and investment. The unemployed do not have the resources to lead a decent life, while the employed do not have the time. Like many ecologists, Gorz proposes a system of part-time work for all based on job sharing and other solutions which will ensure those who want to work a job, and will guarantee everyone, regardless of their occupation, the standard of living necessary to engage in other, more creative, activities.[20]

Gorz concedes that to an extent we continue to live in the realm of necessity, and that a certain amount of alienating and unpleasant work will exist for some time. The point, however, is that there is no objective reason why anyone should perform such labour for long hours throughout their working life. Whichever of these tasks could not be assumed by the Eco-State could be shared at the community level. The giant mistake of the socialist movement across Europe was to promise liberation in a sphere of social activity in which the logic of market exchange, competition and profit will always prevail. Thus in what could be interpreted as a situationist reading of Hannah Arendt, Gorz claims that work will always assume a technical, means-ends character. As such, the world of work has inherently limited potential for personal growth, dialogue with others and creative thinking. The real goal should have been to free people

---

[19] Gorz, *Capitalisme, Socialisme, Écologie*, p.38. This has been published in English with the title *Ecology as Politics*.
[20] Gorz, *Capitalisme, Socialisme, Écologie*, p. 39.

from work, and to create more autonomous public spaces for intrapersonal visibility and authentic communication.[21] This is possible today, though only on condition that people abandon the consumerism that fuels the business cycle and destroys the environment. But environmental safety is not enough; thus Gorz distinguishes between Environmentalism and Ecologism.[22]

Environmentalism is a necessary but not sufficient step in the direction of Ecologism. Environmentalism limits itself to calls for renewable sources of energy, recycling and preservation. Ecologism, for Gorz, is a more global contestation which demands an end to the fetishism of commodities and the logic of greater happiness through greater consumption. It is in this context that he adds an important caveat to the GMI, maintaining that such a step is positive only if new possibilities for creative interaction are established simultaneously. That is, it is no good to give people a GMI if this means nothing more than the right to stay home in front of a larger television in the grip of the passive consumption of vicarious experiences. Thus the Eco-State should not only redistribute wealth, it must promote dialogue between the diverse interests within Civil Society. Rather than claiming to be a workers' State dedicated exclusively to the protection of workers' interests, the Eco-State should respect the plurality of social actors in Civil Society in their search for new forms of public life. Gorz is receptive to the ideas of Bruno Trentin and other Italian trade unionists who would like to see a resurgence of the non-economic support functions of the trade union. Gorz believes that the resurgence of the left requires that the unions reach out to youth organisations, pensioners and a wide range of community groups not immediately involved in the world of work.[23]

While promoting dialogue between various social actors, Gorz also insists that differences must be respected, and that the Eco-State should not impose a sense of community on society as a whole. When the State imposes its vision of community on the rest of society the result can only be dictatorship, which is exactly what happened under State Socialism. Gorz regards this idea of community as a mistaken form of left-wing nostalgia still rife among certain anarcho-communitarian ecologists, to whose ideas we now

---

[21] Gorz, *Capitalisme, Socialisme, Écologie*, pp. 96–102; Shipway, 'Situationism', pp. 156–9. See Arendt's distinction between labour, work and action in *The Human Condition*, chapters 2–6.

[22] Gorz, *Capitalisme, Socialisme, Écologie*, pp. 171–2.

[23] Gorz, *Capitalisme, Socialisme, Écologie*, pp. 174–6; 181–3; and 212–14.

turn. The anarcho-communitarian response is that a large measure of communitarian sentiment is necessary for the organisation of a system of production that can be democratically controlled and immediately responsive to people's needs.[24]

The Green socialist vision (ii): Anarcho-communitarianism

Green anarcho-communitarians and eco-socialists share several important criticisms of existing political and economic institutions. Both camps agree on the pernicious effects of the division of labour, the wastefulness of consumerism and the need to create new public forums of discussion and action. Both agree on the need to distinguish between Environmentalism and Ecologism, and the imperative to elaborate the insights of the former in a distinctly socialist direction. Here the similarities stop however, as Green anarcho-communitarians take up more resolute positions against the market and in favour of local economies. These positions have been consistently articulated by a number of visionaries, though the contributions of Murray Bookchin and Rudolf Bahro merit particular attention.

Like ecologists of many persuasions, Bookchin notes that the impending ruin of our natural world has fundamentally changed the nature of political discourse. While many of the political struggles in both the capitalist and communist world have been concerned with the distribution of wealth and power, he says that we now have no choice but to abolish the industrial system itself. Whether in contemporary capitalist countries or the former communist countries of Eastern Europe, the incessant large-scale exploitation of nature in both systems has brought people of all political opinion to the brink of disaster – Chernobyl being a case in point. On the one hand, the theory of historical materialism has justifiably emphasised the importance of the expansion of the forces of production in modern industrial societies. On the other, the theory says little about how to subordinate this expansion to human needs. Indeed, Marx suggested that these forces unfold according to their own 'laws of motion'. Thus the Bolsheviks and their followers assumed that attaining the largest possible material abundance was the path to emancipation. The persistent problems of crime, drug abuse and alienation in prosperous societies demonstrate that this is not the

---

[24] Gorz, *Capitalisme, Socialisme, Écologie*, p. 21.

case. Moreover, neither the theory of historical materialism nor the doctrine of class struggle really offer insights into how we should treat our fellows. Class struggle motivated by greed or envy is as unlikely to lead to emancipation as any other form of politics. In this sense Bookchin argues that Marxism lacks a reconstructive dimension that is present in the combined forces of Anarchism and Ecologism:

> Just as the ecologist seeks to expand the range of an ecosystem and promote a free interplay between species, so the anarchist seeks to expand the range of social experience and remove all fetters to its development. Anarchism is not only a stateless society but also a har-monized society which exposes man to the stimuli provided by both agrarian and urban life, to physical activity and mental activity, to unrep-ressed sensuality and self-directed spirituality, to communal solidarity and individual development, to regional uniqueness and worldwide brotherhood.[25]

Bookchin argues that the exploitation of the environment precedes the historical emergence of capitalism. He traces our instrumental attitude towards the environment back to the initial exploitation of women as the patriarchal family emerged. From then on, human beings were treated as potential objects of domination rather than subjects in their own right. Not only class domination, but hier-archies based on gender and status were sanctioned in complex legal codes. This made domination in the widest sense a legitimate social practice. From there, Bookchin argues, the tendency to exploit people and treat them as objects was directed towards the natural world. While 'the patriarchal family planted the seed of domination in the nuclear relations of humanity', the Industrial Revolution dis-solved all peasant and feudal relations into market relationships. At this point both people and nature became the objects of the most brutal exploitation ever witnessed. In an age of nuclear weapons, however, an ecological revolution is not a choice but a necessity. Bookchin maintains that far more than 'the good life', our very survival itself depends crucially on our ability as a species to behave ecologically. This means moving beyond the environmentalist demand that we respect the natural world, to actually becoming part of it. In order for the human world to achieve true progress rather than the bogus progress of industrialism, it must emulate the natural world in two fundamentally important respects: (1) by being self-sufficient; and (2) by evolving towards ever greater degrees of

[25] Bookchin, *Post-Scarcity Anarchism*, p. 79.

diversity and complexity. Both of these imperatives are linked with Bookchin's conception of the complementarity of Ecology and Anarchism, as we shall now see.[26]

For Bookchin there can be fewer more striking contrasts than the example of the self-sufficiency of the natural world, on one hand, and the human proclivity towards war, exploitation and despoliation, on the other. Self-sufficiency has enabled the natural world to reproduce the conditions of its existence for thousands of years, whereas people tend to encroach on the land and dignity of other people whenever possible. This tendency has reached its acme in the twentieth century, with two world wars and the threat of nuclear annihilation. In addition, the post-war growth consensus and concomitant environmental ruin has been largely responsible for pushing the eco-system to the outer limits of its ability to carry on the natural cycles of its reproduction. Air pollution disrupts photosynthesis, while water pollution creates chemical imbalances affecting fish and marine plant life, thus endangering our water supply at the same time. In order to attain maximum rates of profit and growth, we have ignored the balance of forces at work in a given territory (what ecologists like Brian Tokar refer to as a bioregion), in order to extract the greatest quantity of what can be most cheaply produced there.[27] In so doing we lose the balance of natural forces that enables a bioregion to survive solely on the energy and nutrients of the sun, soil, wind and rain. Such behaviour jeopardises the region's ability to be self-sufficient, and also makes the existence of autonomous human communities on that terrain impossible. Instead, a world market driven by private or State capital forces large numbers of people off the land into noxious cities, and makes the economy of entire countries dependent on their ability to sell one or two cash crops. That is, rather than respecting natural complexity, modern forms of commerce and industry look for the quickest possible profit. The consequences are devastating for both the human and natural world. In *Post-Scarcity Anarchism* Bookchin writes that:

> The manipulated people in modern cities must be fed, and to feed them involves an extension of industrial farming. Food plants must be cultivated in a manner that allows a high degree of mechanization – not to reduce human toil but to increase productivity and efficiency, to maximize investments, and to exploit the biosphere. Accordingly, the

[26] Bookchin, *The Ecology of Freedom*, p. 342; *Toward an Ecological Society*, pp. 40–1; *Post-Scarcity Anarchism*, p. 63.

[27] Tokar, *The Green Alternative*, p. 31.

terrain must be reduced to a flat plain – to a factory floor, if you will – and natural variations in topography must be diminished as much as possible. Plant growth must be closely regulated to meet the tight schedules of food-processing factories . . . Large areas of the land must be used to cultivate a single crop – a form of plantation agriculture that not only lends itself to mechanization but also to pest infestation.[28]

The lesson Bookchin draws is that the survival of the planet and humanity depends on our ability to emulate nature's propensity to be anarchic, which for Bookchin means self-organising. The natural world has existed for longer than we can imagine with no need for a State to regulate it, so why can not humans, as a natural species, do the same? If we think of the State as the set of institutions that assumes the functions that society will not do for itself – at society's cost – we can then imagine a stateless society to be cheaper and more efficient. Thus anarchy is not chaos but, in fact, quite the opposite: it implies self-regulation and autonomy. The corollary is that self-sufficiency and autonomy can only be realised in quite small, decentralised communities where the ideal of self-regulation is realistically possible. Obviously communities working within bioregions will have much less sophisticated machinery at their disposal than the average multi-national corporation. This will not be a problem, since they will have abandoned the growth-crazed scramble for profits, and instead aspire towards autarchy. As such, they will have to adapt their practices to the conditions offered by the land, and use the much smaller scale technology at their disposal. Rather than thriving on consumerism and waste, autonomy demands the greatest possible conservation and use of renewable energy sources.[29]

Bookchin and others insist that the local, no growth, ecologically sound economy is entirely possible. Indeed, they urge that we combine some aspects of modern technology with the more time-tested practices of older and predominantly agricultural societies to devise new forms of food, shelter, transport, energy and medicine, all of which could make use of local materials. In the sphere of food production, for example, the advocates of such economies follow Kropotkin in emphasising the need to return to systems of organic farming, in which animal and other organic waste is used instead of industrial chemicals to fertilise the soil. Rather than representing a backward step, it is emphasised that small-scale gardening continues to offer some of the highest crop yields known.

[28] Bookchin, *Post-Scarcity Anarchism*, p. 66; Dickson, *Alternative Technology*, pp. 123–5.
[29] Bookchin, *Towards an Ecological Society*, pp. 44–5.

High yields are attributed to the practice of crop rotation and the personal care of the agricultural worker, which help surpass the results achieved with the techniques of monoculture and mechanisation. Alternative models of food production include 'three-dimensional agriculture' using a variety of plants growing both above and below ground. Some tribal societies actually achieved high levels of agricultural productivity in this manner. As David Dickson observes, the systems of agriculturual production employed by tribal societies have often developed over a period of centuries. In many cases the result has been the maintenance of soil fertility, generic variety in plants and a very short working day. Experiments with alternative forms of shelter, medicine, transport and energy which are produced for local use are also being tested.[30]

The alternative to decentralising into autonomous, ecologically-sound local economies is to continue with the present world market and the cash crop economy. This, argues Bookchin, would be to go against the grain of evolutionary development by imposing human simplicity on natural complexity. Writing once again in *Post-Scarcity Anarchism*, he summarises the argument thus:

> The point is that man is undoing the work of organic evolution. By creating vast urban agglomerations of concrete, metal and glass, by overriding and undermining the complex, subtly organized ecosystems that constitute local difference in the natural world – in short, by replacing a highly complex, organic environment with a simplified, inorganic one – man is disassembling the biotic pyramid that supported humanity for countless millennia.[31]

Bookchin stresses that the combined forces of Ecology and Anarchism do not represent some kind of nostalgic yearning for the uncomplicated noble savage. This sort of 'blood and soil' romanticism often has very racist and sexist implications. Rather, his anarchic humanism is a plea for the restoration of the many-sidedness of the human personality which has suffered a tremendous levelling effect under the strain of industrialisation and bureaucratisation. The rise of urban conglomerations accompanying the concentration of industry and capital not only extinguished thousands of rural communities. The urban masses needed centrally organised forms of housing, transport, education and entertainment which, to be provided on a mass scale, were necessarily standarised in character. Like a cook who has to prepare the same meal for

[30] Pearce, Markandya and Barbier, *Blueprint for a Green Economy*, pp. 30–2; Dickson, *Alternative Technology*, pp. 124–47; Pepper, *Communes and the Green Vision*, pp. 136–9.
[31] Bookchin, *Post-Scarcity Anarchism*, p. 67.

thousands of inmates in an institution, the State has actively discouraged individual tastes and opinions so that uniformity and order – prerequisites of a disciplined workforce – could prevail. Thus all forms of spontaneous, creative, individual behaviour have to compete with the stultifying repression of a faceless bureaucracy prescribing standard rules, regulations and norms of 'proper' conduct. Combining the insights of Tocqueville and Kafka on mass society, Bookchin provides a devastating critique of modern industrial society. Yet by arguing for the respect of human complexity and individual difference, he aspires to move beyond this critique towards positive reconstruction.[32]

This notion of a universal species emancipation rather than a limited revolution in the interests of the working class has also informed the life and work of Rudolf Bahro. Bahro began his political career as an activist in the former East German Communist Party (SED). During the 1950s and 1960s he had some reservations about SED policy, though he believed that the Party was doing its best to practise the principles of Marxism-Leninism. He thus accepted standard articles of Marxist-Leninist theory on the dictatorship of the proletariat, the leading role of the vanguard and the desirability of a centrally planned economy. Initially, the Party-State did indeed achieve the reconstruction of East Germany and rapid industrialisation. However, it became increasingly clear to Bahro that the price for such rapid growth was an unprecedented ravaging of the countryside and cities of East Germany. Moreover the East German Party-State was authoritarian and bureaucratic, and its secret police (STASI) attempted to infiltrate all areas of social life, including the arts and sciences. After meditating on the significance of the Warsaw Pact invasions of Hungary in 1956 and former Czechoslovakia in 1968, Bahro became more critical of the SED regime. When he finally published his views in a book entitled The Alternative in Eastern Europe in 1977 in Frankfurt, Bahro himself became a victim of the State's anti-democratic politics. He was arrested by the STASI in August 1977, and in June 1978 he was condemned to eight years in prison. As a result of international campaigns on his behalf Bahro was freed in October 1979, after which he emigrated to former West Germany. He maintained contacts with opposition groups in

---

[32] Bookchin, The Ecology of Freedom, pp. 342, 350–3; Post-Scarcity Anarchism, pp. 65–6; Eckersley, Environmentalism and Political Theory, pp. 146–53; Vincent, Modern Political Ideologies, pp. 220–4.

the German Democratic Republic, and returned as a citizen of a re-unified Germany in December 1989.[33]

The sub-title of The Alternative is A Critique of Real Existing Socialism, but in fact Bahro goes beyond to explore the possibilities of a 'Communist Alternative' to State Socialism. The strategy to realise this alternative forms the third section of the book. He is in broad agreement with Gorz and Bookchin to the extent that he believes that Socialism, whether conceived as Social Democracy or State Socialism, cannot be considered a force for revolutionary change. He re-affirms this position in his later work as well. In the Postscript to the 1990 edition of The Alternative Bahro reminds us that like it or not, the political reality of Eastern Europe since the end of World War II is the only concrete example we have of State Socialism. It was largely inadequate then, and represents nothing to aspire to now. Similarly, despite its ability to palliate the most exploitative aspects of capitalism, Social Democracy remains committed to the politics of growth and industrialisation that is inexorably leading towards the destruction of the planet. What, then, should contemporary revolutionaries be struggling for? Bahro's communist alternative is a Green anarcho-communitarianism, which he hopes will come about through the initiative of a cultural revolution.[34]

Bahro argues that it is not sufficient to change the relations of production, for this would mean merely changing the leaders in charge of what he calls the 'Megamachine' of industrial production. This would be akin to changing the captain and crew of the Titanic. Instead of changing the relations of production, we must change the way we produce. In order to change the way we produce, however, we must alter our relation with the environment, our fellows and ourselves. Emancipation in the widest sense comes not through wealth and consumption, but in seeing how our individual existence is actually an integral part of a much greater whole. Living in harmony with the truth of our inseparability from all forms of life on the planet means respecting life in all its manifestations. In attempting to colonise the natural world for trade and industry, we become enmeshed in an upward spiral of material needs which eventually becomes impossible to satisfy. This inability to satisfy our material needs in turn provokes frustration, aggression and conflict. Thus Bahro concludes that we must find a new stable 'life-form' in which

[33] Bahro, Die Alternative, pp. 10–16. This book was published by New Left Books in 1978 as The Alternative in Eastern Europe.
[34] Bahro, Die Alternative, Part III.

forward development takes the form of an inward journey rather
than external expansion.[35]

The demand for new forms of social organisation has arisen as a
direct result of the collapse of State Socialism and the manifest failure
of capitalism to solve the problems of widespread alienation,
environment and Third World poverty. Bahro argues that there is a
growing consensus for a new economy geared towards producing
no more than is needed to attain subsistence. Such an economy
would be constructed in conformity with the natural capacity of
individual bioregions and would aim at maximum use of local
resources and renewable forms of energy. The use of small-scale
technology would be unthinkable in terms of satisfying the
requirements of large urban populations, but if people were to
federate into associated Communes, large steps in the direction of
autarchy and local control could be taken:

> Let us take an area fifty by a hundred kilometres wide. It must be
> possible to organize reproduction at this level: food, homes, schools,
> clothing, medicine, perhaps as much as ninety per cent of what we
> need. For another nine per cent we could deal on a national or prov-
> incial level, and for the further one per cent we would be dependent on
> a world market.[36]

A subsistence economy would be based on the principle of the
auto-limitation of needs. Scaling down needs would allow a massive
reduction in the number of hours spent working, thus enabling
people to spend time acquiring the spiritual awareness that is both
the presupposition and eventual goal of Bahro's cultural revolution.
He stresses that the cultural revolution takes us beyond the terms of
debate delineated by plan/market dichotomies, towards a more
fundamental change in our collective way of life. For Bahro plan/
market debates centre largely on proposals for the most efficient
forms of producing, on one hand, balanced against considerations
of consumer choice and political democracy, on the other. Yet in all
those debates what is almost always forgotten is that *however* our
material needs are satisfied, real life begins *after* their satisfaction.
That is, we strive to fulfil our potential as learning, loving and
creating beings. The power struggle between competing firms on
the market, or the clash between various factions of the Eco-State or
Party-State's planning elite, is of trifling importance when compared

---

[35] Bahro, 'Zeit für den Neubau von Rettungsbooten', pp. 1–2; *From Red to Green*, p. 221.
[36] Bahro, *From Red to Green*, pp. 179–80; 'Konsens für Subsistenz?', pp. 2–3.

to our ultimate aims: to love, be loved and to engage in various forms of creative activity.[37]

Bahro's suggestions on decentralised Communes reveal his awareness that certain socio-economic and political conditions are necessary in order that our more fundamental needs can be addressed. Since we cannot hope to abolish work, it is reasonable that we work no more than the number of hours necessary to allow us the time to make the inward journey of self-discovery. This commits us to a subsistence economy geared towards satisfying our basic requirements for food, shelter, medicine, energy, transport and education. The more that can be produced locally, the less that organised external interests such as banks, private enterprise or the State can intervene in the affairs of the community. Given the propensity of such institutions to demand 40-hour work weeks, hierarchical management and fiscal austerity, it is imperative that individual communities safeguard their autonomy. This will enable members to govern their own affairs, and to pursue the many activities corresponding to the vast range of human experience. Since we learn through dialogue, self-discovery is only possible when there is the appropriate setting to know the ideas, needs and dreams of others. When our life consists of commuting to jobs that consume the greater part of our physical and mental energy, our possibilities for growth are stunted. This is especially true once we see no alternatives to the rituals of spending and consumption that dominate the lives of many people in the so-called 'advanced' industrial societies.[38]

Bahro thus advocates a tripartite scheme of communal production, radically decentralised government and spiritual regeneration. Production is to be carried out by small teams of work crews within a community. The citizens of the community settle their affairs in a local, decentralised polity, the Commune. Presumably they will do this knowing that certain forms of production should be avoided if the environment is to be protected. Finally, the small-scale, decentralised community will provide the ideal setting for the spiritual growth that Bahro regards as indispensable for human happiness and survival. As Eco-State critics have pointed out, however, this leaves crucial questions concerning the co-ordination of

---

[37] Bahro, *Die Alternative*, pp. 349–55, 451, 477; 'Alles kommt auf eine ökologische Alternative an', pp. 115–16; Vilmer, 'Eine klassenlos Arbeitsorganisation', pp. 123–5.

[38] Bahro, Postscript to *Die Alternative*, pp. 557–9; *Critical Responses*, pp. 169–70; Fleischer, 'Bahro's Contribution to the Philosophy of Socialism', pp. 68–9.

different Communes unresolved. How will co-ordination occur
without some kind of State to perform this function? In a related
vein, we wonder how less favoured bioregions will be able to
maintain their autonomy when they simply cannot attain subsistence with the resources at their disposal. Since there is no State to
redistribute resources, will the less favoured regions simply languish
in isolation? Such questions bring us back to our starting point –
the fundamental schism within Green Socialism – thus necessitating
a concluding assessment of the Green socialist ideal.

Concluding remarks

Eco-State socialists regard the anarcho-communitarian position as
incoherent and unrealistic. They correctly point out that in addition
to the urgent question of co-ordination between Communes, the
'post-industrial utopians' do not demonstrate why Communes will
necessarily be more democratic, or even more environmentally
sensitive. Bookchin argues that our instrumental attitude towards
nature derives from an exploitative attitude towards our fellows. But
it is not difficult to imagine a small environmentally conscious community that also fosters a cult of the personality towards its leadership. It is possible that in such communities dissenting voices will be
regarded as pollutants. If it is reasonable to expect that small communities will not contaminate the air and water they rely on to attain
self-sufficiency, what will prevent them from 'dumping down-
stream', so to speak? Finally, in today's world environmental
issues have assumed a global dimension that stretches well beyond
the boundaries of bioregions, nations and even continents: what
happened at Chernobyl affected farmers in Scotland. This situation
demands some kind of extra-national institution with the authority
to intervene locally. Moreover, the complexity of environmental
protection will necessarily require some kind of planning of a supra-
national kind.[39]

These objections would seem to point towards the necessity for
some kind of Eco-State. But the Eco-State position is itself not without problems. The most obvious is the question of the economy.
Who will finance the Eco-State? The anarcho-communitarians
argue for a no-growth self-sufficient economy based on local
materials and renewable resources. While this raises problems of

[39] Frankel, The Post-Industrial Utopians, pp. 195–6; Ryle, Ecology and Socialism, pp. 24–5;
Eckersley, Environmentalism and Political Theory, pp. 151–3; Weal, The New Politics of
Pollution, pp. 145–50.

feasibility, it is certainly coherent. As we noted earlier, in most predominantly capitalist economies, the State is financed by taxing the revenue of private interests. Redistribution of any kind, whether it be for public housing or environmental protection, depends on private profits. If private interests are too heavily taxed or controlled, they can seek to transfer their capital to more lucrative markets abroad when this is expedient. Examples of this practice abound, though the first years of the Mitterrand government in 1981–82 are particularly striking. During periods of economic recession, it will be extremely difficult to secure the co-operation of private interests for public spending. For the most part, Eco-State proposals do not move beyond the social democratic solution of taxing the military-industrial complex, and are thus seriously deficient. Like many eco-statists, Gorz likes the fact that capitalism has reached a very high level of productive capacity, and he would seek to make this productive capacity work in service of a more well rounded ecological humanity. But it is this very economy that is enmeshed in the politics and production of arms for export, countless automobiles, etc. The economy that gives us nuclear energy and the military-industrial complex forms an intricate web of interests and investment decisions. It is absurd to imagine that we could divide this economy into the sectors we approve of and disapprove of, and then simply jettison the latter. How could the functioning of this megamachine possibly be limited to some well circumscribed economic sphere, and at the same time provide the material foundation for future generations of emancipated individuals? Here the incoherence lies with the Eco-State theorists, not the anarcho-communitarians. In this context it is difficult to see how Gorz's proposals to restrict the logic of private accumulation and instrumental reason to the economy could possibly be implemented. Here the anarcho-communitarians surely have a point: they remind us that capitalism entails more than the production of commodities and private ownership of the means of production. The ideologies of consumerism, commercial success and competitive individualism which dominate the world of work also invade our non-market projects and friendships.[40]

There can be no doubt that Green socialists have made an important contribution to modern political theory. They remind us that the world of equally valid conceptions of the good life – if it ever existed – is now gone forever. There are simply objective limits on

[40] Vincent, Critique du Travail, pp. 130–1; Hartsock, Money, Sex and Power, pp. 96–116; Dunford, Capital, the State, and Regional Development, pp. 362–3.

the natural world that make some forms of industrial society dangerous for human life. Moreover, these theorists have challenged us to rethink the centrality of class interests in an overall project of social transformation. Class struggles continue to play an important role in the conflicts of modern and post-modern industrial societies. But it is also true that the reformist trade union and parliamentary struggles of the working class have not contested the presuppositions of industrialism, consumerism and unrelenting growth. These struggles have largely been concerned with a more equal division of the fruits of the same economy that devastates the environment and impoverishes the Third World. Together with certain socialist feminists, the Green movement continues to represent a more global contestation of industrial society. Indeed, that is the enduring legacy of 1968.

Despite such important contributions to our understanding of the economy and society, the question of the appropriate political economy for a pluralist and socialist Civil Society remains. In this chapter we have seen that the positions of Eco-State socialists and anarcho-communitarians do not adequately provide the contours of this political economy. At a time when both Social Democracy and State Socialism have failed, this remains the most important problem in the theory and practice of Socialism. It is to this issue that we turn in our conclusion.

Conclusion

As the twentieth century draws to a close there are numerous voices proclaiming the 'end of history'. The collapse of the Soviet Union has been celebrated in some quarters as the end of any serious threat to the political and ideological hegemony of capitalism. Meanwhile, political elitism is widely regarded as the worthwhile price to pay for the 'smooth functioning' of our increasingly unaccountable State bureaucracies. Yet this book tells a very different story. There are those who have argued and continue to argue that there are alternatives to both capitalism and the authoritarian Socialism of the former Soviet Union and its allies. At present they are certainly a minority, but there is reason to believe that this may rapidly change in the near future. In this conclusion I would like to draw together some of the arguments that have been made during the course of the book. In so doing I will sketch what I consider as vital themes for the future direction of socialist thought and action.

In a sense, there has indeed been an 'end of history' for socialists. Perhaps unexpectedly, however, there is some cause for optimism. For things are clearer than they have ever been before. That is, there is a rallying point for all opponents of triumphant capitalism. *With the collapse of State Socialism, the single most important task for socialists today is to define the contours of a non-authoritarian socialist alternative to capitalism.* The basis of this alternative exists in the writings of some of the theorists considered in this book, though of course many of their insights need further elaboration in the light of recent events. Briefly stated, the construction of a socialist Civil Society represents the aspiration for a non-authoritarian alternative to capitalism. Theoretically, such a society would be informed by Marx's original critique of the separation of the State and Civil Society. However, it would depart quite substantially from Marxism by denying that the State and Civil Society can be re-unified in an organic totality. A socialist Civil Society could function alongside a decentralised and substantially democratic State. Indeed, a socialist Civil Society is the indispensable presupposition of the very possibility of a democratic State. I will briefly discuss possible responses to the current state of affairs before concluding with a look at the idea of a socialist Civil Society.

This discussion will proceed in two stages. First, I will argue that the apparent triumph of capitalism is illusory. Second, I will consider what is living and what is dead within the libertarian left tradition that has been the focus of preceding chapters.

The end of history revisited

The failure of State Socialism has elicited a series of possibilities, each of which must be examined closely. The first is that there is no alternative to capitalism, that is, the 'end of history' thesis. Within the parameters defined by this thesis there are certainly important distinctions to be made, such as between advocates of monetarist liberalism and defenders of Keynesian Social Democracy. But the institutional framework of such a society will remain more or less faithful to Marx's original critique. That is, a civil sphere characterised by competing private economic interests and rampant inequality shall belie any claims of an equal citizenry in the political community of the State. This point has been argued in the introduction and in chapter 5 on Market Socialism. However, for the purposes of this conclusion, it is important to briefly re-state certain basic realities about contemporary capitalist societies.

Proponents of the 'end of history' thesis tend to be adherents of one of three basic positions: (1) advocates of a return to free market capitalism; (2) defenders of some version of Social Democracy; (3) theoretical supporters of Market Socialism. In the first instance we have the political allies of monetarism and the right-wing interests backing politicians like Thatcher, Major, Helmut Kohl in Germany and most recently Edouard Balladur in France. In the second instance we have supporters of Scandinavian and Dutch style Social Democracy. Finally, there are the market socialist theorists in favour of combining the market with socialist positions on equality and just distribution. We could characterise the first position as a forlorn attempt to return to the early days of free market and minimal State capitalism. This pristine vision of capitalism is also being advocated as the appropriate economy for the de-stalinisation of Eastern Europe. We can summarise positions two and three as an attempt to establish 'capitalism with a human face'. Let us look at these positions for a moment.

With regard to the first position, it is certainly the case that each European country is confronted with a very particular set of problems and prospects. Generalisations are thus risky, but a few basic trends are nonetheless discernible. The German example is inseparable from the problems resulting from the reunification process which began in 1989. Rising unemployment in former East Germany is casting a very doubtful shadow on Helmut Kohl's promises of a speedy and smooth transition to a market economy. At the same time, there is a growing tide of protest against the inordinate power wielded by the Treuhand, the German board of industry, which makes vital decisions about resource allocation and the future employment of human and material resources. A small number of unelected people from a highly unrepresentative sector of German society are thus in a position to decide on the future of millions of workers. That this is not in any way compatible with democracy is too obvious to merit a detailed discussion here.[1]

France and Britain are not able to boast of greater successes. It is as yet too early to clearly assess the new government in Paris. Nonetheless, the French case resembles the German case to the extent that steadily rising unemployment is proving to be an explosive issue threatening the political stability of the country. Balladur's right-wing government assures the French that the turn from socialist economic mismanagement is the key to restoring prosperity. Austerity is preached to millions of unemployed men and women, while projects like Euro-Disney continue to enjoy pride of place amongst the government's economic advisers! With regard to the English attempt to restore economic growth through the politics of monetarism, the results are clear: Britain's industrial decline continues despite many years of Tory government. As if this was not enough time to prove that monetarist policies have been disastrous, government spending cuts in vital areas such as health, education and job training cripple the country further. These measures have ostensibly been taken to reduce inflation, keep sterling strong abroad and to attract investment at home. Yet the devaluation of sterling in the spring of 1993 indicates that the government has lost control of the situation. To date the results of monetarism have been an inexorable destruction of the NHS and British industry, on one hand, and an unprecedented exacerbation of inequalities in wealth and privilege, on the other. There is no reason to expect this to change in the immediate future. What will become worse, however, are the social tensions resulting from this situation. Thus we can expect rising levels of industrial unrest, capital flight and urban violence. Such developments will undoubtedly produce change.

[1] Priewe, 'Treuhandreform', pp. 165–80; Kammerer, 'Die alte DDR', pp. 128–36.

The immediate possibilities will be a return to Social Democracy or a more or less unveiled move to an authoritarian State.[2]

With regard to Social Democracy, the Dutch and Scandinavian models have certainly performed far better than their monetarist counterparts. They are likely to last longer, though it is uncertain for how much longer. As we saw in chapter 6, Social Democracy is the first casualty in times of recession. It was observed that the political consensus for Social Democracy can only be sustained under conditions of economic growth. The fruits of the economy during its upward cycle can be taxed and redistributed. That is, it is a matter of redistributing the profits accrued by private interests within the framework of competitive market competition. In the 1970s the economic growth of the immediate post-war years evaporated. In the wake of the oil crises and the combined effects of unemployment and inflation, Social Democracy was considered an unaffordable luxury. When capitalism ceases to record economic growth, it is not private enterprise and market competition that come under attack - it is Social Democracy.[3] In the long-run this experience has offered two salutary lessons for the forces of Socialism. First, all concessions from capitalism have only been won through organised struggle. Second, they will be taken away just as fast when capitalism falters. The resounding defeat of French Socialism in the March 1993 elections shows that this is applicable to both monetarist regimes in crisis and ostensibly stable social democratic governments. As the world recession shows little signs of abating, this does not augur well for the future of Social Democracy. There is no doubt that Social Democracy still enjoys mass support in Holland and Scandinavia. But this does not refute the point made in chapter 6 – entire industrial sectors and important components of the Welfare State can be dismantled when the capitalist economy slides into recession. At this point 'capitalism with a human face' can demand one of several (depending on the country's political traditions) more authoritarian political forms to restore the growth of private enterprise. Moreover, if the current plans for a European monetarist economy come to fruition, individual social democratic

[2] Kemp and Wall, *A Green Manifesto for the 1990s*, pp. 82–5. The level of violence and anger that erupted over the poll tax controversies suggests that people are going to demand more control over their lives. Whether or not this happens peacefully and democratically will depend vitally on what people think is politically possible.

[3] Hirst, *Representative Democracy*, pp. 85–6; Holland, *The Socialist Challenge*, chapter 1.

governments will have to drastically re-orient their spending priorities.[4]

Finally, the market socialist response to the current political and economic crisis also poses a number of urgent questions. It has been argued that the disastrous end of Market Socialism in Yugoslavia had much more to do with the ethnic divisions in the country than with any inherent flaws in the idea itself. But chapters 5 and 6 demonstrated that: (1) after a period of impressive growth, the market exacerbated existing tensions in Yugoslavia; (2) like social democrats, market socialists have few answers to the perennial problems of capital flight, lack of political accountability and under-investment that besiege a predominantly capitalist economy during recession; (3) where worker co-operatives and self-management initiatives have flourished, this has happened *despite* the presence of the market. That is, in places like Emilia Romagna and the Basque country, there are political, social and cultural factors that support the development of an autonomous and democratic Civil Society. Where such factors exist, a democratically controlled economy can operate; such an economy is the most important attribute of a socialist Civil Society. Where such factors are lacking or in a state of decline, they must be invented or reinvigorated.[5]

For a time the Yugoslav experiment in self-managed Market Socialism inspired faith in the ability of workers' co-ops to solve the problem. It was thought that collectively controlled enterprises could compete on the market, while a federation of Communes would be capable of adjudicating conflicting interests between firms. Yet we also saw that such competiton was likely to produce the same battlefield of winners and losers as normally occurs in any competitive market situation. The winners, when organised politically, dictate the terms of future competition on terms that favour their interests. The usual problems of economic inequality and political elitism ensue, thus undermining the possibilities for an 'equal' competition. Thus neither Market Socialism nor Proudhon's version of Mutualism provide the bases of a viable alternative (chapters 2 and 5). The future of the left surely lies with a more democratic and socialist alternative to the proposals offered by State Socialism, Social Democracy and Market Socialism. Let us conclude by looking at the possibilities for such an alternative.

---

[4] Weiske, 'Maastricht', pp. 102–6. Jessop, *State Theory*, pp. 133–5; Bertramsen, Peter, Thomsen and Torfing, *State, Economy and Society*, pp. 163–4, 188–92.
[5] Michaud, *L'Avenir de la société alternative*, pp. 26–9, 252–3.

Towards a socialist civil society

In various ways all of the theories and movements covered in this book have attempted to forge a non-authoritarian socialist alternative. In chapter 1 we saw how the syndicalists believed that the workers' trade union provided the basis for such an alternative. The works of Georges Sorel armed the doctrine of Revolutionary Syndicalism with a powerful critique of bourgeois society and the State that seemed to point in the direction of a radically decentralised vision of Socialism. Sorel believed that the instinctive violence of the proletariat and its revolutionary myths like the General Strike would bring the capitalist system to its knees. After that, the unions would assume society's productive and educational functions. Yet for all its power and insight, Sorel's excoriation of reformism leaves too many unanswered questions. How would spontaneous acts of proletarian violence be co-ordinated and channeled into a revolutionary movement with clear and precise objectives? Sorel was against such blueprints. But of course there must be a careful consideration of the ultimate aims of any revolutionary transformation. How would the unions co-ordinate their productive activities without the professional politicians of the party and State? Neither Sorel nor his Italian followers could think of any alternative to the market; the problems inherent with this vision have already been discussed. How would syndicalists represent those members of the community not directly involved in the production process? Fernand Pelloutier offered some important ideas on the subject. Pelloutier's involvement with the Bourses du Travail led him to the conclusion that union activity had to be co-ordinated with local political and cultural bodies which united workers above trade distinctions. But his untimely death and the separation of the Bourses from the French trade union movement precluded any further articulation of the syndicalist vision. In any case, the syndicalist glorification of work and the virtuous producer will strike many as absurd in light of the many valid criticisms of this position made by Gorz, Bookchin and Bahro.[6]

As we saw in chapter 3, the Council communists were opposed to both the syndicalist exaltation of the union and the anarchist belief in spontaneous co-operation. They argued that the great strength of the Council form of organisation was its ability to unite workers of various trades in a single institution. This united highly

---

[6] Laclau and Mouffe, *Hegemony and Socialist Strategy*, pp. 36–42; Keane, *Democracy and Civil Society*, pp. 120–4.

skilled, skilled and un-skilled workers in a single force against capital. In so doing, the Factory Council also offered a ready institution for the organisation of production after a communist seizure of power. Pannekoek, Korsch and Gramsci thus posited the importance of Council activity well before the decisive moment of armed struggle. Militants were to organise for the recognition of the Councils in order to prepare the working class for its tasks in a revolutionary situation. Eventually, the Councils would increase their control over all aspects of production. This would make the capitalist class superfluous and deprive the bourgeois State of the material basis that sustained it. Thus Council communists hoped to liberate Socialism from the theoretical strait-jacket that endless debates on reform versus revolution had imposed.[7]

However, the Council vision was itself flawed in two important ways. First, like the syndicalists and anarchists, the Council communists had no use for professional politicians or the parliamentary State. But unlike the former groups, the councilists were not opposed to the State as such. Indeed, they envisaged a hierarchy of producers' Councils which in practice would have been highly centralised and bureaucratic. While Pannekoek and Korsch were aware of this problem, their responses were elliptical and vague. Second, their theoretical writings placed great emphasis on the preparatory importance of politics and cultural revolution. But in practice, the councilists tended to neglect concrete institutional questions unless they happened to be linked with producers' interests. Thus like the syndicalists, they had little to offer to other members of the community.[8]

Despite these flaws, the Council communists were on the right track. They perceived that: (1) the realisation of genuine democracy demands the democratic control of society's material resources; and (2) such control presupposes a certain measure of planning. They did not fully understand the difficulties involved in this, and they greatly underestimated the authoritarian political implications of commmand central planning. That is not reason enough to abandon the principle of decentralised democratic planning, as market socialists have done. Nor is it reason enough to believe social democrats who argue that planning can function well in some parts of the economy, when other vital sectors are controlled by private interests. Decentralised and democratic planning embodies the principle of consulting all affected interests wherever the allocation of

[7] Shipway, 'Council Communism', pp. 111–24.
[8] Cornisso, *Workers' Control under Plan and Market*, chapter 1.

resources is concerned. In the sphere of production, this means devising a form of planning that will take producers' interests into consideration, as the councilists envisaged. But in general it entails moving considerably beyond the councilist vision. Planning must also embrace the interests of consumers and members of the community where production takes place. In chapter 4 it was seen how this larger vision informed the Guild socialist notion that planning, as a function of democracy, should pervade not only economic life, but political and cultural life as well.[9]

The Guild socialist notion of planning is quite distinct from the planning in State Socialism. The latter is based on the idea that a group of experts can analyse vital statistics concerning the housing, health, transport, etc., needs of a population, and then inform the producers what to produce in specific quantities. In the former Soviet Union this amounted to the control of a planning bureaucracy over the material and creative needs of a country. By contrast, Cole and the Guild socialists articulated a non-authoritarian vision of planning. The ideas of dialogue, political transparency and communication are at the centre of this vision. It is precisely this goal of decentralised and democratic planning that socialists must update and defend today.

Cole's support for dialogue followed his defence of functional representation and his attack on the concept of State sovereignty. He showed that the notion of political representation in the abstract is incoherent – you cannot represent someone 'in general'. People could be represented only in terms of some concrete activity, that is, production, consumption, community membership, educational training, artistic activity, etc., where there can be a genuine dialogue between all those participating. In order for there to be political legitimacy, there has to be the ongoing consent of the governed. As in any non-authoritarian relationship, consent is unthinkable without a constant, that is, daily dialogue between the participants. Notions of representation in general or a generic dialogue between governers and governed were simply vacuous abstractions. Thus Cole demonstrated that 'consent in general' was a chimera – and so were existing theories of the citizen and State sovereignty. In refuting State sovereignty, Cole rejected both Bolshevik and Fabian forms of State Socialism. These were simply 'socialist' versions of the practice of general representation. Both implied a non-dialogic relationship between the State and the individuals in Civil Society.

[9] Cole, *Social Theory*, p. 89.

A similarly unacceptable relationship obtained between the citizens and government of the parliamentary State. Here was a 'bourgeois' version of the non-dialogic relationship. Thus Cole shared Marx's belief that parliamentary elections did little more than decide which members of a privileged political class would exploit the people for four or more years running. From an original reading of Rousseau, Cole deduced that both State socialist and bourgeois societies were different examples of an authoritarian implementation of the General Will. Yet Rousseau had reminded his readers that the English people were only alive when electing their government, that is, when in dialogue with their fellow citizens. After this they figuratively ceased to exist. The question then became how to combine Rousseau's insight on the necessity of constant dialogue with Cole's refutation of State sovereignty. Cole concluded that there was no General Will as such, but as many general wills as there were important dialogic relationships. This reality had to be reflected in the economic and political institutions of a democratic society. Such a society was necessarily characterised by a plurality of many-sided and constantly changing relationships, not simply that between the citizen and the State. Most people supposed that the fundamentally important tension in democratic theory was that between direct democracy and representative democracy. Cole argued that finding the right balance between functional representation and territorial representation was the real problem.[10]

Thus the notion of citizenship based solely on territorial 'representation in general' violated the complexity of our lives as producers, consumers, members of families and communities, etc. The *New Age* theorists demanded that politics be re-conceptualised in order to capture that complexity. They saw that what we call politics is the struggle of exploited groups to institutionalise their dialogic relationships with greater transparency and accountability. Democratising Civil Society would result from separating the component parts of the deconstructed citizen, and allowing each constituent part to articulate its specificity. The Guild socialists were particularly concerned with the specifity of the relationship between groups of producers and individual consumers, on the one hand, and between the producers and the entire community, on the other. To complete their work we must also stress the importance of the relationships between men and women, different races and different sexual orientations. This is especially true in contemporary

[10] Cole, *Social Theory*, pp. 101–2.

Europe, where conflicts over questions of ethnicity and cultural identity are assuming the same importance as the struggle between capital and labour.[11]

The democratisation of politics today means the introduction of dialogue and transparency not only in the domain of resource allocation, but in the spheres of race, gender and cultural relations as well. Dialogue and transparency do not signify the end of conflict in these spheres, for where there are differences there will inevitably be the clash of interests and opinions: such conflict is a necessary feature of pluralism. Yet it is also clear that such communication is a necessary step towards reaching common understandings. Indeed, this is the only possibility for transforming the slogan 'living with difference' into a reality. But it is also clear that 'living with difference' requires a solid material basis, that is, a democratically controlled economy. Many contemporary advocates of pluralism fail to discuss the political economy of a democratised Civil Society.[12]

By contrast, it is socialist and bourgeois authoritarianism that conceals conflict and thereby protects powerful interests. The demise of socialist authoritarianism has had the catastrophic effect of providing bourgeois authoritarianism with greater credibility. In this respect Marx's critique of Hegel retains all of its critical force. That is, the so-called 'political revolution' has mystified our real life in Civil Society by reducing politics to the relationship between a chimerical citizen and a speciously sovereign body called the State. Thus our question is, how can we transform our present economic and political institutions in order to give the concept of dialogue real content? The new institutions would form the core of a socialist Civil Society.

We have seen that the capitalist market economy and the parliamentary State do not provide the bases for such a transformation. Moreover, the New Social Movements such as Feminism, Ecologism, the peace movement, the gay rights movement, movements for regional autonomy etc., have demonstrated that traditional vehicles for transformation such as political parties embody the principle of general representation. Parties will have a continuing role in articulating interests and opinions. But it cannot be the

---

[11] Rödel, *Autonome Gesellschaft und libertäre Demokratie*, pp. 19–22.

[12] This is the real shortcoming of the otherwise very impressive work of Cohen and Arato in *Civil Society and Political Theory*, and of Habermas in *Faktizität und Geltung: Beiträge zur Diskurstheorie des Rechts und des demokratischen Rechtstaats*. Frankfurt: Suhrkamp, 1993. This weakness in much contemporary theorising on Civil Society has also been pointed out by Hirsch in 'Das Ende der Zivilgesellschaft', pp. 46–9, and by Honneth, 'Conceptions of Civil Society', pp. 19–22.

leading role that parties enjoy within social democratic and State socialist systems.[13] Yet without a material basis to sustain their activities, the New Social Movements are doomed to the same fate as the Welfare State during times of recession. *Establishing a democratically controlled economy within Civil Society is therefore the most immediate theoretical and strategic issue.* Let us approach it by briefly recalling the ideas of the communitarian anarchists and Guild socialists on the subject.

Being non-capitalist and non-statist, Communitarian Anarchism offers the most coherent theoretical solution. The doctrine has also registered important practical successes in the Spanish Civil War and in Communes around the world. Contemporary communitarian anarchists such as Bookchin and Bahro urge us that a democratically controlled economy within Civil Society is completely feasible. It would normally entail small teams of producers living and working together in the same neighbourhood, city or bioregion. It would also require that people restrict their consumption to basic things needed by everybody. To the greatest extent possible, this should be accomplished with environmentally safe materials that are available within the region in question (chapters 2 and 6).

There are four standard objections to this vision; the last two must be taken most seriously: (1) it is absurd to talk about local economies when people need goods and services that must be imported from all over a continent or perhaps even further away; (2) the model is based on a very strong sense of community which is inexorably disappearing in modern industrialised societies; (3) without some form of political authority there is no way to link and co-ordinate the productive and distributive activities of various bioregions; (4) without some form of political authority there is no way to help urban districts and bioregions that have historically been exploited and are simply incapable of autarky. With the insights of Guild socialist theory we can add two extremely important points: (1) The principle of consulting all affected interests requires that consumers and the community have some measure of real control over what is produced. One could not hope to base a democratically controlled economy on either worker co-ops or market competition. What is needed is the institutionalisation of dialogue between producers, consumers and representatives of the community. This could be accomplished through a network of revitalised trade unions, consumer Councils and civic Councils. Together these forces could provide the basic structure of a decentralised and

---

[13] Keane, *Democracy and Civil Society*, chapter 4; Tester, *Civil Society*, pp. 138–42.

democratically planned economy. They would be capable of collectively deciding on vital issues such as price, need and distribution. (2) We do indeed need political institutions to co-ordinate producer, consumer and community interests and to aid disadvantaged regions. However, this could be done by a series of communes from the local, regional, national and eventually international level. The authority of the National Commune would not be based on the notion of State sovereignty. Rather, it would exist as a high level co-ordinating body based on a democratised economy. The National Commune would thus have very little in common with the existing State, which is a Leviathan crushing powerless 'general' citizens. Thus we need Cole's non-anarchist and pluralist critique of the State to supplement Marx's initial ideas on the separation of the State and Civil Society. We will then be better able to integrate functional and territorial representation from the local to the international level.[14]

Some anarchist insights are certainly important, though they need to be integrated within a broader conceptual framework. As we saw in chapter 6, there are many reasons why local economies are desirable. Nonetheless, we will continue to need large-scale production for the means of transport, communication networks and the utilisation of certain natural resources. The regional and national federal structure adumbrated above is more suitable to these tasks than the local community. Cole realised that the co-ordinating function of politics at the regional, federal, national and even international level was indispensable in a complex world. Chapter 6 also demonstrated that environmental problems have reached global proportions, and we need international bodies capable of enforcing protective legislation. Adapting Marx's notion of base and superstructure to his own theoretical framework, Cole insisted that political life would change dramatically once the democratised economy he envisioned was in place. But only then would national-level authorities and international political bodies be able to serve the environmental and other needs of the public, rather than the particular needs of finance and private industry.[15]

The role for local economies and community control will have to be maintained within this internationalist and functional-territorial model. But as the examples of China and Cuba illustrate, self-sufficiency is not necessarily synonymous with democratic control of the economy. The State socialist retreat from internationalism

[14] Galtung, 'Self-Reliance', pp. 161–4; Cole, *Social Theory*, pp. 100–7.
[15] Cole, *Social Theory*, pp. 106–7.

to 'Socialism in one country' in the former USSR and elsewhere was a complete rejection of Marx's ideas. Within a national framework, communist party elites can exercise power comparable to that of the business elites of various national bourgeoisie. Real internationalism requires departing from both the notions of (world-level or single-country) central planning and universal capitalism. Instead it embraces the ideal of a world with many centres and regions, and a politics of international co-operation.[16]

But we cannot ignore Green theorists and activists who quite rightfully remind us that an international perspective on the environment is only possible by an understanding of specific local realities. Solutions to such problems must be researched and discussed; the results can then be published and disseminated. While we will need to retain some of the advantages of large-scale industry, moves towards more localised economies and a greater degree of community are entirely possible. It will require the political consensus for a no-growth economy and a marked reduction in our consumption. This will provide us all with much more free time for the pursuit of various activities in the home and community. It will be objected that this runs counter to 'common sense', since we live in atomised and competitive societies in which economic prosperity has become the single most important goal for the vast majority of the population. But it is this 'common sense' that provides the crucial support for our present political and economic instituions. There is little doubt that our growth-crazed economy destroys the environment and continues to impoverish the Third World. These will soon be unavoidable problems for those living in the industrialised countries. If we do not object to the politics of securing the conditions of unrelenting economic growth, we will have little ground for complaint when further and perhaps more decisive steps towards the strong State are taken to accomplish just that. In order to avoid such a catastrophe 'everyday life' and 'common sense' must be changed.[17]

To this end, the institutional structures of a democratically controlled economy must be developed with far greater detail than is

---

[16] Galtung, 'Self-Reliance', pp. 166–73.
[17] Michaud, L'Avenir de la société alternative, p. 140; Kolm, La bonne économie, pp. 9–11; Plant, The Most Radical Gesture, pp. 183–7. I wholly support Plant's defence of radical politics in an era of post-modernist doubt and self-contemplation.

possible within the scope of this conclusion.[18] This conclusion has attempted to sketch an answer to the central theoretical question in the introduction of this book: What measures should be taken in order to bring about the re-politicisation of Civil Society, that is, the reappropriation of its political and universal content? The construction of a democratically controlled economy will inevitably be the fundamentally important objective in this political project. It cannot begin to take shape without strong ties between a revitalised trade union movement in a relationship of frank dialogue with all the major actors in the civil sphere. It will require that people take an active role in shaping their own lives, which are currently in the hands of corporate managers, financial elites and State bureaucrats. It will undoubtedly be a long struggle. But the alternative to struggle is the current state of barbarism, which in the end will be much harder on all of us.

[18] See Devine's proposals in *Democracy and Economic Planning*, pp. 236–7; 'Economy, State and Civil Society', pp. 208–15. At present I would argue that Devine's model implies too much centralisation. However, I share his general orientation and believe that the model could be revised in the direction of greater regional and local autonomy. See also Diane Elson, 'The Economics of a Socialized Market', pp. 310–14.

Bibliography

Abrate, Mario. *La lotta sindacale nella industrializzazione in Italia.* Milan: Franco Angeli, 1967.

Adler, Max. *Demokratie und Rätesystem.* Vienna: Verlag der Wiener Volksbuchhandlung, 1919.

Andreasi, Annamaria. *L'Anarchismo in Francia, Italia e Spagna: il filo rosso del movimento operaio,* Volume I. Milan: La Pietra, 1981.

Anthony, P. D. *John Ruskin's Labour.* Cambridge: Cambridge University Press, 1983.

Appel, Jan. *Grundprinzipien kommunistischen Produktion und Verteilung.* Berlin: Kollektivarbeit der Gruppe internationale Kommunisten, 1930.

Apter, David E. and Joll, James (eds.). *Anarchism Today.* London: Macmillan, 1971.

Arato, Andrew. 'Civil Society against the State: Poland 1980–81', *Telos,* 47, 1981.

Arato, Andrew. 'Empire vs. Civil Society: Poland 1981–1982', *Telos,* 50, 1981–82.

Arato, Andrew. 'A Reconstruction of Hegel's Theory of Civil Society' in Drucilla Cornell, Michael Rosenfeld and David Gray Carlson (eds.), *Hegel and Legal Theory.*

Arendt, Hannah. *The Human Condition.* Chicago: University of Chicago Press, 1958.

Arfe, Gaetano. *Storia del socialismo italiano, 1892-1926.* Turin: Einaudi, 1965.

Arfe, Gaetano, (ed.). *Socialismo e socialisti dal Risorgimento al fascismo.* Bari: De Donato, 1974.

Avrich, Paul. *Kronstadt, 1921.* New York: Columbia University Press, 1970.

Bahro, Rudolf. *From Red to Green.* London: Verso, 1984.

Bahro, Rudolf. *Building the Green Movement.* London: GMP, 1986.

Bahro, Rudolf. 'Alles kommt auf eine ökologische Alternative an', in Frank Blohm and Wolfgang Herzberg (ed. and intro.), *Nichts wird mehr so sein wie es war: Zur Zukunft der beiden deutschen Republiken.*

Bahro, Rudolf. *Die Alternative.* Berlin: Verlag Tribune, 1990.

Bahro, Rudolf. 'Konsens für Subsistenz?', *Junge Welt,* I, 1992.

Bahro, Rudolf. 'Zeit für den Neubau von Rettungsbooten' *Junge Welt,* I, 1992.

Bakunin, Michael. *Marxism, Freedom and the State.* London: Freedom, 1950.

Baldassarre, Antonio. *I limiti della democrazia.* Bari: Laterza, 1985.

Baldwin, Roger N., (ed.). *Kropotkin's Revolutionary Pamphlets.* New York: Dover, 1970.

Bancal, Jean. *Proudhon: pluralisme et autogestion,* Volume II. Paris: Aubier Montaigne, 1970.

Bauer, Otto. 'Die Sozialisierung im ersten Jahre der Republik', *Gesammelte*

Werke, Volume 2. Vienna: 1919.

Bauer, Otto. 'Rätediktatur oder Demokratie?', *Werksausgabe*, Volume 2. Vienna: 1919.

Bellamy, Richard. *Liberalism and Modern Society: An Historical Argument*. Cambridge: Polity Press, 1992.

Bellamy, Richard and Schecter, Darrow. *Gramsci and the Italian State*. Manchester: Manchester University Press, 1993.

Berkman, Alexander. *What is Communist Anarchism?* New York: Dover, 1972.

Berkman, Alexander. *ABC of Anarchism*. London: Freedom, 1973.

Berti, Giuseppe. Introduction to the Quaderni of Angelo Tasca, *Gli annali del istituto Giangiacomo Feltrinelli*, 10, 1968.

Bertramsen, Rene B., Peter, Jens, Thomsen, Frolund and Torfing, Jacob. *State, Economy and Society*. London: Unwin Hyman, 1991.

Beyer, Hans. *Die Revolution in Bayern, 1918–1919*. Berlin: VEB, 1982.

Black, Antony. *Guilds and Civil Society in European Political Thought from the Twelfth Century to the Present*. London: Methuen, 1984.

Blackburn, Robin (ed.). *After the Fall*. London: Verso, 1992.

Blohm, Frank and Herzberg, Wolfgang (eds.). *Nichts wird mehr so sein wie es war: Zur Zukunft der beiden deutschen Republiken*. Frankfurt: Luchterhand Literaturverlag, 1990.

Bobbio, Norberto. *Studi hegeliani: diritto, società civile, stato*. Turin: Einaudi, 1981.

Bock, Hans Manfred. *A. Pannekoek, H. Gorter: Organisation und Taktik der proletarischen Revolution*. Frankfurt: Suhrkamp, 1969.

Bock, Hans Manfred. *Syndikalismus und Linkskommunismus von 1918–1923*. Meinenheim am Glan: Verlag Anton Hain, 1969.

Bock, Hans Manfred. *Geschichte des Linken Radicalismus in Deutschland: Ein Versuch*. Frankfurt: Suhrkamp, 1976.

Bookchin, Murray. *Post-Scarcity Anarchism*. Montreal: Black Rose Books, 1970.

Bookchin, Murray. *The Spanish Anarchists: The Heroic Years, 1868–1938*. New York: Free Life Editions, 1977.

Bookchin, Murray. *Toward an Ecological Society*. Montreal: Black Rose Books, 1980.

Bookchin, Murray. *The Ecology of Freedom: The Emergence and Dissolution of Hierarchy*. Paolo Alto: Cheshire Books, 1982.

Bookchin, Murray. 'New Social Movements: The Anarchic Dimension', in David Goodway (ed.), *For Anarchism*.

Bookchin, Murray. *Remaking Society*. Montreal: Black Rose Books, 1989.

Bookchin, Murray. 'The Meaning of Confederalism', *Society and Nature*, 3, 1993.

Borkenau, Franz. *The Spanish Cockpit*. London: Faber, 1937.

Bradley, Keith and Gelb, Alan. *Co-operation at Work: The Mondragon Experience*. London: Heinemann, 1983.

Braverman, Harry. *Labour and Monopoly Capitalism: The Degradation of Work in the Twentieth Century*. New York: Monthly Review Press, 1974.

Breitbart, Myrna Margulies. 'The Integration of Community and Environment: Anarchist Decentralisation in Rural Spain, 1936–39', in A. Buttimer and D. Seamon (eds.), *The Human Experience of Space and Place*.

Brenan, Gerald. 'Anarchism in Spain', in Irving Horowitz (ed.), *The Anarchists*.

Brus, Wlodzimierz. *Socialist Ownership and Political Systems*. London: Routledge & Kegan Paul, 1975.

Buber, Martin. *Paths in Utopia*. New York: Macmillan, 1950.

Bunyan, James, and Fisher, H. H. (eds.). *The Origins of Forced Labour in the Soviet State, 1917–21: Documents and Materials*. Paolo Alto: Stanford University Press, 1934.

Buttimer, A. and Seamon, D. (eds.). *The Human Experience of Space and Place*. London: Croom Helm, 1980.

Cahill, Tom. 'Co-operatives and Anarchism: A Contemporary Perspective', in David Goodway (ed.), *For Anarchism*.

Capouja, Emile and Thomas, Keitha (eds.). Introduction to *The Essential Kropotkin*. London: Macmillan, 1976.

Carpanelli, S. F. (ed.). *L'autogestione nell'industria: analisi di alcune esperienze delle imprese cooperative in Italia*. Bari: De Donato, 1978.

Carpenter, L. P. *G. D. H. Cole: An Intellectual Biography*. Cambridge: Cambridge University Press, 1973.

Cavallari, Giovanna. *Classe dirigente e minoranze rivoluzionarie*. Camerino: Jovene Editori, 1983.

Cerrito, Gino (ed. and Intro). *Malatesta: scritti scelti*. Rome: La Nuova Sinistra, 1970.

Chaulieu, Pierre (Cornelius Castoriadis). 'La voie polonaise de la bureaucratisation', *Socialisme ou Barbarie*, 21, 1957.

Clark, Martin. 'Factory Councils and the Italian Labour Movement, 1916–1921', Ph.D. Thesis, Department of History, University of Reading, 1966.

Clark, Martin. *Antonio Gramsci and the Revolution that Failed*. New Haven: Yale University Press, 1977.

Cohen, Jean L. *Class and Civil Society: The Limits of Marxian Critical Theory*. Amherst: University of Massachusetts Press, 1982.

Cohen, Jean L. and Arato, Andrew. *Civil Society and Political Theory*. Cambridge: MIT Press, 1992.

Cohn-Bendit, Daniel and Gabriel. *Obsolete Communism: The Left-Wing Alternative*. London: Andre Deutsch, 1968.

Cole, G.D.H. *The World of Labour*. London: G. Bell & Sons, 1913.

Cole, G. D. H. *Self-Government in Industry*. London: G. Bell & Sons, 1917.

Cole, G. D. H. *Labour in the Commonwealth*. London: Headley Brothers, 1918.

Cole, G. D. H. *Guild Socialism Re-stated*. London: Leonard Parsons, 1920.

Cole, G. D. H. *Social Theory*. London: Methuen, 1920.

Cole, G. D. H. *A History of Socialist Thought, Volume IV: Communism and Social Democracy, 1914–1931*. London: Macmillan, 1958.

Comisso, Ellen Turkish. *Workers' Control under Plan and Market*. New Haven: Yale University Press, 1979.

Cornell, Drucilla, Rosenfeld, Michael and Carlson, David Gray (eds.). *Hegel and Legal Theory*. London: Routledge, 1991.

Crowder, George. *Classical Anarchism: The Political Thought of Godwin, Proudhon, Bakunin and Kropotkin*. Oxford: Clarendon Press, 1991.

Debord, Guy. *La société du spectacle*. Paris: Buchet-Chastel, 1967.

Debord, Guy. English translation to the Introduction of the fourth Italian edition of *La société du spectacle*, in Italy: *Autonomia, Post-Political Politics*. New York: Semiotexte (e), 1980.

De Felice, Franco. *Serrati, Bordiga, Gramsci e il problema della rivoluzione in Italia*. Bari: De Donato, 1971.

Demoustier, Daniele. *Les Coopératives de Production*. Paris: Editions La Decouverte, 1984.

Devine, Pat. *Democracy and Economic Planning: The Political Economy of a Self-Governing Society*. Cambridge: Polity Press, 1988.

Devine, Pat. 'Economy, State and Civil Society', *Economy and Society*, 20, 1991.

Dickson, David. *Alternative Technology and Technical Change*. Glasgow: Fontana/Collins, 1974.

Dolgoff, Sam, (ed.). *Bakunin on Anarchy*. London: Allen & Unwin, 1973.

Dolgoff, Sam, (ed.). *The Anarchist Collectives*. Montreal: Black Rose Books, 1974.

Dollèans, Edouard. *Proudhon*. Paris: Gallimard, 1948.

Dollèans, Edouard. *Histoire du mouvement ouvrier*, Volume 2. Paris: Colin, 1957.

Drulovic, Milojko. *Self-Management on Trial*. Nottingham: Spokesman, 1978.

Dunford, M. F. *Capital, the State and Regional Development*. London: Pion, 1988.

Dunford, M. F. 'Theories of Regulation', *Environment and Planning D: Society and Space*, 8, 1990.

Eckersley, Robyn. *Environmentalism and Political Theory: Toward an Ecocentric Approach*. London: UCL Press, 1992.

Elliot, Gregory. 'The Cards of Confusion: Reflections on Historical Communism and the "End of History" ', *Radical Philosophy*, 64, 1993.

Enbergs, Helmut Müller, Schulz, Marianne and Wielgohs, Jan (eds.). *Von der Illegalität ins Parliament: Werdegang und Konzept der neuen Burgerbewegungen*. Berlin: Links Druck Verlag, 1991.

Femia, Joseph V. *Marxism and Democracy*. Oxford: Clarendon Press, 1993.

Fleischer, Helmut. 'Bahro's Contribution to the Philosophy of Socialism' in Ulf Wolter (ed.), *Rudolf Bahro: Critical Responses*.

Fowkes, Ben. *Communism in Germany under the Weimar Republic*. London: Macmillan, 1984.

Frankel, Boris. *The Post Industrial Utopians*. Cambridge: Polity, 1987.

Fraser, Ronald. *Blood of Spain*. London: Penguin, 1981.

Furiozzi, Gian Biaggio. *Sorel e l'Italia*. Messina-Florence: Casa Editrice Giorgio D'anna, 1978.

Galassi, Nazario. *La cooperazione imolese dalle origini ai nostri giorni (1859–1969)*. Imola: Grafiche Galeati, 1968.

Galtung, Johan. 'Self-Reliance: Strukturveränderungen auf internationaler, nationaler, lokaler und persönlicher Ebene', in Joseph Hüber (ed.), *Anders arbeiten, anders Wirtschaften*.

Gentile, Emilio. *La Voce e l'età giolittiana*. Milan: Pan Editore, 1972.

Gentile, Emilio. *Il mito dello Stato nuovo: dall'antigiolittismo al fascismo*. Bari: Laterza, 1982.

Gerber, John. *Anton Pannekoek and the Socialism of Workers' Self-Emancipation, 1873–1960*. London: Kluwer Academic Publishers, 1989.

Gilbert, Michael (ed.). *A Century of Conflict*. London: Hamish Hamilton, 1966.

Ginsborg, Paul. *A History of Contemporary Italy: Society and Politics, 1943–1988*. London: Penguin, 1990.

Glass, S. T. *The Responsible Society: The Ideas of Guild Socialism*. London: Longman, 1966.

Gombin, Richard. 'The Ideology and Practice of Contestation seen through Recent Events in France', in David E. Apter, and James Joll (eds.), *Anarchism Today*.

Gombin, Richard. *The Origins of Modern Leftism*. London: Penguin, 1975.

Goodin, Robert E. *Green Political Theory*. Cambridge: Polity Press, 1992.

Goodway, David (ed.). *For Anarchism*. London: Routledge, 1989.

Gorter, Hermann. 'Offener Brief an den Genossen Lenin', in Fritz Kool (ed. and intro.), *Die Linke gegen die Parteiherrschaft*.

Gorz, Andre. *Farewell to the Working Class*. London: Pluto, 1982.

Gorz, Andre. *Capitalisme, socialisme, écologie: désorientations, orientations*. Paris: Éditions Galilée, 1991.

Gorz, Andre. *Métamorphoses du travail: quête du sens*. Paris: Éditions Galilée, 1991.

Gramsci, Antonio. *L'Ordine nuovo*. Turin: Einaudi, 1975.

Grave, Jean. *L'Anarchisme: son but: ses moyens*. Paris: Librarie Stock, 1924.

Grünenberg, Antonio (ed. and Intro.). *Die Massenstreikdebatte*. Frankfurt: Europäische Verlaganstalt, 1970.

Guarnieri, Maurizio. *I Consigli di fabbrica*. Città di Castello: Il Solco, 1946.

Guerin, Daniel. *L'Anarchisme*. Paris: Gallimard, 1976.

Guillaume, James. 'Ideas on Social Organisation' in George Woodcock (ed.), *The Anarchist Reader*.

Gunn, Christopher Eaton. *Workers' Self-Management in the United States*. Ithaca: Cornell University Press, 1984.

Gysi, Gregor. 'Wird es einen demokratischen Sozialismus in der DDR geben?', in Frank Blohm and Wolfgang Herzberg (eds. and intro.), *Nichts wird mehr so sein, wie es war: Zur Zukunft der beiden deutschen Republiken*.

Habermas, Jürgen. *Antworten auf Herbert Marcuse*. Frankfurt: Suhrkamp, 1968.

Habermas, Jürgen. *Erkenntnis und Interesse*. Frankfurt: Suhrkamp, 1968.

Habermas, Jürgen. *Faktizität und Geltung: Beiträge zur Diskurstheorie des Rechts und des demokratischen Rechstaats*. Frankfurt: Suhrkamp, 1993.

Hamon, Hervé, and Rotman, Patrick. *Génération (I): les années de rêve*. Paris: Éditions du Seuil, 1987.

Hampel, Anne. 'Das Wahlbündnis Die Grünen/Büdnis 90 – BürgerInnenbewegung' in Helmut Müller Enbergs, Marianne Schulz and Jan Wielgohs (eds.), *Von der Illegalität ins Parlament: Werdegang und Konzept der neuen Burgerbewegungen*.

Hartley, David. 'Communitarian Anarchism: A Contemporary Reconstruction and Assessment', University of Oxford, Ph.D. thesis, 1994.

Hartsock, Nancy C. M. *Money, Sex and Power: Toward a Feminist Historical Materialism*. London: Longman, 1983.

Hegel, G. W. F. *Philosophy of Right*. Oxford: Oxford University Press, 1967.

Heller, Agnes. *The Theory of Need in Marx*. London: Allison & Busby, 1976.

Hindess, Barry. 'Marxism and Parliamentary Democracy', in Alan Hunt (ed.), *Marxism and Democracy*.

Hirsch, Joachim. 'Das Ende der Zivilgesellschaft', in *Diskus*, 4, 1992.

Hirst, Paul Q. (ed. and Intro.) *The Pluralist Theory of the State: Selected Writings of G. D. H. Cole, J. N. Figgis and H. J. Laski*. London: Routledge, 1989.

Hirst, Paul Q. *Representative Democracy and its Limits*. Cambridge: Polity Press, 1990.

Hobson, S. G. *National Guilds: An Inquiry into the Wage System and the Way Out*. London: G. Bell & Sons, 1914.

Hobson, S. G. *National Guilds and the State*. London: G. Bell & Sons, 1920.

Holland, Stuart. *The Socialist Challenge*. London: Quartet Books, 1975.

Holmstrom, Mark. *Industrial Democracy in Italy*. Aldershot: Avebury, 1989.

Honneth, Axel. 'Conceptions of Civil Society', *Radical Philosophy*, 64, 1993.

Horowitz, Irving. *Radicalism and the Revolt Against Reason: The Social Theories of Georges Sorel*. London: Routledge & Kegan Paul, 1961.

Horowitz, Irving (ed.). *The Anarchists*. New York: Dell, 1964.

Horvat, Branko. *The Political Economy of Socialism*. New York: M. E. Sharpe, 1982.

Houseman, Gerald L. *G. D. H. Cole*. Boston: Twayne Publishers, 1979.

Hüber, Joseph (ed.) *Anders arbeiten, anders Wirtschaften*. Frankfurt: Fischer Taschenbuch Verlag, 1979.

Hugenroth, Reinhold (ed.). *Kein leichter Weg nach Eurotopia*. Bonn: Pahel-Rugenstein Verlag, 1993.

Hughes, H. Stuart. *Consciousness and Society: The Reorientation of European Social Thought, 1890–1930*. New York: Vintage, 1977.

Hulse, James. *The Forming of the Communist International*. Stanford: Stanford University Press, 1964.

Hunt, Alan (ed.). *Marxism and Democracy*. London: Lawrence & Wishart, 1980.

Hunt, R. N. *The Political Ideas of Marx and Engels*, two Volumes. Pittsburgh: University of Pittsburgh Press, 1974.

Jennings, Jeremy. *Georges Sorel: The Character and Development of His Thought*. London: Macmillan, 1985.

Jennings, Jeremy. *Syndicalism in France: A Study of Ideas*. London: Macmillan, 1990.

Jessop, Bob. *State Theory: Putting Capitalist States in their Place*. Cambridge: Polity Press, 1990.

Joll, James. *The Anarchists*. London: Methuen, 1979.

Julliard, Jacques. *Fernand Pelloutier et les origines du syndicalisme d'action directe*. Paris: Éditions du Seuil, 1985.

Julliard, Jacques. *Autonomie ouvrière: Etudes sur le syndicalisme d'action directe*. Paris: Éditions du Seuil, 1988.

Kammerer, Peter. 'Die alte DDR: der Mezzogiorno des neuen Deutschland?', in Thomas Klein et al. (eds.), *Keine Opposition. Nirgends?*

Kardelj, Edward. *Democracy and Socialism*. London: Sommerfield, 1978.

Kautsky, Karl. *The Class Struggle*. New York: Norton, 1971.

Keane, John. *Civil Society and the State: New European Perspectives*. London: Verso, 1988.

Keane, John. *Democracy and Civil Society*. London: Verso, 1988.

Kemp, Penny, and Wall, Derek. *A Green Manifesto for the 1990s*. London: Penguin, 1990.

Kinna, Ruth. 'George Crowder's *Classical Anarchism* and the Uniqueness of Kropotkin's Political Thought', *Anarchist Studies*, I, 1993.

Klein, Thomas, Vordenbäumen, Vera, Wiegrefe, Carsten and Wolf, Ugo (eds.). *Keine Opposition. Nirgends?* Berlin: CH Links Verlag, 1991.

Kolm, Serge Christophe. *La bonne économie: la réciprocité générale*. Paris: Presses Universitaires de France, 1984.

Kool, Fritz (ed. and intro.), *Die Linke gegen die Parteiherrschaft*. Olten: Walter Verlag, 1970.

Kornai, Janos. *The Socialist System: The Political Economy of Communism*. New Jersey: Princeton University Press, 1992.

Korsch, Karl. *'Was ist Sozialisierung?'*. Hanover: Freies Deutschland, 1919.

Korsch, Karl. *Rätebewegung und Klassenkampf* (ed. and intro. by Michael Buckmiller). Frankfurt: Europäishe Verlaganstalt, 1980.

Kremendahl, Hans and Meyer, Thomas (eds.). *Menschliche Emancipation: Rudolf Bahro und der demokratische Sozialismus*. Frankfurt: Europäische Verlaganstalt, 1981.

Kropotkin, Peter. *The Conquest of Bread* (1892). London: Elephant Editions, 1985.

Kropotkin, Peter. *Fields, Factories and Workshops*. London: Hutchinson, 1899.

Kropotkin, Peter. *Mutual Aid* (1902). Harmondsworth: Penguin, 1939.

Kropotkin, Peter. 'The Wages System', in George Woodcock (ed.), *The Anarchist Reader*.

Kropotkin, Peter. 'Anarchist Communism: Its Basis and Principles', in Roger N. Baldwin (ed.), *Kropotkin's Revolutionary Pamphlets*.

Kropotkin, Peter. 'Modern Science and Anarchism', in George Woodcock (ed.), *The Anarchist Reader*.

Kymlicka, Will. *Contemporary Political Philosophy: An Introduction*. Oxford: Clarendon Press, 1990.

Labriola, Arturo. *Sindacalismo e riformismo*. Florence: G. Nerbini Editore, 1905.

Labriola, Arturo. 'Sindacati e socialismo', in *Il Divenire Sociale*, 2, 1906.

Labriola, Arturo. 'L'Onesta polemica contro Giorgio Plekhanoff e per il sindacalismo', in *Pagine Libere*, 2, 1908.

Labriola, Arturo. *Storia di dieci anni 1899–1909*. Milan: Casa Editrice "Il Viandante", 1910.

Laclau, Ernesto and Mouffe, Chantal. *Hegemony and Socialist Strategy: Toward a Radical Democratic Politics*. London: Verso, 1985.

Lanzillo, Agostino. *La rivoluzione del dopoguerra: critiche e diagnosi*. Città di Castello: Il Solco, 1922.

Laqueur, Walter. *Europe in Our Time: A History, 1945-1992*. London: Penguin, 1992.

Lefebvre, Henri. *Critique de la vie quotidienne (II): fondements d'une sociologie de la quotidienneté*. Paris: L'Arche Editeur, 1961.

Lefort, Claude. 'L'Insurrection hongroise', *Socialisme ou Barbarie*, 20, 1957.

Le Grand, Julian and Estrin, Saul (eds.). *Market Socialism*. Oxford: Clarendon, 1989.

Lenin, V. I. *Collected Works*, Volume 25. Moscow: Progress Publishers, 1975.

Leone, Enrico. 'L'Azione elettorale e il socialismo', in *Il Divenire Sociale*, 2, 1906.

Leone, Enrico. *Il sindacalismo*. Milan: Remo Sandron Editore, 1910.

Leone, Enrico. 'Per uno secondo congresso sindacalista', in *Il Divenire Sociale*,

4, 1910.

Leval, Gaston. *Collectives in the Spanish Revolution*. London: Freedom, 1975.

Levrero, Antonio. *La formazione del PCI*. Rome: Editore Riuniti, 1971.

Linse, Ulrich (ed. and Intro.). *Gustav Landauer und die Revoluzionszeit 1918–1919*. Berlin: Karin Kramer Verlag, 1974.

Louzon, Robert (ed. and Intro.). *Georges Sorel: lettres à Paul Delesalle, 1914–1921*. Paris: Editions Bernard Grasset, 1947.

Lumley, Robert. *States of Emergency: Cultures of Revolt in Italy from 1968 to 1978*. London: Verso, 1990.

Luxemburg, Rosa. *The Mass Strike*. New York: Pathfinder, 1970.

Lydall, Harold. *Yugoslavia in Crisis*. Oxford: Clarendon, 1989.

Maitron, Jean. *Histoire du mouvement anarchiste en France (1880–1914)*. Paris: Société Universitaire d'Éditions et de Libraire, 1955.

Maione, Giuseppe. *Il biennio rosso: autonomia e spontaneità operaia nel 1919–1920*. Bologna: Il Mulino, 1977.

Malatesta, Errico. *Scritti*, Volume I. Geneva: Edizioni del Risveglio, 1934.

Mantica, Paolo. 'Mentre si attua il suffraggio universale', *L'Internazionale*, 3, 1913.

Marcuse, Herbert. *Counterrevolution and revolt*. London: Allen Lane, 1972.

Marshall, Peter. *Demanding the Impossible: A History of Anarchism*. London: Harper Collins, 1992.

Martell, Luke. *Ecology and Society: An Introduction*. Cambridge: Polity Press, 1994.

Martin, David E. and Rubinstein, David (eds.). *Ideology and the Labour Movement*. London: Croom Helm, 1979.

Marucco, Dora. *Arturo Labriola e il sindacalismo rivoluzionario in Italia*. Turin: Einaudi, 1970.

Marx, Karl. 'Critique of Hegel's Philosophy of Right', in the *Collected Works of Marx and Engels*, Volume 3. Moscow: Progress Publishers, 1977.

Marx, Karl and Engels, Friedrich. *Marx and Engels Selected Works in 1 Volume*. London: Lawrence & Wishart, 1980.

Mason, David. 'Solidarity as a New Social Movement', *Political Science Quarterly*, 1, 1989.

Mastnak, Thomas. 'From the New Social Movements to Political Parties', in James Simmie and Joze Dekleva (eds.), *Yugoslavia in Turmoil*.

Mathews, Frank. 'The Ideology of Becoming: A. R. Orage, A. J. Penty, and the Origins of Guild Socialism in England', in David E. Martin and David Rubinstein (eds.), *Ideology and the Labour Movement*.

Mattick, Paul. 'La prospettiva della rivoluzione mondiale di Anton Pannekoek', in *Storia del marxismo contemporaneo*. Milan: Feltrinelli, 1973.

Mattick, Paul. *Spontaneität und Organisation: Vier Versuche über praktische und theoretische Probleme der Arbeiterbewegung*. Frankfurt: Suhrkamp, 1975.

Melis, Renato (ed. and Intro.). *Sindacalisti italiani*. Rome: Volpe Editore, 1964.

Mellor, Mary, Hannah, Janet, and Stirling, John. *Workers' Co-operatives in Theory and Practice*. Milton Keynes: Open University Press, 1988.

McLellan, David. *Marxism after Marx*. Boston: Houghton Mifflin, 1979.

Michaud, Dominique Allan. *L'Avenir de la société alternative: des idées 1968–1989*. Paris: Éditions L'Harmattan, 1989.

Miller, David. 'Kropotkin', *Government and Opposition*, 18, 1983.

Miller, David. *Anarchism*. London: J. M. Dent & Sons, 1984.

Miller, David. *Market, State and Community: Theoretical Foundations of Market Socialism*. Oxford: Clarendon, 1990.

Miller, Robert F. (ed.). *The Developments of Civil Society in Communist Systems*. Sydney: Allen & Unwin, 1992.

Morris, William. *News from Nowhere*. London: Routledge & Kegan Paul, 1970.

Nove, Alec. *The Economics of Feasible Socialism*. London: George Allen & Unwin, 1983.

Oakeshott, Robert. *The Case for Workers' Co-Ops* (second edition). London: Macmillan, 1990.

Olivetti, A. O. 'Ripresa', *Pagine Libere*, 1, 1920.

Olivetti, A. O. 'Il Manifesto dei sindacalisti', *Pagine Libere*, 8, 1921.

Olivetti, A. O. 'La fiaba del governo ed altre sciocchezze', *Pagine Libere*, 8, 1921.

O'Neill, John. 'Exploitation and Workers' Co-operatives: A Reply to Alan Carter', *Journal of Applied Philosophy*, 8, 1991.

O'Neill, John. 'Markets, Socialism and Information: A Reformulation of a Marxian Objection to the Market', *Social Philosophy and Policy*, 6, 1991.

O'Neill, John. *Ecology, Policy and Politics: Human Well-Being and the Natural World*. London: Routledge, 1993.

Ophuls, William. *Ecology and the Politics of Scarcity: Prologue to a Political Theory of the Steady State*. San Francisco: W. H. Freeman, 1977.

Orano, Paolo. 'Perché il sindacalismo non è populare in Italia', *Il Divenire Sociale*, 2, 1907.

Orano, Paolo. 'Decentramento e lotta di classe', *Pagine Libere*, 7, 1920.

Orano, Paolo. 'Il controllo operaio', in *Pagine Libere*, 7, 1920.

Paggi, Leonardo. *Gramsci e il moderno principe*. Rome: Editori Riuniti, 1970.

Pannekoek, Anton. *Lenin als Philosoph*. Frankfurt: Europäische Verlaganstalt, 1969.

Pannekoek, Anton. 'Marxistische Theorie und revolutionäre Taktik', in Hans Manfred Bock (ed.), *A. Pannekoek, H. Gorter: Organisation und Taktik der proletarischen Revolution*.

Pannekoek, Anton. 'Massenaktion und Revolution', in Antonio Grünenberg, *Die Massenstreikdebatte*.

Pannekoek, Anton. 'Weltrevolution und kommunistische Taktik', in Fritz Kool (ed. and intro.), *Die Linke gegen die Parteiherrschaft*.

Pannekoek, Anton. *Les Conseils ouvrières*. Paris: Éditions Belibaste, 1974.

Panunzio, Sergio. 'Socialismo, liberismo, anarchismo', *Il Divenire Sociale*, 2, 1906.

Panunzio, Sergio. *La persistenza del diritto*. Pescara: Casa Editrice Abruzzese, 1910.

Panunzio, Sergio. 'Per la revisione di socialismo: criteri preliminari circa il metodo', *Vie Nuove*, 1, 1917.

Panunzio, Sergio. 'Il socialismo in ritrato', *Pagine Libere*, 8, 1921.

Parkin, Frank. *Class Inequality and Political Order*. London: Granada, 1972.

Pastori, Paolo. *Rivoluzione e continuità in Proudhon e Sorel*. Milan: Giuffre, 1980.

Pateman, Carole. *Participation and Democratic Theory*. Cambridge: Cambridge University Press, 1970.

Pearce, David, Markandya, Anil, and Barbier, Edward B. *Blueprint for a Green*

Economy. London: Earthscan Publications, 1989.

Peirats, Jose. *La CNT en la revolucion espanola*, 3 Volumes. Paris: Editions Latran, 1971.

Peirats, Jose. *Los anarquistas en la guerra civil espanola*. Madrid: Ediciones Jucar, 1976.

Pelcynski, Z. A. 'Solidarity and the Rebirth of Civil Society in Poland', in John Keane (ed.), *Civil Society and the State: New European Perspectives*.

Pelloutier, Fernand. *Histoire des Bourses du Travail*. Paris: Schleicheur Frères, Editeur, 1902.

Pengan, Alain. 'Anarcho-Communism', in Maximilien Rubel and John Crump (eds.), *Non-Market Socialism in the Nineteenth and Twentieth Centuries*.

Penty, A. J. *The Restoration of the Gild System*. London: Swan Sonnenschein, 1906.

Penty, A. J. *Old Worlds for New: A Study of the Post-Industrial State*. London: George Allen & Unwin, 1917.

Pepper, David. *Communes and the Green Vision*. London: Green Print, 1991.

Pierson, Christopher. *Marxist Theory and Democratic Politics*. Cambridge: Polity Press, 1986.

Plant, Sadie. *The Most Radical Gesture: The Situationist International in a Postmodern Age*. London: Routledge, 1992.

Portis, Larry. *Georges Sorel*. London: Pluto, 1980.

Prezzolini, Giuseppe. *La teoria sindacalista*. Naples: Francesco Perrella Editore, 1909.

Priewe, Jan. 'Treuhandreform: von der Kritik der Treuhandanstalt zu industrie-politischen Alternativen', in Werner Schulz and Ludger Volmer (eds.), *Entwickeln statt abwickeln: Wirtschaftspolitische und ökologische Umbau-Konzepte für die neuen Lander*.

Procacci, Giorgio. *La lotta di classe in Italia agli inizi del secolo xx*. Rome: Editori Riuniti, 1971.

Proudhon, J. P. *De la capacité politique des classes ouvriéres*. Paris: Librarie Internationale, 1873.

Raz, Joseph. *The Morality of Freedom*. Oxford: Oxford University Press, 1986.

Redmond, John. Introduction to William Morris, *News from Nowhere*. London: Routledge & Kegan Paul, 1970.

Richards, Vernon. Introduction to G. D. H. Cole, *Guild Socialism Re-Stated*. London: Transaction Books, 1980.

Richter, Rudolf. 'A Socialist Market Economy – Can it Work?', *Kyklos*, 45, 1992.

Riosa, Alceo. 'Alcuni elementi dell'ideologia sindacalista rivoluzionaria in Italia all'indomani dello Sciopero Generale del 1904', in Gaetano Arfe, (ed.), *Socialismo e socialisti dal Risorgimento al fascismo*.

Ritter, Alan. *The Political Thought of Pierre-Joseph Proudhon*. New Jersey: Princeton University Press, 1969.

Ritter, Alan. *Anarchism: A Theoretical Analysis*. Cambridge: Cambridge University Press, 1980.

Roberts, David D. *The Syndicalist Tradition and Italian Fascism*. Manchester: Manchester University Press, 1979.

Rödel, Erich (ed.). *Autonome Gesellschaft und Libertäre Demokratie*. Frankfurt: Suhrkamp, 1990.

Romano, S. F. *Storia della questione meridionale*. Palermo: Edizioni Pantea, 1945.

Roosevelt, Frank. 'Marx and Markets', *Dissent*, 4, 1992.

Rosmer, Alfred. *Le mouvement ouvrier pendant la guerre*. Paris: Librarie du Travail, 1920.

Rubel, Maximilien, and Crump, John (eds.). *Non-Market Socialism in the Nineteenth and Twentieth Centuries*. London: Macmillan, 1987.

Rühle, Otto. 'Die Räte', in Fritz Kool, (ed. and Intro.), *Die Linke gegen die Parteiherrschaft*.

Russel, Bertrand. *Roads to Freedom*. London: Allen & Unwin, 1977.

Ryle, Martin. *Ecology and Socialism*. London: Radius, 1988.

Salvadori, Massimo. *Il mito del buongoverno: La Questione Merdionale da Cavour a Gramsci*. Turin: Einaudi, 1960.

Salvadori, Massimo. *Kautsky e la rivoluzione socialista, 1880–1938*. Milan: Feltrinelli, 1976.

Salvemini, Gaetano. *Scritti sulla Questione Merdionale, 1896–1952*. Turin: Einaudi, 1958.

Schecter, Darrow. *Gramsci and the Theory of Industrial Democracy*. Aldershot: Avebury, 1991.

Schmidt, Alfred. 'Existential Ontologie und historischer Materialismus bei Herbert Marcuse', in Jürgen Habermas (ed.), *Antworten auf Herbert Marcuse*.

Schulz, Marianne. 'Neues Forum', in Helmut Müller Enbergs, Marianne Schulz and Jan Wielgohs (eds.), *Von der Illegalität ins Parliament: Werdegang und Konzept der neuen Bürgerbewegungen*.

Schulz, Werner and Volmer, Ludger (eds.). *Entwickeln statt abwickeln: Wirtschaftspolitische und ökologische Umbau-Konzepte für die neuen Lander*. Berlin: CH Links Verlag, 1992.

Selucky, Radoslav. *Marxism, Socialism and Freedom: Toward an Essential Democratic Theory of Labour-Managed Systems*. London: Macmillan, 1979.

Shapiro, Leonard. *The Origins of the Communist Autocracy*. Cambridge: Cambridge University Press, 1972.

Shipway, Mark. 'Council Communism', in Maximilen Rubel and John Crump (eds.), *Non-Market Socialism in the Nineteenth and Twentieth Centuries*.

Shipway, Mark. 'Situationism', in Maximilen Rubel and John Crump (eds.), *Non-Market Socialism in the Nineteenth and Twentieth Centuries*.

Simmie, James and Dekleva, Joze (eds.), *Yugoslavia in Turmoil: After Self-management*. London: Pinter, 1991.

Sirianni, Carmen. *Workers' Control and Socialist Democracy: The Soviet Experience*. London: Verso, 1982.

Smart, D. A. (ed. and intro.). *Pannekoek and Gorter's Marxism*. London: Pluto, 1978.

Smidovnik, Janez. 'Disfunctions of the System of Self-Management in the Economy in Local Territorial Communities and in Public Administration', in James Simmie and Joze Dekleva (eds.), *Yugoslavia in Turmoil: After Self-management*.

Soldani, Franco. *La struttura del dominio nel sindacalismo rivoluzionario e nel giovane Gramsci*. Milan: Edizioni Unicopli, 1985.

Sorel, Georges. 'Étude sur Vico', *Le Devenir Social*, 11–12, 1896.

Sorel, Georges. *La Décomposition du marxisme*. Paris: Marcel Rivière, 1908.

Sorel, Georges. *Les Illusions du progrès*. Paris: Marcel Rivière, 1908.

Sorel, Georges. *Matériaux d'une theorie du proletariat*. Paris: Marcel Rivière, 1919.

Sorel, Georges. *Réflexions sur la violence* (fifth edition). Paris: Marcel Rivière, 1921.

Spriano, Paolo. *Storia del Partito comunista italiano (I): da Bordiga a Gramsci*. Turin: Einaudi, 1967.

Steele, Tom. *Alfred Orage and the Leeds Arts Club, 1893-1923*. Aldershot: Gower, 1990.

Steenson, Gary P. *Karl Kautsky, 1854–1938: Marxism in the Classical Years*. Pittsburgh: Pittsburgh University Press, 1978.

Sternhell, Zeev. *La Droite révolutionaire: 1885–1914*. Paris: Maspero, 1978.

Sternhell, Zeev. *Ni droite ni gauche*. Paris: Maspero, 1983.

Taylor, Michael. *The Possibility of Cooperation*. Cambridge: Cambridge University Press, 1987.

Tester, Keith. *Civil Society*. London: Routledge, 1992.

Thomas, Henk, and Logan, Chris. *Mondragon: An Economic Analysis*. London: George Allen & Unwin, 1982.

Thomas, Hugh. 'Anarchist Labour Federations in the Spanish Civil War', in Irving Horowitz (ed.), *The Anarchists*.

Thomas, Hugh. 'Anarchist Agrarian Collectives in the Spanish Civil War', in Michael Gilbert (ed.), *A Century of Conflict*.

Thomas, Hugh. *The Spanish Civil War*. London: Penguin, 1977.

Thomas, Paul. *Karl Marx and the Anarchists*. London: Routledge & Kegan Paul, 1980.

Thompson, E. P. *William Morris: Romantic to Revolutionary*. London: Lawrence and Wishart, 1955.

Thornley, Jenny. *Workers' Co-operatives: Jobs and Dreams*. London: Heinemann, 1982.

Tokar, Brian. *The Green Alternative: Creating an Ecological Future*. San Pedro: R. and E. Miles, 1977.

Tucker, Robert C. (ed.). *The Marx-Engels Reader* (second edition). New York: W. W. Norton & Company, 1978.

Vaneigem, Raoul. *Traité de savoir-vivre à l'usage des jeunes générations* (second edition). Paris: Gallimard, 1992.

Vanek, Jan. 'The Worker-Managed Enterprise as an Institution', in Jaroslav Vanek (ed.), *Self-Management: Economic Liberation of Man*.

Vanek, Jaroslav. *General Theory of Labour-Managed Market Economies*. Ithaca: Cambridge University Press, 1970.

Vanek, Jaroslav. *Self-Management: Economic Liberation of Man*. Harmondsworth: Penguin, 1975.

Vico, Giambattista. *La scienza nuova* (1744). Milan: Garzanti, 1983.

Vincent, Andrew. *Modern Political Ideologies*. Oxford: Blackwell, 1992.

Vincent, Jean-Marie. *Critique du travail: le faire et l'agir*. Paris: Presses Universitaires de France, 1987.

Vilmer, Fritz. 'Eine klassenlos Arbeitersorganisation: Bahros Alternative geht auch uns an', in Hans Kremendahl and Thomas Meyer (eds.), *Menschliche Emancipation: Rudolf Bahro und der demokratische Sozialismus*.

Ward, Colin (ed. and Intro). *Fields, Factories and Workshops Tomorrow*. London: George Allen & Unwin, 1974.

Ward, Colin. *Anarchy in Action*. London: Freedom, 1982.

Weale, Albert. *The New Politics of Pollution*. Manchester: Manchester University Press, 1992.

Weiske, Christine. 'Maastricht: so nicht, europäische Sozialpolitik?', in Reinhold Hugenroth (ed.), *Kein leichter Weg nach Eurotopia*.

Williams, Gwyn. *Proletarian Order*. London: Pluto, 1977.

Williams, Raymond. *Sources of Hope: Culture, Democracy, Socialism*. London: Verso, 1989.

Wolff, R. P. *In Defence of Anarchism*. New York: Harper & Row, 1970.

Wolffheim, Fritz. 'Gewerkschaftsprobleme', *Arbeiterpolitik*, 12, 1917.

Wolter, Ulf (ed.). *Rudolf Bahro: Critical Responses*. White Plains: M. E. Sharpe, Inc., 1980.

Woodcock, George (ed.). *The Anarchist Reader*. London: Fontana, 1977.

Wright, A. W. *G. D. H. Cole and Socialist Democracy*. Oxford: Clarendon Press, 1979.

Zukin, Sharon. *Beyond Marx and Tito: Theory and Practice in Yugoslav Socialism*. Cambridge University Press, 1975.

Index